SOCIALIST LABOR AND POLITICS
IN WEIMAR GERMANY

Socialist Labor
and Politics
in Weimar Germany

THE GENERAL FEDERATION
OF GERMAN TRADE UNIONS

by

GERARD BRAUNTHAL

ARCHON BOOKS
1978

Library of Congress Cataloging in Publication Data

Braunthal, Gerard, 1923-
    Socialist labor and politics in Weimar Germany.
    Bibliography: p.
    Includes index.
    1. Trade-unions—Germany—Political activity—History.
2. Allgemeiner Deutscher Gewerkschaftsbund. 3.
Sozialdemokratische Partei Deutschlands. I. Title.
HD8455.B7   322'.2'0943   77-29131
ISBN 0-208-01740-2

© Gerard Braunthal 1978
First published 1978 as an Archon Book,
an imprint of The Shoe String Press Inc,
Hamden, Connecticut 06514

For Peter and Stephen

CONTENTS

[7]

Appendixes

Tables

PREFACE

LABOR MOVEMENTS in European countries have always been deeply involved in politics. This study concentrates on one country, Germany; one time segment, Weimar (1918-1933); and the politics of one major labor federation, the socialist General Federation of German Trade Unions. It is not designed to provide a complete overview of the German labor movement, which before 1933 was ideologically and politically fragmented primarily into socialist, Christian, and liberal unions. Rather it is designed to fill one lacuna in the literature on German trade unionism, by dealing specifically with the socialist or "free" labor unions' politics, organization, and linkage to the Social Democratic Party (SPD) and the Weimar governments.[1] It focuses on these unions because they served as prototypes for other European socialist unions, their high membership and large-scale apparatus gave them significantly more power at the national level than the other German unions possessed, and their relationship to the SPD fit into a union-party pattern typical in a number of European countries.[2]

The socialist unions then constituted one of the two largest labor movements in the world (the British Trades Union Congress was the other) and the largest organized secular group in Germany. They were composed of three central federations, not subsumed under one peak organization but encompassing the major social and occupational strata. These were:

(a) the General Federation of German Trade Unions (Allgemeiner Deutscher Gewerkschaftsbund, ADGB), created in 1919 from national craft and industrial unions of manual workers, with a membership of about 4.7 million in 1930;

(b) the General Free Federation of Salaried Employees (Allgemeiner freier Angestelltenbund, AfA), founded in 1921, with over 460,000 members by 1930;

(c) the General Federation of German Civil Servants (Allgemeiner Deutscher Beamtenbund, ADB), created in 1922, with about 170,000 members by 1930.

This study deals basically with the most powerful of the three, the ADGB, and its predecessor.[3] The purpose is to dissect the ADGB as an associational interest group operating in the political realm of parties, the executive branch, and legislature. It aims at contributing to the understanding of a social movement with an impact far transcending the boundaries of Weimar Germany.

Interest groups, such as trade unions, are important in politics. They seek maximum benefits for their clientele membership. But each issue, whether higher wages, profits, or prices, is resolved within the framework of a political setting that may be hostile or friendly to the interest group. Therefore, it is imperative for the group to broaden its horizon and influence the political sphere if it expects economic gains. Time and location make little difference in techniques. Whether one focuses on the German unions in the Empire or Weimar eras or in the 1970s matters little, since pressures upon the policy makers are similar in all cases.

This is essentially a "history from the top down" study of a national organization and its leadership rather than a study of the rank and file—history's "silent majority." No elitist bias exists in the choice of this approach: it was made on the basis of concentrating on the principal policy makers who affected the destiny of the movement, but who were rarely affected by pressures from the base. This imbalance in the power relationship between an entrenched leadership and a quiescent membership was not unique to Germany, but it did reflect a social pattern of obedience to authority that is consistent through that nation's history.[4] It would be valuable to understand more about the inner dynamics of the organization, but relevant data are incomplete; however, archival materials and personal interviews were informative.

[10]

The study is arranged first historically-chronologically and then analytically-topically, an unorthodox approach designed to give the reader continuity in the historical narrative. Its disadvantage is that the death of the unions in 1933 is followed by topical chapters each beginning with the birth of the Weimar era. The author suggests that specialists on German politics who are familiar with the historical material plunge immediately into the topical chapters.

The historical survey accents the unions' involvement in national politics, beginning with a brief chapter on the growth of the socialist unions and their ties to the SPD in the Imperial era. Then there follows a more detailed chronological account of the unions' political involvement in several Weimar crises: the Revolution of 1918 and 1919, the Kapp Putsch of 1920, the political turmoil from 1921 to 1923, the Ruhr occupation of 1923, the demise of the Müller cabinet in 1930, and the authoritarian cabinets of Brüning, Papen, Schleicher, and Hitler. Many authors have already dealt with each crisis, but none has given an overall account of the ADGB in Weimar politics.

The approach then becomes topical, starting with a survey of the ADGB: its organization, leadership, bureaucracy, decision-making process, and factionalism; as well as short surveys of the AfA, ADB, and the nonsocialist federations. The following chapters examine the targets of union pressure in the Weimar era, and concentrate first on the socialist unions' ideological ally, the SPD. The important union linkage to the party ranged from institutional collaboration, membership and voter support, to the financing of campaigns and organizational expenses. A second target was the Reichstag, to which union candidates sought nomination on the SPD tickets. Emphasis is put on the extent of union representation during the several Reichstag periods, in both the SPD parliamentary groups and the parliamentary committees, and its effect on bills passing through the legislature. A third target was the executive branch, where unions were represented at the chancellor, cabinet, and administrative agency levels, and influenced legislation in an era when the state became increasingly involved in labor affairs.

Next, the study deals with major economic policies of concern to the unions in the Weimar period, such as the eight hour day, unemployment insurance, reparations, socialization, works councils, economic democracy, and socialism, assessing in each case the role of the unions in fulfilling their objectives. The concluding chapter analyzes the part the socialist unions played in the political sphere during their decades of growth, decline, and death—a life cycle of trials and triumphs, failures and achievements, crises and stability.

ACKNOWLEDGMENTS

I WISH to express my gratitude to the Labor Relations and Research Center, University of Massachusetts, Amherst, for granting me financial support to pursue field research in Germany and to complete the manuscript; and to the library staffs of the Federation of German Trade Unions, Duesseldorf; the Friedrich Ebert Archives, Bonn; the National Archives, Koblenz; the Frankfurt University; the Institut für Weltwirtschaft, Kiel; the Free German Trade Union Federation, East Berlin; the International Institute for Social History, Amsterdam; and the Buttinger Library, New York, who directed me to valuable and original source materials.

I am especially indebted to a number of veteran union and socialist leaders who in interviews both in the early postwar period and more recently provided vivid recollections of the Weimar era, and added insightful information not available in the literature. I am thankful to the late Professor Franz Neumann for the inspiration for this study; to Herr Hans Gottfurcht, a former staff official in the AfA, and to my father, Dr. Alfred Braunthal, formerly an economist on the staff of the SPD-union sponsored research institute in Berlin, for having made valuable suggestions in their reading of the entire manuscript; to Professor Solomon Barkin for being kind enough to read one section; to Janet Bowden Colombo for most helpful editorial assistance; and to my wife, Sabina, for the constant encouragement and aid during the long preparation of the manuscript.

ABBREVIATIONS

ADB	Allgemeiner Deutscher Beamtenbund (General Federation of German Civil Servants)
ADGB	Allgemeiner Deutscher Gewerkschaftsbund (General Federation of German Trade Unions)
AfA	Allgemeiner freier Angestelltenbund (General Free Federation of Salaried Employees)
AFL	American Federation of Labor
DBB	Deutscher Beamtenbund (German Federation of Civil Servants)
DGB	Deutscher Gewerkschaftsbund (German Trade Union Federation)
IFTU	International Federation of Trade Unions
KPD	Kommunistische Partei Deutschlands (Communist Party of Germany)
NSDAP	Nationalsozialistische Deutsche Arbeiter Partei (German National Socialist Workers Party)
NSBO	Nationalsozialistische Betriebszellen Organisation (National Socialist Works Organization)
SPD	Sozialdemokratische Partei Deutschlands (Social Democratic Party of Germany)
USPD	Unabhängige Sozialdemokratische Partei Deutschlands (Independent Social Democratic Party of Germany)

Part One

HISTORICAL OVERVIEW

I

THE FORMATIVE YEARS

THE MANUAL SKILLED and unskilled worker was at the center of the
modern organizing efforts of European trade unions and socialist
parties in the second half of the nineteenth century. He was most
directly affected by the harsh economic and social conditions produced by the industrial revolution and governments and employers
unsympathetic to his plight. His lot differed little from country to
country. He was poorly paid, worked long hours in dangerous
surroundings at a hectic pace, lived in unsanitary, cramped housing,
spent up to 60 percent of income on food (much of it starch), had
poor health, and little recreation. His status in society was low; his
human dignity unrecognized by those above him.

As one observer of factory life in Saxony noted:

> Think for a moment what it is to spend the week, day after
> day, in the monotonous routine of the ugly factory, often at
> uninteresting work, in dirt and sweat, no comfortable resting-
> place at the noon hour, no resource at evening save the street
> before the door, the court-yard of the lodging-house or its
> small and crowded living-room with noise of children and
> smell of cookery; to spend the nights in wretched sleeping-
> quarters; to earn no more than enough for all daily needs; to be
> without oversight, without control, without parental care and
> love . . . [1]

No wonder then that most class-conscious, skilled workers in Europe gravitated toward the political Left, in many countries consisting of the trinity of a socialist party, a socialist union federation, and a consumers' cooperative. In the first decades, the main vehicle of the workers on the Continent was the socialist part whose long-range aim was the radical transformation of society and the political system. The party opposed the feudal class order and the conservative elites, and stood for universal suffrage, public education, and equal opportunities in the social and cultural fields.

An increasing number of workers supported unions to achieve their economic objectives. Overshadowed in the formative years by the socialist parties, the unions became more powerful as industrialization proceeded and soon their leaders challenged the supremacy of the socialist parties.

The European union movements faced common problems: economic crises, lack of financial support for workers in times of need, and the hostility of governments, courts, and employers. But their internal makeup and political profile differed in membership recruitment, militancy of workers, organizational structure, ideology, and attitude toward the state.[2] Although diversity existed, a numerical and a developmental pattern emerged, each consisting of two types. In the first pattern, a single central socialist trade union federation was created, which either flourished without serious competition, as in Great Britain and Scandinavia; or had to compete with federations based on other political, religious, and ideological foundations, as in most Continental countries.

In the second pattern, in those Continental countries with a strong Marxist influence, socialist parties surfaced first and then created the central union federations, mainly because the party leaders wanted to create unions as a revolutionary weapon. Conversely, in Great Britain the unions emerged first and then spawned the Labour Party to gain a power base in Parliament.

But regardless of pattern, the Left in most countries, including Germany, did not have the political punch to match that of the business elite in the period before World War I. An elitist model of a strongly entrenched and interlocking conservative governing and business group prevailed rather than a pluralist model of well-balanced interest groups seeking to gain their objectives under the benevolent patronage of a neutral government. We must turn now to

[18]

an analysis of the German socialist labor movement during two time segments: the formative period to World War I, and the consolidation period during the war.

GERMAN UNIONS: FROM BIRTH TO 1914

German unionism started late because of the preindustrial socioeconomic pattern of the early nineteenth century in which four-fifths of the population was engaged in agriculture. In the small nonagricultural sector, artisans, craftsmen and journeymen had long been organized in guilds for self-protection and the provision of social insurance for their members. In the 1830s, when a small industrial base for unionization was visible, workers' educational associations were founded to substitute for unions that could not be formed legally. But industrialization lagged for two more decades because of capital losses from wars, pillage, and levies; British and French competition in the textile, iron, and mining industries; and the inexperience of the new German entrepreneurs, many of whom were former craftsmen.

By 1850, however, the preconditions for unionization were ripe as a result of the rapid population increase to 35.4 million, railroad and industrial plant construction, expansion of trade, and emergence of a nascent industrial labor force of 1 million workers whose working conditions were as harsh as those in Great Britain and France where industrialization had begun much earlier.[3] Although German industry still was in its infancy then, and did not expand significantly until after 1871, that made little difference to the worker on the job for thirteen to fourteen hours a day with inadequate provisions against sickness, accident, and the insecurity of old age.

The Socialist Unions

In 1848, a German revolution failed. Yet that year trade unions emerged. A printer, Stephan Born, who had met Karl Marx and Friedrich Engels in Paris, founded the first national workers' organization, which soon enrolled 12,000 members.[4] But the movement was doomed two years later when several state governments passed anticoalition laws, and when most workers were not yet willing to strike against their bosses, saw no advantage in unionization, or were unable to shed the ideologies of the dominant culture.

Thus, socialist leaders (Ferdinand Lassalle, August Bebel, and Wilhelm Liebknecht, among others) embarked on a strategy to raise the political and class consciousness of the workers. This was a difficult task. Apathetic and resigned to their lot, workers had been socialized at home, in schools, and at church to believe in traditional conservative values. To gain a foothold among them, the leaders emphasized the political rather than the economic struggle against an authoritarian monarchy among the most reactionary and backward on the continent. With an accent on the class struggle, they sought social and political equality for the workers. But isolated in a political subculture, they faced a bitter struggle to gain any of their goals.

Not until 1875, after decades of struggle and rivalries between competing political movements, did they succeed in founding the Socialist Workers' Party of Germany (later renamed the Social Democratic Party, SPD). By then the party was willing to build up a union movement as long as it could control the movement. The party shored up the weak local unions existing since the 1850s. It sought to establish a central union federation, but economic crises and police harassment frustrated that plan. Instead rival unions coalesced at the local level only to be faced with a new crisis. In 1878, Chancellor Bismarck, afraid of its increasing power and rapid growth, outlawed the party. Although he promised to spare the unions, the Prussian High Court declared them to be political organizations. As a result, the police moved against all unions under the slightest suspicion of an association with the party.[5]

With the expiration of the antisocialist legislation in 1890, the party and unions were free to organize again. By then industrialization had grown swiftly. In a few decades Germany had changed from an agricultural to a powerful industrial nation outdistancing its competitors on the Continent. Coal, iron and steel, textile, and chemical industries became the base for expansion of the railroad system, merchant fleet, armaments industry, and foreign trade. Financial and banking organizations gained more power. Such radical changes in the economy were bound to produce changes in the labor force. An exodus from the rural to the urban sector took place. The pace of industrialization finally produced a labor force that was later increasingly willing to join the socialist and union movements.

In 1890 the socialist national unions (Zentralverbände) created the first major central federation, the General Commission of German Trade Unions (Generalkommission der Gewerkschaften Deutschlands), with headquarters in Hamburg. The General Commission aimed to win government and employer recognition of the right of unions to organize workers, to stop government harassment of unions by labeling them political organizations, and to gather statistics and issue information bulletins on union developments in Germany for the labor movement.

The founders set up a powerful seven-member national executive committee, which centralized decision making to the point at which most union statutes specified that the committee could veto elections to branch executives.[6] The executives of the affiliated unions (Konferenz der Vorstandsvertreter) met periodically to share in decision making. Carl Legien (born in 1861), then head of the Lathe Workers Union, became president of the General Commission. A pragmatist at heart, the somber young man also became an SPD deputy in the Reichstag (Lower House of Parliament) in order to represent union interests directly in the legislature.

In a move typical of interest groups anywhere, the General Commission emphasized the need to build a strong organization as a way of gaining access to government leaders. Legien noted at the 1896 SPD convention, "In our society, everything is a matter of naked force. The power of the workers lies in their organization. If they strengthen their organization, they increase their power."[7] Political parties adopted as a model the impressive organizational structure of the General Commission, including the use of full-time paid officials.

The General Commission received support from its affiliated unions in the mining, metal, textiles, lumber and construction, paper, leather, and clothing industries. The unions, representing a mixture of skilled craft and industrial workers employed in small and medium-sized plants, emphasized membership recruitment rather than strikes. In early 1890, the General Commission membership stood at about 250,000, a small fraction of the total labor force.[8] The low membership may be explained by the country's late industrialization, Bismarck's antisocialist laws, the uncertainty concerning the legal right to organize, and workers' continuing resistance to unionization. As a consequence, power remained in the hands of the authoritarian state and the employer community, by then well organized in associations.

In 1892, at the first General Commission Congress in

Halberstadt, delegates adopted resolutions proclaiming the unions' independence from parties, political neutrality, and readiness to admit members regardless of political or religious conviction. The resolutions were passed for tactical reasons to avoid repressive government action against the unions for engaging in illegal partisan politics, and to gain equality with the SPD. The unions did not hide their socialist sympathies, but were eager to establish a "two-pillar" relationship with the SPD in which the party would strive to achieve the political and the General Commission the economic base of socialism.

SPD leader August Bebel, backed by Ignaz Auer and other party chiefs, opposed union aspirations. Bebel admitted the usefulness of the unions' membership recruitment function for the party, but he did not consider them as independent carriers of socialism. He urged the trade unionists to become party members, demanded their active participation in politics, and assailed those labor leaders who insisted that the union movement have primacy over the political movement.[9] In fact, he feared that the unionists would neglect the revolutionary struggle, attempt to free themselves from the party, and concentrate instead on bread-and-butter problems.

The power struggle waged by party and union leaders reflected in part the generation gap between older party leaders who clung faithfully to Marxist theory and younger union leaders who in their pragmatic orientation were more influenced by the day-to-day problems of the workers. The struggle, which provoked bitter feelings, revolved around the observance of May Day and the use of the general strike as a political weapon. SPD leaders took a positive position and the union leaders a negative one on both issues, but after years of discussion arrived at relatively satisfactory compromises.[10]

Signs of a rapprochement between the two organizations were visible around the turn of the century. At the 1899 General Commission Congress, Legien reminded his audience that the majority of union members were also party members, that several union leaders were members of the SPD Reichstag Fraktion (Group), and that the two organizations had parallel aims.[11] By 1906 union membership had increased meteorically to almost two million, rapidly approaching the British Trades Union Congress membership. At last, the members had realized that their dreams of a better life—higher wages and better working conditions as a minimum—could be fulfilled only if they became part of an organized movement pitted against one of the most powerful industrial elites in Europe.

The SPD was aware of the unions' mounting strength, especially since its vote had risen correspondingly.[12] Hence Legien's strategy of maintaining an independent stance to prevent the union movement from becoming an appendage of the party paid off, although he knew that the unions needed the SPD if they were to achieve legislative objectives. The stage was set, after several joint meetings, for the proclamation of the historic Mannheim Agreement at the 1906 SPD Convention. The SPD recognized the General Commission as an equal partner, expressed willingness to cooperate rather than seek to control it, and to arrive at joint decisions on issues affecting both. The SPD and the General Commission concurred in the "two-pillar" doctrine to promote common political and economic aims, such as democratization of the state, reforms in the Prussian franchise, the furtherance of collective agreements, and the lifting of the prohibition on strikes.[13]

The Mannheim Agreement did more than produce equality between the erstwhile feuding partners: it tipped the balance toward the unions in the new power relationship. In effect, it signified union control or veto over those SPD decisions in which the unions had a stake. Rosa Luxemburg (a leader of the SPD radical wing) noted that the new relationship of parity was comparable to the arrangement by which a peasant woman sought to regulate her life with her spouse, "On matters of question between us, when we agree, you will decide; when we disagree, I shall decide."[14]

The agreement also strengthened the linkage between the two organizations. More party members joined the unions, rose in union ranks as functionaries, and spread the socialist gospel.[15] As a result, a powerful socialist or working subculture emerged. The life of the workers revolved around the ancillary organizations set up by party and union ranging from youth groups to mandolin and sports clubs. The workers' secular activities and their faith in a socialist utopia substituted for their lost religious faith. Their immersion in union and party work gave them a sense of satisfaction missing in their daily routine. As one miner aptly put it, "The modern labour movement enchants me and all my friends by its ever brighter beam of knowledge. We realize that we are no longer the anvil, but rather the hammer forging the future of our children. This feeling is worth more than riches."[16]

During this time the lot of the workers improved as a result of gains made by the pragmatic and politically conservative union leaders who, in acquiring more influence within the SPD, strengthened the revisionist or right wing of the party. The revisionists, led by Eduard Bernstein, argued that Marxist theories had to be revised because the pauperization of the workers and the collapse of the capitalist system could not be expected. Therefore socialism would have to be achieved by evolutionary means, transforming the capitalist system stage by stage. Bernstein praised the dynamic union movement which fulfilled vital social tasks, set in motion a reaction against exploitative capital, and served as an important instrument to achieve socialism.

Although in sympathy with the revisionist forces, the majority of union leaders remained neutral in order to gain support from all party wings and not to exacerbate the already serious ideological intraparty schism. This schism pitted the revisionists against the centrist majority wing (led by Karl Kautsky), and against the radicals (led by Luxemburg and Karl Liebknecht). The latter were hostile to the unions for dimming the chance of an early revolution through their adaptation to the capitalist system and their "betrayal" of the class struggle. The centrists were critical of the unions' emphasis on the nonideological, pragmatic economic struggle. However, the outbreak of World War I soon eclipsed the limited warfare of unions and party wings.

In summary, the development of the socialist unions up to World War I reveals their steadily growing power and influence upon the SPD. The period up to 1906 was marked at first by party dominance over the unions and by interorganizational cleavages, followed by the union struggle for equality with the party, a goal finally attained in 1906. Thereafter the unions dominated the SPD, which could no longer counter their objectives. Curiously, what emerged in this tug-of-war was what union leaders had wanted all along—a party, becoming revisionist and evolutionary, which would defend their rights in the Reichstag and support their legislative goals. Hence the leaders de-emphasized strikes as economic weapons and stressed instead their organization's readiness to become politically involved. But they could score only limited improvement in the standard of living of the workers in face of an entrenched business-government elite. The pluralist theory of countervailing groups making claims on a neutral government did not apply to Imperial Germany.

As an extension of its involvement at the national level, the General Commission also devoted time and resources to international matters. Its representatives were delegates to the congresses of the Socialist International (the Second International), founded in 1889, which in its first years also represented the national trade union centers. But the union drive for a separate identity grew swiftly. As organized labor gathered momentum in the 1880s and 1890s in several countries, national craft and industrial unions, beginning with the typographical and mine workers' unions, formed international trade secretariats encompassing unions from the same craft or trade. By the turn of the century twenty-eight existed. Reflecting the power and organizational know-how of German unions, twenty-four had headquarters in Germany and were chaired by German labor leaders. They were established to exchange information on labor conditions in their countries, to help journeymen crossing borders to find jobs, and to halt international strikebreaking activities by employers.[17]

The creation of a trade union international was the next logical step, but it was delayed because of General Commission objections. Legien was wary of such an ambitious plan given the weakness of many national union centers and their clashing views on the eight-hour day, the general strike, antimilitarism, and ideological questions, which might wreck the International at its birth. But in 1901, after pressures from other leaders, he offered to support the creation of the International Secretariat of Trade Union Centers. One year later it was set up with headquarters in Berlin; Legien was elected secretary-general. The secretariat became primarily a center gathering statistics from the affiliated national federations, which before World War I claimed 7 million members in nineteen countries, with the German the numerically strongest, followed by British, French, and Italian federations.[18] Congresses were held every two years from 1903 to 1913. Legien's continued opposition to their discussing ideology and politics meant that the Socialist International congresses handled such issues.

After Samuel Gompers visited Europe in 1909, the American Federation of Labor (AFL) joined the International Secretariat, which was renamed in 1913, at his urging, the International Federation of Trade Unions (IFTU). With the exception of the AFL, all member federations were socialist and based in Central and Western Europe. Gompers had joined his European brethren in the hope of their ideological conversion, but the possibility seemed remote even though they were beginning to shed their radical dogma. The IFTU adopted a constitution, opened headquarters in Berlin, and elected Legien as chairman, but German hospitality was short-lived as World War I soon rent the international organizations, and the IFTU relocated in Amsterdam.

The Non-Socialist Unions

While the German socialist unions moved to center stage of the national and international labor movements before World War I, two rival German union movements emerged from the wings. Like those in other Continental countries, German workers, split along ideological and religious lines, could not be organized into a single labor federation. This schism reflected the historic fragmentation of the German polity, and weakened the role of labor within the political and economic spheres.

The Christian trade union movement was the principal rival of the socialist unions. By 1868, a number of local Christian workers' groups were formed, although the movement did not gain momentum until the 1890s. The Christian unions were founded by clerical and intellectual members of the Catholic-oriented Center Party. They based their appeal on the Pope's 1891 encyclical "Rerum Novarum" (on the condition of the working classes), expressed their concern with the economic and social problems of the workers, and called for the peaceful resolution of labor-management disputes. The conservative Catholic hierarchy, still imbued with preindustrial and antistrike attitudes, but influenced by the social concerns of Bishop Wilhelm Emanuel von Ketteler, gave its reluctant blessing because it was especially worried that the workers would be weaned away from the Church and into the camp of the "intolerant free-thinkers" in the SPD.

Within the unions, tensions developed between the conservative and the liberal wings. The conservatives wanted unions restricted to Catholics and tied closely to the Church and the Center Party. The liberals wanted them to become more independent and to explore the feasibility of amalgamation with the socialist unions should the latter be willing to cut their ties to the SPD. The conservatives received the support of the German Catholic hierarchy and of the Pope who in 1912 issued a new encyclical "Singulari quadam" emphasizing the religious nature of social questions and giving moral support to Catholic workers' associations rather than to interconfessional Catholic-Protestant trade unions.[19]

The year 1868 also marked the establishment of a nonsocialist liberal union federation founded by social reformer Max Hirsch and publisher Franz Duncker. Impressed by a first-hand look at British trade unions, Hirsch, with Duncker's help, drafted a master statute for this nonideological German federation in which power rested with the local unions. The federation reflected the British Manchester type of liberalism, and was meant to serve as a harmonious link between the interests of capital and labor, producers and consumers. It opposed strikes, urging arbitration to resolve labor disputes. It also rejected state aid for the workers because it wanted to help its own members in times of need. But when the Bismarck government launched a social welfare program, the ground was cut from under the Hirsch-Duncker federation.

In the 1890s an insurgent wing surfaced, de-emphasizing liberalism and instead stressing government obligations to workers in the social and economic spheres. After the death of Hirsch in 1905, this wing triumphed, but was still unable to mobilize the majority of the manual workers whose socialist views remained firm. Its strength, no more than 100,000 members in the early 1900s, lay rather among the growing number of salaried employees whose hostility to the bosses was less marked than that of the workers. The federation did engage in some political action by allying itself with the Progressive Party and putting up candidates for the Reichstag.

Thus, as war clouds loomed on the European horizon, German organized labor was dominated by three rival federations (socialist, Christian, and liberal), vying for support among the same social strata, but with the socialist unions still numerically on top. By then an organizational merger was but a distant dream.

WORLD WAR I

The imminent outbreak of war in 1914 was a crucial test for the European socialist parties and unions. In late July it could not be predicted with certainty whether they would be strong enough to prevent hostilities or to refrain from supporting their nation once war erupted. Although Socialist International members, including the SPD, had taken an antiwar position at a number of congresses from 1907 to 1914, the international bonds between them were too fragile to overcome strong nationalist feelings surfacing everywhere in Europe in the wake of the Sarajevo incident.

In this volatile situation, the position of the General Commission became critical. Would it call a general strike anticipatory to any war declaration by the German government? Or would it support its government? A few days before the outbreak of the war, the General Commission was swamped with telegrams from other European and United States labor federations urging it to do its part to prevent hostilities. It responded negatively to these appeals. Legien justified his support for the war by blaming the imperialist policies of the allied governments, pointing out the weakness of the international proletariat, and citing the threat of the immediate dissolution of his organization should it fail to support the war. But equally important were his fear that a Czarist victory over Germany would lead to the crushing of the unions, and his emergent nationalist feelings. ("We claim the same right for us as other nations naturally view as theirs, the right to support one's own country.")[20]

As a result of Germany's declaration of war on Russia on August 1, the union leaders resolved not only to support the war, but also to end all strikes, desist from further wage demands, and aid government efforts to relieve the high unemployment.[21] The SPD position was more ambivalent. When party leaders failed to agree on whether or not to support war credits in a pending Reichstag vote, union leaders convinced their wavering colleagues in the SPD Fraktion to sustain the prowar union position in the crucial Reichstag session of August 4.[22] On that day, the entire Fraktion, maintaining party discipline, voted for war credits. Thus the vote partly reflected union pressure on the SPD. No wonder that Legien, who headed the union bloc in the SPD Fraktion, boldly contended on the basis of this and other votes that the SPD was "the agency of the political interests of the trade unions."[23]

Patriotism and jingoism sprouted among unionists. The leaders assailed demonstrations, protest strikes, and other opposition efforts against the war that were soon beginning to crop up. The union press unstintingly lauded the nation's military victories. As a consequence, the unions gained national prestige and legal status, a psychological boost after having been attacked so long by Establishment forces. In June 1916, the ever present threat of being tagged as a political association ended when the Reichstag passed a supplementary section to the Law on Associations declaring unions to be nonpolitical bodies. In December 1916, the unions gained further benefits with the passage of an Auxiliary Service Law. It provided for joint employer-employee boards and workers' shop representation, but also mobilized all workers from 17 to 60 years of age, assigned them jobs, and deprived them of any opportunity to change employment. It left workers embittered by taking away their freedom while failing to impose similar burdens upon the upper classes. Nevertheless, the unions reluctantly agreed to the law because its rejection might have meant military control of all industries.[24]

Although the national stature of the General Commission was enhanced during this period, it still had no decisive policy-making voice at the governmental level. True, public officials, in order to maintain union support for the war, engaged in discussions with the unions, visited their headquarters, and gave labor leaders minor positions in the government, but did not call one labor leader into a key administrative position. The unions had only limited influence within the conservative Army General Staff and regional defense posts.

Many workers and middle-level union leaders were dissatisfied with the General Commission's support of government policy. They coalesced with a few prominent socialist leaders to form the nucleus of a dissident group within the SPD, and in 1915 issued a manifesto condemning the party and the General Commission for their prowar stance.[25]

The schism mirrored different ideological perceptions of the role labor organizations should play in this critical period. A reconciliation seemed impossible between the dissident leaders who wanted to radicalize the workers as a prelude to an overthrow of the system, and the conservative leaders who viewed the dissidents as targets for government repression which would be followed by a threat to their own organization. The conservatives waged a strong campaign against the dissidents. Legien was one of the first to demand that the SPD expel Liebknecht and other SPD deputies who had committed a breach of party discipline by their refusal from December 1914 on to vote for war credits. Legien also requested union officials to be more active in the SPD in order to weaken the radical opposition.[26]

In January 1917, the SPD Board, supported by its union members, voted to oust the dissident bloc from the party. In April, the bloc constituted itself into the Independent Social Democratic Party, USPD (Unabhängige Sozialdemokratische Partei Deutschlands). Not unexpectedly, the majority of General Commission leaders maintained their support of the SPD and easily defeated a resolution introduced by the left wing at a general union conference in July calling on the General Commission "to cooperate in all political matters with both Social Democratic parties."[27] The General Commission leaders were able to maintain organizational unity, not because they were more tolerant toward their own opposition than was the SPD, but because they did not have to participate directly in national politics and to make important decisions in the Reichstag.

As workers' dissatisfaction mounted, however, the left-wing opposition in the General Commission became more important. It was composed of union locals in such major cities as Berlin, Leipzig, and Munich, and groups in the powerful Metal and Textile Workers Unions, whose ranks were swollen by workers in defense industries.[28] Among the groups were the Revolutionary Shop Stewards who represented class-conscious skilled craftsmen in the Berlin metal trade. Long active in the union movement, they became increasingly disenchanted with the General Commission leadership. Joined by the USPD, the left-wing opposition endorsed the large-scale strikes of 1917 and 1918 directed against the government's war policy. Although many strikes were caused primarily by insufficient food for the workers, the work stoppages became political in some cities. The strikers called for immediate peace negotiations, workers' representation at the peace table, and democratic reforms by the government.[29]

They did not receive any support from the hard-line General Commission, which assumed no responsibility for the strikes, especially when not notified that they would be called. On the occasion of the 1917 strike, the General Commission leaders sent an urgent warning to lower-level officials, "Germany is not Russia. The revolutionary games of the Independents (USPD) and the Spartacists (radicals) endanger the German labor movement, especially our union organization and the defensive strength of the country."[30]

The General Commission chiefs took a no less conservative stance on the twin issues of war and peace. When Gompers wired Legien in February 1917, "Can't you put pressure on the German government that a break with the United States and thereby a general conflict be avoided?," Legien responded that the German working class was opposed to an extension of the war, but that his intervention would be successful only if the United States could stop Great Britain and the other Allies from continuing their "war of famine" against Germany.[31]

In May 1918, the General Commission Executive passed a resolution denouncing Allied peace proposals as an "imperialistic peace by force," in which 70 million people will become "helots and slaves" of the Allies. Asserting that an Anglo-French victory followed by a dishonorable peace must be prevented, it chose to continue resistance.[32] It also participated in the founding of the League for Freedom and Fatherland, an organization supporting the war but mildly critical of government colonial policies.

The General Commission maintained a consistent attitude toward the nation's war policy, but became more critical of the government's failure to initiate domestic political reforms. It endorsed the SPD's unsuccessful effort for the dissolution of the Prussian diet and for electoral reforms in Prussia designed to grant greater equality to workers. In September 1918, Legien informed Chancellor Count von Hertling of the workers' dissatisfaction with the government's failure to decide on the electoral reform question. The Chancellor promised such reforms, but none were enacted to stem the revolutionary tide threatening Germany.

In conclusion, the war was a transitional phase in the history of German trade unionism. Repressed in the early Imperial years, the unions gradually rose to a respectable "Establishment" position during the war. Their crucial decision to sustain the government's war effort was made largely to preserve their organization, created painfully over the decades. Their support of the revisionist wing in the SPD was proof of their willingness to work for moderate reforms within the capitalist system; their opposition to the USPD demonstrated their distaste for revolutionary upheavals and experimentation. Their attitudes toward the government and the political parties were conditioned by pragmatic considerations, to the dismay of a minority within and outside the labor movement.

II

THE WEIMAR ERA

THE INIMICAL POLITICAL surroundings of the Imperial era notwithstanding, the socialist unions had grown strong and gained economically. Yet their natural expectation of still greater gains in the
democratic atmosphere of the Weimar Republic proved too optimistic—as their own destiny paralleled the political and economic
course of successive governments. During the stable period from
1924 through 1929 they fared relatively well, their political activity
confined to supporting the SPD and to fostering favorable economic
legislation.

In the unsettled years from 1918 through 1923 and 1929 through
1933, however, not only their economic progress but their very
continuance was imperiled. Their leaders, now on the defensive,
tried to affect those political events immediately bearing on the
fortunes of the union movement. Their maximum attention was
concentrated on domestic policy, but they could not neglect foreign
policies of concern to them. An investigation of the socialist unions'
cyclical involvement in German politics should help us evaluate more
accurately the depth of their impact on national history. In this
chapter, we deal primarily with major developments in the first
unsettled period from 1918 to 1923, emphasizing the role unions
played during the Revolution of 1918-1919, the Kapp Putsch of 1920,
the political turmoil from 1921 to 1923, and the Ruhr occupation of
1923. We also note briefly the birth of the ADGB in 1919, and its

[32]

position on the Versailles Treaty and the 1926 Hohenzollern referendum.

REVOLUTION

The end of World War I and the November 1918 Revolution marked the first stage of political instability and union involvement. It gave labor leaders new opportunities, but caught them by surprise. Their plans for the postwar era were not ready; the future held too many uncertainties. Faced by a leftist movement seeking political power, General Commission leaders desperately tried behind the scenes to stop the creation of an ideologically and pragmatically unacceptable radical system. When the movement could not be stopped they wanted to divert it onto the least radical path in order to remain viable and to achieve their goals in the social and economic spheres blocked too long in the prewar era by conservative governments and unresponsive employers.

In the last days of the monarchy, General Commission leaders took part in political discussions between military and civilian chiefs. To the union leaders, it was immaterial whether Germany would remain a monarchy or become a republic if only a democratic form of government with labor participation were established. Specifically, they demanded the creation of a parliamentary regime headed by a regent who would govern until the eldest son of the Crown Prince became of age, the establishment of a constitutional court, and civilian control over the Army.[1] In the meantime, radical shop stewards in the Berlin branch of the Metal Workers Union, who had formed the spearhead of a revolutionary organization under the leadership of Richard Müller, planned an uprising for November 11. Most of the Revolutionary Shop Stewards and their union followers were left-wing USPD adherents; the others were Spartacists (the forerunners of the Communists). During the fevered revolutionary days these trade unionists had an influence within the radical parties disproportionate to their numbers.

Their plan for an uprising became obsolete when a naval revolt broke out in Kiel on November 3 and spread rapidly to other cities fanned by mounting military and civilian dissatisfaction with the old order. On November 6, General Ludendorff's successor, General

Groener, consulted SPD and union leaders, with whom he had been on friendly terms for more than a year, about plans to reorganize the tottering Imperial government. SPD chief Friedrich Ebert and Legien, with somewhat changed attitudes, urged Groener to convince the Kaiser that abdication was necessary to prevent more bloodshed. Groener rejected this attitude, arguing that he could not deprive the army of its commander-in-chief.[2] Thereupon the SPD, but not the General Commission, threatened a general strike unless the Kaiser abdicated by November 9.

The General Commission still hoped that a government reorganization would suffice to prevent a revolution. Afraid of a radical workers' uprising, union agents circulated proclamations in Berlin on November 8 instructing workers to remain at work. But the workers, influenced by the Revolutionary Shop Stewards, the USPD, and the Spartacists, stayed away from their jobs the following day and called for the establishment of a republic. As a consequence, the SPD asked its members to join the strike. In the afternoon the SPD Executive and a newly-formed Workers' and Soldiers' Council issued a flysheet (significantly not signed by the General Commission) proclaiming the abdication of the Kaiser and nomination of Ebert as provisional Chancellor.[3]

The General Commission, not very reluctantly, avoided political action at the explicit wish of the SPD leadership, but was assured of participation in economic policy decisions. While claiming to regret its subordinate political role, it asked the SPD to use the advice and experience of unionists, and began to press the Council of People's Representatives (the new SPD-USPD provisional government) for immediate social reforms. The Council, in sympathy, issued decrees fulfilling virtually all the union demands, such as the reinstatement of social insurance laws and the introduction of the eight-hour day.[4]

The General Commission and the other labor federations won additional demands sought for decades by their leaders as they negotiated privately with top employers during and immediately after the war. In the winter of 1917-1918, at the behest of Walther Rathenau, then a leader in the electrical industry, several employers from the electrical and chemical industries met informally with labor leaders to discuss general problems, including war aims. The bosses in the coal, steel, and iron industries were at the time opposed to any links with the unions, but by October 1918 they knew that the increasingly incompetent government would not be able to win the war. They were willing to form an alliance with the strong unions as a way of preserving the capitalist system. In a series of secret meetings in October and early November, interrupted only briefly by the Revolution, labor leaders Legien, Alexander Schlicke, Theodor Leipart, Robert Schmidt, and Gustav Bauer met with steel magnate Hugo Stinnes and other industrialists. Initially both sides discussed only demobilization and measures for the transition to a peacetime economy, but once the Revolution erupted the employers were ready to make major concessions to the unions which they viewed as a bulwark against the threat of anarchy, bolshevism, and the social-ization of industry, and because they wanted to keep state interven-tion to a minimum. The labor leaders were willing to sign an agreement with the employers not only because they would make substantive gains but also because they too were frightened by the revolutionary political situation and feared a collapse of their own organization as well as an economic breakdown unless employers helped to shore up the economy.

On November 15, 1918, both sides signed the "Stinnes-Legien Agreement," viewed by the General Commission as a Magna Carta for labor intended to produce a harmonious relationship between the erstwhile adversaries. Employers pledged to recognize the unions; conclude collective agreements with them on wages and working conditions; disband "yellow" company unions; stop discrimination against union members; recognize an eight-hour day subject to its introduction in the major industrial nations; and establish jointly managed employment exchanges, arbitration agencies, and shop committees in plants employing more than fifty workers. On Decem-ber 4, the Central Joint Labor Council (Zentralarbeitsgemeinschaft), having equal representation of management and labor, was created. It consisted of two central committees at the national level and, eventually, joint councils for each industry and region. The councils were to discuss demobilization and other common problems, and advise the government on economic and social legislation.[5]

The union leaders' signature to this agreement demonstrated their intention to work within the existing but shaken capitalist system and their opposition to its revolutionary transformation. Their action was bound to cause dissension among workers when millions favored the socialization of industry rather than collaboration with it. In later months, the General Commission-affiliated Metal Workers Union (by then left-controlled), the USPD, and the Spartacists began to campaign against the councils and assailed the General Commission for failing to support the workers' revolutionary aspirations and the class struggle. They were critical of Legien's class collaboration policy and his willingness to let the industrial elite once again assume political power and influence in the nation. In reply, Legien argued that it was only an extension of earlier union policy to negotiate with employers for the improvement of conditions for the workers.[6] Dissatisfied with the General Commission position, the Metal Workers Union withdrew in October 1919 from the Central Joint Labor Council. Thereafter, dissatisfaction rose in other unions: by 1922 six of them withdrew, and by 1924 the two socialist federations officially ended their association with the Council.

Thus the policy of official collaboration between the economic associations lasted only five years (1919-1924), a period in which collaboration increasingly turned to collision. Why this shift? The employers who had regained their prewar strength were openly hostile to labor and unwilling to introduce the eight-hour day in their industries. Inflation had produced a lag in wages and salaries and a mounting increase in workers' dissatisfaction. Large numbers of workers who had joined the unions after the war also were disillusioned with their leaders' collaboration with employers and acceptance of a bourgeois-dominated state—in protest, they quit the union movement. Finally, the Central Joint Labor Council had been robbed of its outstanding labor spokesman on Legien's death in 1920 and of its functions when the government established works councils and a national economic council, and intervened in industrial relations.[7]

During the November 1918 uprising, socialist and Left forces had spontaneously formed workers' and soldiers' councils, patterned on the soviets. The General Commission could not stand idly by when the councils assumed governing powers over the nation and fired the imagination of millions of radicalized workers. Although a majority of councils were soon under SPD control, a minority remained in the hands of the USPD and the Spartacists. To ensure that not all councils would be dominated by the radicals, the General Commission reluctantly asked its functionaries to place themselves at the disposal of the councils, and called on its district chapters to participate more in the "revolutionary" activities of the people.[8] The General Commission was afraid that Spartacist-controlled councils would eliminate the unions, that the Revolutionary Shop Stewards would capture the unions from within, and that the syndicalists would replace the unions with decentralized councils at the shop level. The General Commission even discussed moving its headquarters away from turbulent Berlin to a safer city.[9]

When the councils assumed not only political but also economic functions, the General Commission warned them to restrict their activities to politics and to let the unions function freely in the economic sphere in order to maintain production and order in the shops.[10] In late 1918 a majority of SPD officials began to have doubts about the continuing political role of the potentially revolutionary councils since the councils' major support as a permanent institution came from the Spartacists and the USPD. They demanded that a democratic parliamentary government replace the councils. Success came in early February 1919 when the provisional council governments abdicated in favor of a National Assembly responsible for drafting a new constitution. Legien thanked the councils for having "saved Germany from a bloodbath," but he made sure that unionists would participate in large numbers in the election of representatives to the National Assembly convened in the city of Weimar.[11]

As the political role of the councils came to an end union leaders could take credit for helping to quell a potentially radical transformation of the political and economic system, for subsequently shoring up the new parliamentary government, and for ensuring a transformation of the councils into works councils with purely economic functions. But they still had to gain the workers' support for the new political system.

Officially, the General Commission leaders opposed or did not endorse the January, February, and March 1919 political strikes organized primarily by the Revolutionary Shop Stewards, the Communists, and the Independent Socialists. The Left parties were protesting the use of the Reichswehr against demonstrating workers. They were also seeking to oust the SPD-led government, and install a workers' government instead. In some cities, radical workers turned against free union leaders for their wartime collaboration with the government and the signing of the November Agreement. In Hamburg, angry workers repeatedly occupied trade union headquarters, expelled union officials, and closed the treasury.[12] The union leaders maintained their support of the SPD-led government, intent on transforming the former Marxist movement into a socialist reformist movement within a parliamentary democracy.

The new political system which took form at Weimar (described in chapter VII) reflected the views of the three major parties—the SPD, the German Democratic Party, and the Center Party (Catholic)—and a number of minor parties represented in the National Assembly. The Reichstag (Lower House) was empowered to approve and dismiss the chancellor and the cabinet ministers, who were to be the policy makers. The president nominated the chancellor, could dissolve the Reichstag, and could rule by emergency decree. Hence the chancellor and the cabinet were dependent on both the president and the Reichstag for maintaining themselves in power. In such a situation, the chancellor was exceptional who could govern for a long period, especially when faced with a shifting array of political parties in the legislature. The result was a series of cabinet turnovers and political instability.

The multiplicity of parties and splinter groups affected the labor movement. In 1919, the SPD-USPD rivalry damaged the unions. SPD functionaries and workers were ousted from USPD-controlled unions and vice versa. When the union wing favorable to the USPD gained strength because of its radical views and workers' dissatisfaction with political and economic conditions, the conservative labor chiefs knew they could no longer openly retain their alliance with the SPD. They would have to become politically neutral if they expected to preserve the unity of their organization. This was made evident to them at the 1919 Nuremberg Congress where a strong minority opposition (then representing the peak of radical influence within the union movement) was able to muster nearly 30 percent on a resolution rejecting the General Commission's policy of wartime collaboration with the SPD.[13] As a result, the labor leaders backed a declaration of neutrality in party politics, supplanting the Mannheim Agreement of 1906. Their bonds to the SPD were loosened.

In retrospect, the conservative and cautious views of most union leaders were reflected in their activities during the critical Weimar formative years when they tried to suppress radical upheavals by first endorsing a constitutional monarchy, then concluding an accord with employers, and subsequently choosing a parliamentary rather than a council system. They were more concerned with maintaining order and discipline among the working class and making immediate gains than with broad plans for the fundamental democratization of the state. They rejected any plan to alter a system which left powerful archconservative industrial, army, police, judicial, and bureaucratic forces intact. In effect, by not supporting political strikes or pressing for socialization, they helped entrench the increasingly bourgeois order.

THE BIRTH OF THE ADGB

The trend toward conservatism notwithstanding, the government granted the labor movement more freedom than it had ever enjoyed during the Imperial era. New tasks, opportunities and challenges, and a rapid rise in union strength caused the labor leaders in 1919 to decide to reorganize the General Commission. At the tenth Congress in Nuremberg (June 30-July 5), they formed the General Federation of German Trade Unions (ADGB).[14] The change in name reflected a need for structural reforms to allow greater centralization of power in order to coordinate the activities of the national unions, to influence the ever-expanding sphere of economic and social legislation, and to monitor government regulation of the labor sector.

A commission headed by Theodor Leipart, then head of the Wood Workers Union and future ADGB president, drafted a statute containing the principle of centralization and the organization's goals—to disseminate information to members and outsiders, collect statistical and other data pertaining to economic and social questions, publish a weekly journal and pamphlets, preserve and expand protective legislation for workers, establish workers' secretariats, schedule educational programs and elections for workers' representatives, prevent jurisdictional conflicts among union affiliates, support union struggles, and promote links to labor in other countries.[15] In later chapters the extent of the ADGB's achievement of these goals will be seen, but the long list indicated the multiple tasks confronting the unions then compared to before, under the Empire.

INTERNATIONAL DEVELOPMENTS

The ADGB had little time to consolidate its organization before it became involved in dramatic domestic and international developments. It participated once again in the activities of the reconstituted

International Federation of Trade Unions, but because of the effects of the war no longer could expect to be the leading force. The IFTU headquarters remained in Amsterdam, rather than being moved back to Berlin where it had originally been located. A British labor leader replaced Legien as president: indeed, no German labor leader received any policy-making position in the early postwar years even though the German federation again constituted the numerically largest national contingent.

In the first Weimar years, the ADGB leaders also vigorously opposed the Versailles Treaty. They were worried about the disastrous economic effect—mass unemployment and ruined industries— its reparations clauses would have on German workers. Acknowledging Germany's obligation to help in the reconstruction of Belgium and northern France, they called the Versailles accord a war treaty and not a peace treaty. According to Legien, the treaty would produce hate and discord, and "a people of seventy million helots and slaves of the Allied and Associated . . . western states."[16]

Those ADGB leaders representing the "conservative" majority harshly denounced USPD labor leaders who supported the signing of the treaty under all circumstances. The former suggested that Germany should first attempt to change the war-guilt and other provisions of the treaty, and even then sign only under duress. They said that the Allies' charging Germany with sole responsibility in starting the war was an "untenable lie," and called on the Allies to open their secret archives if they expected the German Foreign Office to do the same. They also denounced Allied demands for the extradition of thousands of Germans accused of war crimes, and protested Allied refusal to release German prisoners of war, thereby condemning them to "slave labor."[17] In later years, the ADGB chiefs mellowed in their opposition to Versailles, and passively supported the policy of treaty fulfilment, a policy strongly backed by the SPD as a way of accelerating Germany's return to the international community.

KAPP PUTSCH

The ADGB involvement in domestic politics intensified soon after the Revolution and Versailles as a result of several attempts made by extremist political forces to overthrow the legitimate government. In the nascent Weimar period, the establishment of a parliamentary regime did not produce stability; on the contrary, as a result of defeat in battle and the peace terms imposed on it, the nation became embroiled in acrimonious political, economic, social, and military turmoil. Among the most serious outbreaks of turbulence was the Kapp Putsch. On March 13, 1920, two reactionary leaders, monarchist and founder of the wartime Fatherland Party Wolfgang Kapp, and Reichswehr General Walther von Lüttwitz, made one such attempt. They secretly organized 6,000 Marine Brigade troops in Prussia and marched on Berlin to overthrow the government and install themselves in power.

Success would depend on the attitude of the Reichswehr, the cabinet, and the unions. General von Seeckt and other top officers remained neutral, telling Minister of War Gustav Noske (SPD) that "troops do not fire upon troops."[18] Thus, the coalition cabinet, headed by Chancellor Bauer (SPD), had to seek an alternative to save the Republic. The SPD ministers in the cabinet, at the behest of the party Executive, drafted a call for a general strike which they issued in their own behalf and in the names of the German president and the SPD chairman.[19] Then the cabinet fled from Berlin, eventually to Stuttgart.

At the same time, rebel forces seized the Chancellery and a number of public buildings in Berlin, declared the constitutional government abolished, and proclaimed Kapp chancellor. But the Putschist leaders had little conception of how to gain national power because their plans were incomplete and their staffs incompetent. When the Reichswehr high command, the government bureaucracy, and the Reichsbank failed to cooperate with them, and when the trade unions accepted the government's call to action, their chance of success was slim.

On March 13, the ADGB Executive, after hearing reports from the SPD Executive, proclaimed the general strike, unprecedented in Germany. Union leaders who had been opposed to the strike if it were to be called against a legitimate government did not hesitate to use it for the support of such a government. They were aware that the ADGB's organizational existence was in jeopardy; radical forces might seize the initiative unless they supported the call for a strike. As one historian notes:

It is one of the ironies of history that the successful general strike should have taken place, not in France, the home of the general strike theory, nor in England, where both the earliest and the greatest general strikes were staged, nor even in the lands of more revolutionary tradition, Spain, Italy, and Russia. It is even more ironical that the successful strike should have been conducted, not to destroy a government, but to save it.[20]

To array more support, the ADGB immediately invited the leaders from the Berlin trade unions, salaried employees unions, the SPD, USPD, and later the Communist Party (KPD) to joint sessions, but soon discovered that even in this period of crisis the fragmentation of the Left could not be erased momentarily. USPD leaders refused to collaborate with the SPD because they considered the SPD co-responsible "for the entire affair," responsible for jailing and mis-treating USPD members, and responsible for opposing the immediate formation of a workers' government. In retort, the SPD representative accused the USPD of stirring up revolts against the Weimar governments, which in turn inspired a backlash from the Right. Not unexpectedly, the KPD representative also vetoed an alliance with the SPD. As a result, rival moderate and leftist strike committees were formed.[21] Legien and other labor leaders directed the rapidly spreading national strike from a cellar hideout in Berlin. They received support from the Hirsch-Duncker federation, but the Christian unions held back, ostensibly for fear the strike would damage the economy.

Legien was displeased that he had to step into a political void in Berlin following the departure of the cabinet members. To his chagrin they were beginning to distance themselves from the general strike, fearing that the Reichswehr generals would no longer support the Republic. When the strike became effective, Kapp tried at first to placate its organizers. On March 15, free labor leaders were invited by telephone to a conference at which Kapp was ready to discuss the formation of a grand coalition government willing to extend the rights of labor.[22] The ADGB, refusing to attend the meeting, rejected the offer saying that it would confer only with a legally constituted government. Kapp sent a representative to ADGB headquarters to offer the federation some ministry posts. When it declined, the representative left angrily, remarking, "Now the machine guns will speak."[23] On the following day, Kapp ordered the death sentence for the strike leaders. Because he lacked power, Kapp's threat was futile. Unable to break the strike or to receive support from government organs, he ordered his troops to withdraw from Berlin on March 17.

With the swift end of the Putsch, the SPD-led coalition government, still meeting in Stuttgart, and supported by Reichswehr officers and conservative politicians fearing a revolt of the Left, called for an end to the strike. But the labor leaders, flushed with victory, eager to assert union power, frustrated by unmet demands, and afraid of losing the support of the radicalized members, rejected a return to the old order. They refused to end the strike or permit the Bauer cabinet to take effective command until their nine-point program for reforms had been accepted. They demanded:

(1) Decisive influence of the union organizations on the formation of governments in the Reich and in the states, and also on new economic and social legislation and regulations.

(2) Immediate disarming and punishment of all troops who had participated in the Putsch.

(3) Immediate resignation of War Minister Noske (SPD) and two Prussian ministers.

(4) Complete purge of all reactionaries from public service.

(5) Rapid democratization of administrative services with the assistance of trade unions.

(6) Immediate extension of social laws that would guarantee workers, salaried employees, and civil servants social and economic equality.

(7) Immediate socialization of mines and electric power, with the Reich to take over the coal and potash syndicates.

(8) Immediate introduction of an expropriation law against property owners who fail to release available foodstuffs or to manage their property in the interest of the public.

(9) Dissolution of all counterrevolutionary military formations; takeover of security forces by the organized labor movement.[24]

The government did not accept the program, but on March 20 reached accord with the unions on a revised program, which reflected union concessions on some of the more radical demands.[25] The labor leaders, although not completely satisfied with the revised agreement, signified their support of it, especially because they wanted to facilitate the formation of a socialist-labor cabinet. On March 20, they proclaimed the end of the general strike. As a result of USPD and KPD dissatisfaction with the agreement, most workers in the Berlin area refused to return to work. After union and SPD pressures on the USPD, the latter accepted a proposal to end the strike on March 23. USPD spokesmen regarded the agreement as a minimum program only, but were mollified when the unions promised to renew the strike should government assurances of compliance with the agreement be broken.[26]

The strike was not renewed at the national level, although the agreement produced few results, the most important being the resignation, under Legien pressure, of the unpopular and reactionary Minister Noske, and later the socialist-bourgeois coalition cabinet led by Bauer. When Bauer's resignation was imminent the union leaders demanded that a socialist and labor coalition government be formed, including representatives of the SPD, the USPD, and all trade union federations, but excluding the KPD. This dramatic plan was most likely advanced as a propaganda gesture to appease the ADGB left wing and the radical workers rather than as a genuine plan of the conservative union leaders who in the past had sustained cabinets based on majority support in the Reichstag, and who may have calculated that the political parties would reject the plan.

In any case, the union chiefs needed SPD and USPD backing and KPD toleration for the plan if it were to achieve success. The SPD was not enthusiastic about a union initiative that might incite a revolutionary movement and engender hostile reactions from other governments.[27] Rather, it believed that a new cabinet should be formed on the basis of parliamentary support.

The USPD was split: the majority, including the left wing, rejected the plan because the SPD and the unions had not accepted the more extensive USPD demands made after the Putsch and because it mistrusted Legien's sudden switch to political activism. This negative stance was typical of the disordered German world of the twenties: a radical faction vetoing for reasons which made little political sense a radical proposal made by conservative union leaders. Had the USPD given its approval, then the plan might have been accepted by the SPD.

The KPD, after vehement debate, took a favorable stand. Although its newspaper asserted, "No pure socialist government with parliament as a basis," its leader Wilhelm Pieck said the party regarded a labor government as exceedingly desirable.[28] A conference took place between union and KPD leaders, at which the latter offered their party's "loyal opposition."

Unable to receive full backing for it, the free unions dropped their plan. But before the nation was again governed by the cycle of socialist or bourgeois coalition cabinets, President Ebert, on behalf of the SPD, asked Legien to form a new cabinet. When he declined, Ebert, according to unverified reports, asked Rudolf Wissell, ADGB Executive member, whether he would accept the chancellorship, but he too declined.

Why the veteran labor leaders refused to take political power at the height of their careers has remained a mystery, especially as they had pressed for a socialist-labor cabinet just a few days earlier. Among the reasons may have been Legien's ill health (he died in December, 1920), his lack of interest in the post, his knowledge that he could not command a majority in the Reichstag (a rejection of his cabinet or his program would have been a personal blow to him and to the unions, which might have set off more extraparliamentary actions), and his belief that he should head only a workers' government at a more favorable time in history when the country was not on the verge of a civil war. Whatever the reason, the unions lost their one chance in the Weimar Republic to take command of the government.[29] Whether their legislative objectives could have been achieved if one of their leaders had become chancellor remains doubtful given the political configuration in the legislature.

When the union leaders declined to assume power, Hermann Müller (SPD) on March 27 formed a new coalition cabinet representing the SPD, Democratic, and Center parties. As a final assertion of its residual political power, the ADGB gave prior approval of the new cabinet members. Thus, on the national front, the *status quo ante* had been restored.[30] Workers in the industrial Ruhr region and in sections of central Germany accused their national leaders of failing to "turn the country around." Disappointed at developments, they refused to turn in their weapons to the authorities until a national labor government should be created. Communist-inspired workers' defense battalions (the "Red Army") were formed and occupied numerous Ruhr cities. The stage seemed set for a repetition of the postrevolutionary period when Left radical forces battled government-directed Reichswehr forces. Not surprisingly, the Reichswehr could always be counted on to back the government and the fatherland if a threat from the Left but not from the Right occurred.[31]

Therefore, when the Müller cabinet ordered the Reichswehr and the Free Corps troops to quell the workers' uprising, the military forces did not hesitate to intervene. Ironically, General Seeckt ordered units loyal to Kapp to be used in the bloody fight against the workers. Many SPD adherents, uneasy about the government's alliance with Right forces, disapproved of the party's attempt to crush the Left. Several high ranking Social Democrats vainly did attempt to avert further clashes in the Ruhr. On March 23 and 24, in Bielefeld, representatives from the government, the free unions, the Left parties, and workers' defense battalions accepted a regional agreement expected to ensure peace in the area.[32] But new military skirmishes erupted, and the government issued an ultimatum to the workers, who proclaimed a general strike. The ADGB acted as mediator, but was ineffective. Eventually, the Reichswehr crushed the last workers' units with great brutality, and an uneasy peace spread over the region.

To sum up: the unions were not satisfied with the outcome of the Kapp Putsch, although they must share the blame. Able to extract minor concessions from the government in the nine-point agreement, they were unwilling to assume more power after the Putsch than they had held before. One may speculate that if the SPD had accepted the original union demands embodied in the agreement, or had carried out its revisions, or had accepted the unions' bid for a socialist-labor government, the democratic foundation of the Republic would have been strengthened. The opportunity was missed. No alternative remained but for the unions to support the SPD-led coalition once again in the hope that the trend toward the Right would be arrested—even though the SPD used the Right to crush the Left. In retrospect, the Kapp Putsch represented the zenith of the unions' political power in the Weimar period—their strike had helped to preserve the Republic—but the Putsch also revealed their inability to win major concessions from the governing coalition.

POLITICAL ASSASSINATIONS

Political instability was one of the chief characteristics of Weimar Germany. After the Kapp Putsch and the Left uprising, the extreme nationalists and monarchists turned their ire on the German signers of the Versailles "Diktat," whom they held responsible for the crises besetting the country. From protests at veterans' rallies to antirepublican nationalist press campaigns, some of them escalated their tactics to assassinations of politicians associated with the Weimar regime.

The first major political figure assassinated was Matthias Erzberger, a Center Party deputy and former Finance Minister. After his murder on August 26, 1921, the unions and socialist parties sponsored protest demonstrations and demanded that the government reinforce public security immediately. But the government was slow to act. On June 24, 1922, Foreign Minister Walther Rathenau (Democratic Party), who had tried to produce a policy of reconciliation with the Allies and to meet Germany's reparation debts, was assassinated. The democratic forces in the nation were shocked; they seized this opportunity to once again demand fundamental reforms to erode the strength of the extremists responsible for the wave of terror.

The ADGB spearheaded the political protest movement because, according to Leipart (who succeeded Legien as ADGB president), the three workers' parties were not united, and failure to act might have resulted in incalculable consequences for the Republic.[33] The ADGB Congress, then meeting in Leipzig, called on the workers to strike for one day in a symbolic protest. The strike call was heeded; large demonstrations took place throughout Germany.

The ADGB Executive also urged the socialist parties to join it in seeking ways to uphold the security of the Republic and to safeguard the rights of workers against reactionary attacks. It asked the government to purge civil servants disloyal to the Constitution, demanded judicial and administrative reforms, and called on the workers to stand by the Republic—if necessary, with their lives.[34]

On June 25, leaders from ADGB and the newly formed General Free Federation of Salaried Employees (AfA) met with representatives of SPD, USPD, and KPD. ADGB and AfA leaders succeeded in halting momentarily the fratricidal warfare between the three parties in the face of the common enemy. The parties agreed to issue a joint appeal calling on the conservative Chancellor Wirth and Parliament to approve a law designed to protect the Republic.

But they were unable to agree on an ADGB-AfA plan to reorganize the cabinet, or, in an escalation of union protest, on an additional half-day work stoppage to be held on July 4. The SPD and USPD supported the union proposals, but the KPD was more interested in a long general strike and in the formation of a workers' government. The ADGB rejected the KPD proposals, and accused the party of playing into the hands of the counterrevolutionaries.[35] The ADGB-KPD feud weakened the power of the Left at another stage of political turmoil. Evident in the dispute between a short work stoppage and a long general strike were fundamental differences on tactics and the kind of political system Germany should have.

The ADGB Executive went ahead with preparations for the work stoppage. It met to discuss details reflecting the German penchant for meticulous planning and the yearning for order. Labor leaders spent much time on the questions of whether the trolley cars should stop running between 1 and 5 P.M., whether trains should stop for thirty minutes, and whether the Ministry of Postal Affairs would allow a ten-minute work stoppage. They agreed that the planned demonstrations of workers in the cities must not interfere with traffic, law and order.[36]

While the Left showed a brief atypical spurt of unity followed by the more typical schism, the Chancellor issued a government decree on maintaining the security of the Republic. When union and party representatives expressed dissatisfaction with certain provisions, Wirth promised them that he would consult with President Ebert and the Minister of Justice to see if amendments could be made. Although he issued a new decree on June 30, incorporating some of their suggestions, they asked for additional legislation to include the dissolution of all monarchist and antirepublican organizations, and the dismissal of monarchist officers from the Reichswehr. In the end, the Reichstag did enact a number of laws designed to strengthen the nation's democratic base. The SPD and USPD considered the laws unsatisfactory, but voted for them, aware that a negative vote might lead to a Reichstag dissolution and continued political crises.[37]

Union and socialist leaders looked for additional support from abroad in the struggle against the Right. They convinced Executive members of the IFTU and the two socialist internationals, holding a joint conference in Amsterdam, to issue a manifesto (addressed "To the Workers of the World") praising the German workers for their demonstration of massed strength in the defense of freedom and the fight against reaction.[38]

During this period of instability the German socialist unions had been in the forefront of political action against reactionary forces. But they were not strong enough to counter the powerful Right, the upsurge of nationalism and anti-Versailles sentiment, and the reassertion of power by the conservative industrial community. The assassinations of democratic leaders constituted one more blow against the democratic system.

POLITICAL CRISES: ANOTHER ROUND

Domestic turmoil was paralleled by international turmoil stemming from the aftermath of World War I. Once again the ADGB responded to developments that would adversely affect the interests of its members. One such development was the reparations question, which plagued Allied-German relations for many years. In 1922, because of a devastating inflation, Germany requested a moratorium on reparations payments, but the Allies rejected it. France pressed for occupation of the Ruhr to guarantee German payments. On January 11, 1923, French Premier Raymond Poincaré used the German default on timber and coal deliveries as a pretext for occupying the Ruhr with French and token Belgian forces. Great Britain and the United States disapproved of the French action, and the German government, backed by an aroused and strongly nationalist population, branded it illegal.[39]

German unions and employer associations, with the blessing of the government, started a passive resistance movement against the occupation forces. The industrialists immediately stopped coal and coke deliveries to France. The unions asked the workers to halt work in industries and mines taken over by the French. They took this step despite receipt of a French note warning workers of heavy fines if they disobeyed orders. The unions also called a symbolic half-hour national work stoppage, but decided against a prolonged general strike because of its adverse economic effect on the population.[40]

On January 16, the French generals and the Inter-Allied Control Commission requested German labor leaders to end their passive resistance. When the request was rejected, the French confiscated mines and arrested local labor leaders, but with little effect on coal production. Violence broke out in many places.

The unions sought international support to strengthen their case, urging workers in other nations to protest the "French military dictatorship's action which had resulted in the enslavement of free workers."[41] Many labor federations protested the French occupation, but were unwilling to boycott French goods. The German unions considered a boycott, but abandoned the idea when they realized that such French luxury export goods as wines, liqueurs, and silks would not be bought by German workers in any case.[42] They did dispatch an appeal to the United States Congress urging the establishment of an investigation commission, but the Congress took no action.

In the meantime, the IFTU, the Second International (Socialist), and the International Workers Union of Socialist Parties denounced the military occupation.[43] In February, the IFTU recommended a twenty-four-hour international protest strike, provided that the German workers would join in. Grateful for the offer in principle, the ADGB replied that such a strike would damage the German economy, rather than the nations responsible for the crisis. As a result, all tangible international union action failed, except for collections of money to help the Ruhr workers, whose need was increasingly desperate.[44]

Passive resistance could not last forever as inflation increased in Germany. From April to June, the unions and the SPD noted that their treasuries ran low, unemployment among union members rose to 20 percent of the membership, and fear of extremist uprisings mounted. In July, they submitted a plan to the Allies for a guarantee of reparations payments. According to Leipart, it could have served as the basis for negotiations to end the crisis, but none of the governments replied. Simultaneously, the ADGB rejected the French attempt to obtain special reparations guarantees from the Rhineland and the Ruhr, which would have involved danger of their separation from Germany.[45]

The unions also put pressure on Chancellor Wilhelm Cuno's conservative government to produce a plan acceptable to the Allies for settling the crisis. They accused the government and the industrialists of aggravating the economic debacle by letting prices outpace wages, and denounced Cuno's advice to the population to consume less and save more. They submitted proposals for combating the inflation by tightening Reichsbank credits and changing the fiscal policy, and demanded that the wealthy class be taxed more heavily to accelerate the nation's return to a normal condition. They blasted industry's plan to end inflation by lengthening the work week, its establishment of company unions, and its refusal to end passive resistance.

The ADGB Executive saw little hope for a revision of Cuno's policies. Hence, as early as April, it urged the SPD to enter a grand coalition cabinet, but the timing was premature. In the months thereafter, radical union locals and district councils demanded the resignation of the Cuno cabinet and the formation of a labor government. The ADGB argued that such a government could not rest on a democratic basis because it would not receive a popular majority in an election. This argument was the same one expressed by the SPD during the Kapp Putsch to which the ADGB then objected, but now it reflected the more politically moderate and orthodox course the ADGB was following.

The opposition to Cuno grew; his downfall seemed imminent. On July 30, ADGB leaders, in a conference with the Chancellor, voiced their loss of confidence in his administration, and urged him to resign. On the other hand, they did not endorse the political strikes against the government led by communist-controlled works councils in July. These culminated in a strike in the Reich Printing Office on August 10, and in spontaneous strikes throughout Germany the following days. The restless and frustrated workers were signaling Cuno and the nation that the status quo could not be continued. The SPD took up the cue, warning the Chancellor that Germany needed a leader who would command the support of the masses, and threatening him with a vote of no confidence.

On August 12, Cuno resigned and Gustav Stresemann, head of the People's Party, formed a government with SPD participation. Stresemann claims that he included SPD ministers in order to win the backing of the moderates in the labor movement and to split them from the radical wing.[46] On September 24, after long diplomatic discussions, the new Chancellor announced that further passive resistance would be useless. This marked the end of the Ruhr struggle, but not yet the end of civil discord.

The government was faced by revolutionary threats from the

Left in Thuringia and Saxony, from the Right in Bavaria and among units of the illegal "Black Reichswehr," and from separatists in Bavaria and the Rhineland. During this revolutionary period, an increasing number of workers, disillusioned with the moderate policies of the SPD, joined the KPD—indeed, one expert estimates that the party may have had the support of millions of angry workers.[47] The party, encouraged by the Soviet Union, secretly prepared for a national uprising in October 1923. It expected to make use of the proletarian defense corps units and action committees, consisting of left-wing ADGB, SPD, USPD, and KPD members, which it had organized in many parts of Germany.

At the same time, it tried to gain political power in Saxony and Thuringia by joining the left-wing SPD cabinets. From this power base it expected the revolution would spread over Germany. On October 21, the Stresemann government quickly smothered the incipient uprising by sending the Reichswehr into both states. At a conference in Chemnitz, the KPD called for a general strike, but SPD and union representatives vetoed the proposal on the basis that they did not want to encourage a rightist Putsch against the beleaguered Republic. Not all union leaders concurred. In Hamburg, the ADGB local called a meeting on October 22 of SPD, KPD, and union officials to determine how to support the Left in Saxony and Thuringia. SPD and union members voted to send a resolution to their Berlin central offices urging the proclamation of a nationwide demonstration strike, but the KPD members, eager to see a national uprising, voted negatively.

Ironically, one such uprising did take place on October 23 in Hamburg where Communist participants had not been apprised in time of the KPD leadership's change of mind. After thirty-six hours of fighting, the police suppressed the uprising. It had not received the support of a majority of Hamburg workers who were then more concerned about their low wages.[48] (Less than one month later, on November 8, Hitler launched his short-lived Beerhall Putsch in Munich.)

The challenges from Left and Right stopped after this period, and the national governments could peacefully carry on their more mundane tasks in domestic and foreign policies. The mark was eventually stabilized and the Dawes Agreement, easing German reparations obligations, was signed. Under the leadership of

Stresemann, who became Foreign Minister in November 1
who kept the post until his death in 1929, the period up to the ᴜreat
Depression saw no more external threats to the Republic.

The ADGB relinquished its activist role in national politics and
restricted itself to the narrower pursuit of economic goals—with
some exceptions; one, for instance occured in 1926 at the time of the
proposed initiative and referendum on the expropriation of the large
Hohenzollern estates in East Prussia. At the request of the SPD, the
ADGB approached the KPD to plan joint strategy. The federation
produced a rare working accord between the two feuding parties; in
addition, ADGB unions contributed sizable financial support and
collected millions of signatures for the initiative campaign. In the
end, the referendum failed because of insufficient support.[49]

As will be noted, when the right wing in the USPD merged with
the SPD in 1922, the ADGB could once again endorse the SPD at
election time without worrying about causing an internal split between its SPD and USPD adherents. In the periodic elections thereafter, especially in 1928 when the SPD formed a government again, the
ADGB unions provided strong financial assistance to the party. In
addition, Leipart several times counseled the SPD on the explosive
question whether or not to participate in coalition governments.
Normally, he gave his assent if the workers' economic interests could
be promoted.[50] Thus, the ADGB participated in a range of partisan
activities that intensified during election campaigns and the formation of cabinets, but ebbed in the interval—except for the normal
lobbying for economic objectives.

CONCLUSION

In the formative Weimar years the powerful socialist unions had
little hesitation in venturing into stormy politics in order to gain their
multiple goals. As a consequence they won victories and suffered
defeats. Although they intervened in public affairs primarily when
their own survival or economic welfare was at stake—during the
Revolution and the Ruhr occupation—they were willing to put
pressure on governments concerning political issues if the creation of
a democratic system or its continuance, as in the Kapp Putsch, was
endangered. Nor did they refrain from seeking a change among the

political elite if the direction of policy was injurious to their interests.

Their political activities were typical for any interest group whose welfare is closely linked to the support and maintenance of the political system. This "conserving" role was bound to affect the ideology of the union federation's elite who, under normal circumstances, eschewed radical experimentation and turned instead to moderate incremental actions. True, radical pressure from the rank and file was intense during these formative years, and the labor elite could not help moving slightly to the Left during the Kapp Putsch—to its own ideological discomfort. Yet this was a short-lived period and marked an exception to the reformist or conservative policies pursued on other occasions.

III

THE WEIMAR ERA (II)

UNION INVOLVEMENT in national affairs during political or economic crises resumed in the declining years of the Weimar Republic. The advent of the Great Depression in 1929 threatened the hard-won gains of the unions. To cope with rising unemployment and decreasing state support, the unions began protest actions and lobbied hard to keep their gains. We must examine their degree of political involvement and success or defeat in the kaleidoscope of cabinets ranging from Müller and Brüning to Papen, Schleicher, and Hitler.

OVERTHROW OF THE MÜLLER CABINET

In 1929 and 1930, the Social Democratic-led coalition cabinet of Hermann Müller was overwhelmed with grave economic problems.[1] For the unions, widespread unemployment or underemployment among their members endangered their organizational and financial strength, not to speak of the personal hardships facing jobless members. The unions' strategy lay in fighting legislative measures that would affect their membership adversely. Their resistance symbolically centered on unemployment insurance, an issue of concern to the cabinet and the political parties in the Reichstag as they grappled with overall budget estimates.

In March 1930, the cabinet decided that public expenditures had to be reduced and more taxes raised to cover mounting relief costs and to compensate for lower revenues. The ministers, however, could not come to an accord on the details, especially the rate of benefits to be paid unemployed workers under the provisions of the Unemployment Insurance Act of 1927. The SPD, at the insistence of the ADGB, wanted benefits to be raised from 3.5 to 4 percent, which would have helped maintain the workers' standard of living. The People's Party and other conservative parties, under pressure of employer associations, advocated lower benefits. Thereupon, Heinrich Brüning, then leader of the Center Party in the Reichstag, offered a compromise proposal in which the Reich would raise some taxes so that benefits could remain at 3.5 per cent, but with a possible cut in the future.

The bourgeois coalition parties were willing to accept the compromise, but the ADGB informed the SPD that it was opposed. Since the Depression had instilled in the labor movement great fear and insecurity, the ADGB could not countenance any legislative effort that might result eventually in a lower standard of living for the workers. Thus on a number of occasions the ADGB warned the party that, given the limits of coalition politics, it would criticize government policies whenever they conflicted with the interests of the workers.[2] It also intimated that the SPD Reichstag Fraktion could not support the Brüning compromise without the party suffering a sizable loss of votes (i.e. from workers) at the next election. This implicit threat to a fraternal organization was unusual, but showed how serious was the crisis.

Minister of Labor Wissell supported the ADGB position, Chancellor Müller and two other SPD ministers opposed it. They were ready, with some reluctance, to accept the Brüning compromise given the budgetary stringency and their fear that the coalition government would have to resign if it could not agree on this vital issue. Such a resignation, they argued, could precipitate the formation of a reactionary government, which would really hurt the interests of the workers.[3]

The deadlock among the SPD ministers could be resolved only at the party's top decision-making level. On March 27, 1930, at the height of the Reichstag debate on unemployment insurance, the SPD leaders decided that the Fraktion must meet in a strategy-planning session to determine the party position, to be binding on all SPD ministers. One observer at the session gave a graphic account:

The crucial negotiations in the Social Democratic Fraktion proceeded under nervous tension. . . .one talked only briefly and excitedly. The decision, in fact, had already been reached when several of the trade union leaders who were Fraktion members entered the room; from their midst Hermann Müller of Lichtenberg (ADBG Executive member) asked for the floor. . . . Now Hermann Müller stood against (Chancellor) Hermann Müller. The speaker for the trade unions declared in a dictatorial tone that the compromise over unemployment insurance was completely unacceptable. Should the Fraktion arrive at a different decision, the trade unions would make known their opposing point of view as energetically as possible in the Reichstag, in the press, and in the party. This declaration was the more unfortunate in that it was completely superfluous. As a matter of fact, the decision was as good as made. It was decided almost unanimously to reject the compromise.[4]

According to another observer, Chancellor Müller emphasized before the vote that the SPD and ADGB must continue to make concessions on the unemployment insurance issue, whereupon Otto Wels, SPD Chairman, stated that the trade union movement could not be sacrificed any further.[5]

The decision of the Fraktion, upheld by the SPD Executive and Board, to back the ADGB was a way of avoiding a dangerous confrontation with the labor federation and with the party's own growing left-wing minority, a section of which had already seceded and formed the Socialist Workers Party. As predicted, once the decision was made, the Chancellor and the other SPD ministers resigned from the cabinet immediately, thereby causing its dissolution.

The SPD decision not to support its own chancellor naturally became the object of some controversy in party and nonparty circles. The SPD Executive quickly issued to party members a statement justifying the decision of the Fraktion.[6] A labor journal praised the Fraktion for having adhered to a pledge, made at the 1929 Marburg SPD Convention, not to yield to other parties on the question of unemployment insurance. There was a point in politics at which it was no longer possible to compromise, the journal said.[7]

Others sharply disagreed with this thesis. SPD editor Friedrich

Stampfer argued that the party should have taken the lead in such a crucial political decision because only it could work out the proper balance between trade unionism and the national interest. He admitted that the Fraktion and the unions could not have foreseen the results of their decision (i.e., national governance by emergency decree), and said that the split with other parties over economic questions was inevitable. He noted that this was especially true of the People's Party which was intent on ousting the SPD from the government. Yet, he continued, such factors did not justify hasty action in the face of an unknown future, especially because the Fraktion soon thereafter had to accept as fact the decrease in unemployment insurance benefits, and because it managed to tolerate the Brüning government that enacted this law.[8] Rudolf Hilferding, SPD Minister of Finance in the Müller cabinet until December 1929, also believed that the party should have remained in the coalition since the crisis only worsened after its withdrawal.[9]

This crisis was another illustration of the ADGB pressure and influence on the SPD and the cabinet, and of the dichotomy which arises between interest groups pursuing a narrow interest and a party in power representing a broader interest. True, the governing coalition might have broken up anyhow over fundamental differences between the SPD and the People's Party, but the crisis was certainly precipitated by the union action.

The ADGB position was understandable. It did not want to compromise on an issue considered vital to its economic program, especially since the danger was acute that if it did not stand firm then, other measures more damaging to the workers would follow suit. But the ADGB did not realize at the time that its dramatic victory over the SPD was empty and Pyrrhic. In ousting its political ally from the government, the ADGB contributed to a strain within the union-party alliance, to the end of SPD participation in later cabinets, to an unmistakable turn to the Right, and to the decline of the Weimar Republic and its parliamentary institutions. In 1930, of course, the fateful consequences of the crisis were not yet clearly visible; thus, the democratic Left, pushed into the wings, still clung to the hope that democracy could be saved.

TOLERATION OF BRÜNING

Upon the resignation of the Müller cabinet on March 27, President Hindenburg requested Heinrich Brüning to become chancellor.

When Brüning appointed only members of conservative parties to his cabinet and embarked on a policy injurious to labor to meet the worsening Depression, the socialist trade unions and the SPD moved into the opposition camp and proposed alternative measures to combat the economic crisis.[10] Their symbolic opposition did not last long; on September 19, the German National Socialist Workers Party (NSDAP) made spectacular gains in the Reichstag election. Thereupon the SPD, sustained by the free unions, decided to tolerate the Brüning regime as the lesser evil when compared to a fascist government. Their toleration policy signified that they would not try to overthrow Brüning in a Reichstag vote or challenge his emergency decrees, but they gave the Fraktion carte blanche to suggest policy alternatives whenever necessary.

There was resistance to the new toleration policy among a number of union leaders and rank and file—as there was in the SPD. KPD propaganda fanned this opposition, claiming that starvation under Brüning was as reprehensible as starvation under anyone else. On the other hand, ADGB and SPD, in justification, argued that to oust the Chancellor would be to precipitate another Reichstag dissolution, new elections, and an eventual victory for fascism. In effect, they were willing to tolerate the government's expected unpopular economic measures in the hope that economic conditions would soon improve and that the extremist parties would then present no further menace.

The economic situation did not improve. Foreign loans were halted; industrial production and trade declined; banks failed; unemployment rose swiftly from 2 million in 1930 to 6 million in early 1932; and government tax revenues fell drastically while expenditures, especially for relief and social services, steadily increased. Brüning initiated a deflationary policy to combat the crisis. By a series of controversial emergency decrees, the Chancellor intended to make severe cuts in national expenditures and to raise revenues. He slashed official salaries, wages, and prices; reduced unemployment benefits; imposed additional taxes; and aided agriculture through subsidies and higher tariffs.[11]

Brüning was able neither to ease the serious strain on the economy with these measures nor to halt the dissatisfaction mounting within most strata of the population. The unions claimed that workers were faced with a 13 percent cut in their standard of living. As a remedy, they proposed a balanced budget and price reductions not accompanied by wage reductions, in order to stimulate consumption and increase production.

The unions were critical of Brüning's deflationary policy only when it threatened wages and unemployment benefits. They failed to realize that their support of a high wage level would have ruined many smaller businesses and created even more unemployment, and that their demand for a balanced budget could not have maintained the level of unemployment benefits. Their opposition to any currency manipulation, based on the memory of the disastrous inflation of 1922-1923, indicated their basic support of Brüning's deflationary economic policy.[12] Only in the latter part of his tenure of office, as will be noted, did some union experts set forth counter-proposals, but the SPD did not endorse them.

Labor leaders, without a direct voice in the executive branch, fell back on the use of traditional pressure techniques in attempts to block government measures most injurious to their members. They could rely little on parliamentary support, because Brüning, backed by President Hindenburg, ruled by emergency decree under Article 48 of the Constitution. The Chancellor took this step in order to prevent Parliament from considering—and blocking—his legislation. Union protests were loud and clear, but ineffective. In public statements, the unions claimed Brüning's retrenchment measures intensified the crisis; they urged the government to allow more foreign credits to enter Germany. At conferences with the President and the Chancellor on February 26, 1931, all trade union federations expressed their anxiety about the inadequate actions undertaken to alleviate unemployment. They were told that the government would do its utmost to help. On April 23 and May 30, the free unions requested the government to institute the forty-hour week, to increase the workers' purchasing power, to preserve existing social insurance benefits, and to boost taxes on high incomes.[13]

The appeals had no effect. On June 5, Brüning issued an emergency decree, extremely unpopular with the unions, ordering cuts in government expenditures, wages, and prices. According to the ADGB, the Chancellor refused to meet with protesting labor leaders and the SPD Fraktion, and insisted on the decree becoming effective immediately.[14]

The patience of the leaders with the government and the coali-

tion parties was running out. They complained about workers having
to make the most sacrifices, and about the Center Party's threats of
cabinet dissolution whenever it wanted to ram through unpopular
measures. They insisted the government take measures against fascism, including the veiled fascism of heavy industry and of a segment
of the civil service bureaucracy. They were angry that the government had not sought advice from them, but only from employers. In
sum, they were telling Brüning that if he desired continued SPD and
free union toleration, he should take a stronger stand against the
NSDAP and apportion the economic burden more equitably.[15]

Brüning did not heed the union messages. He next reduced
unemployment insurance benefits from twenty-six to twenty weeks,
although not to eighteen weeks as the employers had urged him—at
best a minor victory for labor and the SPD. On December 8, he
ordered further slashes in wages, salaries, prices, and interest rates.
Once again, labor leaders protested to the Chancellor, warning him
that they assumed no responsibility for the latest decree. But on
December 16, at a mass rally in Berlin held jointly by the unions, the
SPD, and the paramilitary, primarily socialist Reichsbanner, speaker
after speaker reaffirmed the necessity for maintaining the toleration
policy in face of a fascist threat.

To the pleasure of Brüning, labor leaders did not threaten strikes
or other extraparliamentary moves, even though left-controlled
union locals were demanding them. In his memoirs, he asserts, "The
trade union leaders in this year have generally shown a responsibility
for the fatherland, which leaders of other professions and associations have not been able to demonstrate on a single occasion."[16]
There were of course more compelling reasons than patriotism why
the union leaders did not call for strikes. First, they were opposed to
political strikes for ideological reasons. Second, their resources were
depleted: by early 1932, when 45 percent of their members were
unemployed and 22 percent were underemployed, and when more
cuts in wages and unemployment benefits were in prospect, the
union treasuries were running dangerously low.[17]

Labor leaders ruled out political strikes as a protest against the
emergency decrees, but they took some steps to prepare against a
possible fascist takeover. In 1930 and 1931, when rumors of a rightist
putsch were rife, ADGB and SPD leaders met secretly to plan
countermeasures, the details of which were never revealed.[18] In late

1931, the SPD and the free unions created the paramilitary Iron Front to defend the Republic from the growing rightist threat. All unionists were urged to join the Iron Front and contribute funds, and key factory workers were assembled into shock units (Hammerschaften) to be alert for any eventuality. Two top ADGB leaders served on its executive committee. As a propaganda weapon and as a way of arousing the morale of the workers, the Iron Front was initially effective. In ensuing crises, however, it was never called into action; thereby accelerating the workers' apathy and resignation. Evelyn Anderson writes:

> If it was to have any purpose at all, it could only have been that of preparing for a civil war which the Nazis would launch sooner or later. But both Party and Unions were convinced that democracy and Constitution would be destroyed in a civil war, and they were determined to avoid it. There was therefore not much point in forming the "Iron Front."[19]

In summer 1931, the union and SPD toleration policy continued; but as unemployment mounted, the noted economist Wladimir Woytinsky (director of the ADGB research and statistics division) began to formulate a number of unorthodox proposals to counter Brüning's deflationary measures and thereby overcome the Depression. When he submitted them to the ADGB Executive and did not receive immediate backing, he enlisted the support of Wood Workers Union President Fritz Tarnow and SPD agricultural economist Fritz Baade for a more precise formulation. In December 1931, they submitted their plan, entitled a "Program for Creation of Jobs" (more commonly known as the WTB plan, after the initials of its three authors), to the ADGB Executive. The plan called for the creation of a Central Office for Works Procurement, with strong union representation to coordinate the employment of a million jobless men on such public works projects as highway maintenance and improvements, low-cost housing construction and repairs, flood control, agriculture, and railroads. Its cost was calculated at 2 billion marks, to be raised through a Reichsbank loan and borrowing on the private capital market, freed unemployment insurance payments, and taxes from those reemployed.[20] The authors, in demanding an end to the government's deflationary policy, argued that the plan would not be inflationary since it would use the latent productive capacity of the economy. On February 16, 1932, the ADGB Executive approved the plan, launched a press campaign to publicize it, and scheduled an Emergency Congress for April as an additional means of lobbying for its implementation by the governing coalition.[21] The plan, revolutionary at the time, was a precursor to the Keynesian antidepression program of deficit financing launched later by the United States and Sweden.

Yet, many leading SPD economists and theoreticians, adhering in this instance to orthodox Marxist views, were mistrustful of a plan that would rescue the capitalist system from its possible death throes. Rudolf Hilferding (one of the staunchest supporters of Brüning's deflation policy), Fritz Napthali, Rudolf Breitscheid, and Paul Hertz showed little enthusiasm for a plan implying inflation, an end to a balanced budget, a currency devaluation, or abandonment of the gold standard. Some of them argued that the proposals would cost too much to implement and would secure work for only 600,000 persons. They called instead for a broader approach through increased state planning and control of industry, maintenance of wage standards, nationalization of heavy industry and banking, the inauguration of a dynamic business cycle, a rapprochement with France that would ease the financial situation, and a world-wide investment policy.

They packaged some of these proposals into a counterplan and presented them to the ADGB Executive, but by February 1932 the union leaders fully backed the WTB plan.[22] At issue were not only ideological versus pragmatic considerations, but, from the party's point of view, also the question whether it should not have the right to take the lead in what it considered to be primarily a political matter. According to Woytinsky, at the ADGB meeting which voted support of the WTB plan, Leipart stated "now our unions must take full responsibility for the economic policy of German labor." Wels, who had not participated in the discussion, then retorted, "You, the unions, have voted for a program of legislation. This has never been done before. In the past the party developed the program and cleared it with you. Do you intend to clear your program with us?" To which Leipart replied, "We are confident that the party will support us. Am I right, Otto?" Wels did not reply, but was only interested in the question of who should determine party policy.[23]

[63]

Since the answer was obvious to him that the party had this responsibility, the SPD economists had no difficulty in selling their proposals to the SPD Executive, even though party leaders and the economists were not thoroughly committed to increased state planning and ownership, and were aware of the proposals' political impracticality.

To see if the stalemate between ADGB and SPD could be broken, Woytinsky recalls, eighty party and union representatives met in a strategy meeting under the chairmanship of Wels. The two sides, one led by Hilferding and one by Woytinsky, were unable to convince each other of the best means to tackle the Depression. After a heated discussion, "Leipart put the ADGB plan to a vote. All the representatives of the unions raised their hands in favor it it, all the representatives of the party except Baade voted "nay."[24]

The party, not accepting the WTB plan, publicized its own plan, with an emphasis on state planning and nationalization. This tactic was pursued as a means of regaining the support of disillusioned workers who were defecting to the KPD and NSDAP. But it led to more bitterness among union leaders who accused the SPD of forgetting the unemployed workers who had remained loyal to the party. The SPD could not alienate this clientele entirely; hence did not publicly denounce the WTB plan. Indeed, in September 1932, the SPD Fraktion introduced a bill in the Reichstag calling for a works creation program of 1 billion marks (a watered-down version of the WTB plan), as well as a bill calling for the nationalization of key industries. The bills were designed to put the SPD on record as being progressive and to needle the cabinet into action, but they had no chance of adoption. Nevertheless, before their pro forma introduction in the Reichstag, Hilferding and Hertz lobbied hard in the SPD Fraktion to obtain the members' full support (only Tarnow voted in the negative).[25] Both bills being unsatisfactory to the ADGB, it did not lobby strenuously to win popular support for them. In any case, the conservative majority in the Reichstag killed the legislative proposals.

Minister of Labor Adam Stegerwald (Center Party) was aware of the WTB plan's appeal among the working masses. In order to defuse and deflect the appeal he submitted to the cabinet a works creation proposal containing some of the same features. But Brüning and the fiscally conservative ministers (on May 20) approved only a public works bill with a ceiling of 135 million marks. That bill too was never enacted into law. Paradoxically, Hitler's works creation program, begun after he assumed power, contained some of the same basic principles as those of the WTB plan, except that it eventually included defense projects. The success of the Nazi program in eliminating unemployment raises the speculative question whether a WTB plan translated into law would have reduced unemployment enough to have produced a decrease in the votes for the NSDAP.

Brüning was able to ward off the ineffective critique from the democratic Left, which assailed only the wage and unemployment benefit cuts in his program but supported the deflationary program. He had more difficulty in suppressing intrigues from the Right. Power-hungry archconservatives and generals were eager to move into the decision-making posts and in May 1932 were able to convince the President that Brüning must be dismissed.[26]

The unions had followed a tortuous course under the Brüning regime. On the one hand, they tolerated the conservative government; on the other hand, they criticized some of its policies. Their failure to receive support, especially from the SPD, for a bold alternative economic program to provide jobs contributed to the mood of apathy sweeping the working masses and to cooler relations between ADGB and SPD. The SPD must be blamed for backing an orthodox national economic policy when all signs pointed to its failure, but SPD and ADGB both must be blamed for tolerating a regime which could not halt the slide into economic and political catastrophe.[27]

THE PAPEN COUP

President Hindenburg's appointment of the archconservative Franz von Papen as Chancellor on May 31, 1932 ended the SPD-ADGB policy of toleration of a nonsocialist government. The two organizations had little to gain from tacitly supporting a non-party cabinet of barons who held a strong antisocialist and antilabor bias. This ideology was reflected in Papen's government declaration of June 4 denouncing previous governments for having transformed the state into a welfare institution ("state socialism") and for having weakened the moral fibers of the nation.

The declaration was followed by action. Papen dismissed the Reichstag and, in a familiar replay of Brüning's moves, issued a set of emergency decrees lowering wages and unemployment insurance benefits. Most labor officials considered protests to be their only recourse. They appealed to the President to withhold his assent from Papen's decrees, met with cabinet ministers to voice their complaints, scheduled a mass protest meeting in Berlin to which they invited the Chancellor, and condemned the cabinet's strong links to industrialists.[28] But these initiatives did not produce any policy change.

Although the democratic Left suffered one defeat after another at the national level, it still retained political power in the most important state—Prussia. To Papen, this was a cancerous growth that had to be eliminated. On July 20, he staged a coup against the SPD-led coalition cabinet. On the pretext that law and order were not being preserved in Prussia, the Chancellor had himself appointed Commissioner for Prussia by Presidential decree. He threatened to use the Reichswehr if the Prussian police or other groups resisted. Then he dismissed the Prussian cabinet ministers, headed by Otto Braun, and purged a number of bureaucrats. The ousted ministers appealed to the Supreme Court, stating that the federal decree dismissing them was unconstitutional. But the court decision, favoring them, was not rendered until October 25 when it had lost all significance.[29]

Other responses to the coup followed a predictable pattern. The conservative parties supported it and the Left parties and the unions rejected it. Young rank and file union activists staged immediate work stoppages in Berlin and other cities, and then paused for instructions from the ADGB high command. Small formations of the Reichsbanner and Iron Front gathered at their stations in various areas of Germany similarly waiting for directions. They expected as a matter of course that some retaliatory action would be undertaken.[30] They were bitterly disappointed that union or party leaders, then meeting in emergency sessions, did not call for a general protest strike or token demonstration.

The workers had not known that top party and union leaders had already met jointly a few days before the coup to discuss alternative strategies when many rumors of a pending coup were sweeping the capital. At that meeting Wels queried Leipart about the possibility of a strike, to which the latter is said to have replied that "neither would the strike funds (of the unions) be sufficient, nor would the psychological preconditions be present."[31]

When the coup took place, ADGB leaders by coincidence were meeting to discuss other urgent political matters, with Wels and two party colleagues present. According to Wels' later recollections, the union leaders' reaction to the coup was depressing to him. "Not a word of outrage, no visible emotion was to be noticed. I had the impression that they were generally undecided what to do."[32] Thereupon, Leipart asked an equally uncertain Wels for his opinion. The SPD chief argued that even though the situation was not comparable to the Kapp Putsch of 1920, the ADGB ought to seriously consider a general strike, especially since it had repeatedly stated that it would act in an emergency. But he warned that a strike might lead to a bloody civil war, with up to 100,000 casualties. The government would then use the strife as a pretext to postpone the coming July 31 Reichstag election, in which the SPD hoped to make gains and turn the tide against fascism. Leipart underlined the importance of the election, and queried the presidents of the railroad and public service unions on how their members would respond to a strike call. They said that the members would not respond since many unemployed men were ready to step into the jobs of those who would go out on strike.

Thereupon Wels informed Prussian Minister of the Interior Severing of his conversation with the union chiefs. Wels doubted that the union leaders (who were still meeting without him) were ready to call a general strike which could be won. Severing noted that a strike would lead to civil war in which the Reichswehr would crush the Prussian police. After Wels returned to the ADGB meeting to report on his conversation with Severing, all labor leaders apparently concurred that a general strike should not be called.[33]

Thereupon the ADGB publicized its no-strike policy, urged workers to heed only its own decisions and to maintain exemplary discipline, and warned them of provocateurs who in the name of the Iron Front were agitating for a general strike. On June 20 and 21, the SPD policy makers, no doubt influenced by the ADGB decision, also decided against a strike. Iron Front executive members reached a similar decision at their emergency session. They defeated a proposal by Reichsbanner chief Karl Höltermann and Afa President Siegfried

Aufhäuser that at least a demonstration strike be held, and voted instead to deactivate the unofficial Iron Front and Reichsbanner mobilization.[34]

Yet ADGB and SPD leaders prepared cautiously for a future general strike should one become necessary. They discussed a plan in which trusted workers in key industries and services would make discreet inquiries among workers whether they would heed a strike call should one ever be issued. A number of local union leaders, however, doubted that workers would support a strike that was bound to fail. One Reichsbanner and union chief from Frankfort told Wels that the Reichsbanner did not even have enough trucks at its disposal to transport workers to a possible scene of action.[35]

The ADGB stand in the wake of the Papen coup proved once more that the federation had reverted to its typically cautious attitude evident during most earlier political crises. Neither willing to rock the Establishment nor ready to risk a civil war, it failed to take the initiative and preferred instead to await developments. When these came, they were not of the kind the ADGB—or the SPD—had either hoped for or anticipated. In the July 31 election, the NSDAP registered more gains and became an increasing menace to the crumbling government, while the KPD gained votes from workers exasperated by the ADGB and SPD policy of moderation. The vote did not worry Papen as much as did a possible violent reaction on the part of the workers to the election outcome. On the day before the election, he invited ADGB leaders Leipart, Peter Grassmann, and Wilhelm Eggert to his office for a discussion of the election. They appeared reluctantly, obviously not wanting to give the appearance of collaborating with the enemy. The Chancellor asked them whether the ADGB had its members so firmly in its grip that it could unconditionally guarantee law and order regardless of the election outcome. They replied in the affirmative, although they insisted ADGB and SPD would maintain their opposition to the government within the legal bounds. When Papen also inquired whether they were ready to discuss at a later time the position of the unions in the new conservative political order, they agreed.[36] But the volatile political and economic situation made any plans uncertain, including those of the Chancellor whose own term of office was to last just a few more months.

During the brief Papen era, the Chancellor's coup against the socialist Prüssian government was the most brazen flouting of the Constitution. The response of the Left was crucial at that grave moment in German history. In retrospect, whether the no-strike decision was the correct one remains a matter of debate. Had the trade unions decided on a general strike, the SPD, the Iron Front, and apparently the Prussian police, would have backed them. Conversely, the party could not possibly have initiated a strike with the unions opposing it. Which organization made the original decision not to strike is a moot point, although indications are that the unions were responsible.[37]

Nazi leaders expected this outcome. Joseph Goebbels wrote in his diary, "All is moving along according to plan ... One must merely bare the teeth to the Reds, and they lie down. SPD and the unions do not move one finger. The Reichswehr stands ready, but does not have to intervene directly." And, in a comment on a "fairy tale" rumor of a Reichsbanner uprising, he notes, "The Reds are completely tame. But inside they are seething with rage."[38]

Goebbels' characterization of the SPD and unions, shorn of its colorful language, was not far off the mark. A review of arguments expressed in later years defending the no-strike policy shows a streak of caution and a clinging to legality running through them: it was difficult to know what proportion of workers would have participated in the struggle, especially since so many were unemployed; it was impossible to arm them in time; rightist paramilitary organizations would have attacked shops and factories; Papen was still trying to prevent Hitler from taking power. Therefore the constitutional basis of the nation had to be maintained at all costs. Prussian Prime Minister Braun wrote that he had no desire to sacrifice thousands of true republicans in a completely hopeless struggle.[39] SPD editor Stampfer put it just as succinctly: no other decision was possible taking into consideration the SPD mentality and history; "The knack for bloody adventures was not theirs."[40] He could have made a similar remark about the ADGB.

Looking back it is even more astonishing that since rumors of a coup abounded after Papen took power the Prussian government failed to take any measures to ward it off. A feeling of resignation and passivity permeated the Prussian government. It did not strengthen its own police forces or build up a coalition with other Länder governments to safeguard state rights. Whether military and political preparations could have prevented a coup is questionable, but the effort never was undertaken.

In any case, the coup was the precursor to fascism, since it was the first of many illegal acts performed by nonresponsible German governments. Whatever one may have thought of the feasibility of a strike, the decision of the socialist unions and the SPD not to act helped undermine the democratic system. There was only one major force—organized labor—available at that critical hour which could perhaps have saved the situation, but its failure to produce at least an impressive demonstration strike to rally the masses demonstrated its paralysis, irresolution, and fatalism. While its opponents moved outside the constitutional framework, it feared undertaking any political experiment that entailed risks to its members and its organization.

OVERTURES TO SCHLEICHER

On November 17, 1932, Papen resigned. He had aroused the enmity of the army and of all parties, and could not command a parliamentary majority. On December 2, the President appointed General Kurt von Schleicher, Reichswehr leader and Defense Minister in the Papen cabinet, to succeed his chief as chancellor. Before forming the cabinet, the conservative Schleicher, who also lacked an organized party following of his own, approached the various political and trade union organizations to enlist their support for a broad social base for his government.

In his parleys with the trade unions, Schleicher had short- and long-range goals in mind. In private conversations he often expressed the hope that all trade union organizations would sever their links with the political parties, unite under one labor front, and counteract the Nazi menace by exercising more power in the state. He also envisioned the eventual organization of the economy into guilds, and the creation of a corporative government based largely upon the unions.[41]

To this end, Schleicher, when he was still Minister of Defense in the Papen cabinet, and Minister of Interior von Gayl, met secretly on September 9 with top ADGB officers Grassmann and Eggert, and a minor ADGB functionary, and two leaders of the NSDAP moderate faction, Gregor Strasser and the economic theorist Adolf Wagner. The two ministers sought to produce a consensus among the participants for the idea of a corporative state. Strasser and Wagner gave their full support, but ADGB leader Eggert, more hesitant, mentioned difficulties to be faced by a government made up of such heterogeneous forces. First, the unions could not do without their own "revolutionary" elements, which would be strongly opposed to any assimilation attempt. Second, union power would have to be strengthened before any incorporation into the state. Third, time was needed for the unions to discuss such a new idea. Schleicher retorted that as holder of actual power he could easily control revolutionary elements and urged the participants at this meeting to promote corporatism within their organizations.[42]

The readiness of some ADGB chiefs to meet with Nazi officials and to consider the concept of corporatism indicates how far the unions had withdrawn from class struggle and socialism. These union leaders were willing to accept corporatism if it meant a rescue of their organization. This attitude may explain their earlier furtive attempt to meet with Strasser directly. Maintaining a façade of public criticism of Strasser, in July and August 1932 they had approved plans for union intermediaries to make secret contacts with the Nazi leader. Strasser, it must be noted, had been wooing the unions for some time. He denounced capitalism and supported the unions' work creation plan, but he also warned them that the NSDAP would cooperate with them only if they severed their ties with the SPD.[43]

As labor chiefs began secret contacts with one wing of the NSDAP, they had to deal with Schleicher's imminent rise to the chancellorship. On November 28, Schleicher invited Leipart and Eggert to a personal conference. When they accepted, SPD Executive members, who had heard of the invitation, were angry. According to one account, "Leipart was asked to come to party headquarters. . . . There Breitscheid (SPD leader) told him that the party rejects any collaboration with the reactionary Schleicher, and expected the same attitude of him (Leipart)."[44]

Not heeding the party request, Leipart and Eggert met with Schleicher. The participants avoided discussing corporatism, and plunged into a discussion of government policy should Schleicher become chancellor. The General bid for the labor officers' support by acknowledging that Papen's wage cuts had been too drastic and the financial support of the Prussian Junker estates too generous. The ADGB leaders told Schleicher that he would have to initiate an employment policy and scrap Papen's emergency decree on wage cuts if he expected their support. Schleicher asked them to submit their demands to him in written form.[45]

Schleicher, in attempting to form a cabinet, met with representatives of parties and other organizations. In discussions with them he soon gave up some of his more grandiose schemes. One called for the creation of a labor government based on a "trade union axis," to be headed by Reichswehr generals. Apparently, Schleicher believed that such a coalition would preclude the rise of Hitler, but no such combination was possible then since the two forces were antagonistic to each other. The General reportedly also considered a rightist coalition of Reichswehr- Papen- Göring-Hitler, but it is doubtful that this plan was ever fully discussed.[46] Schleicher did hold new conversations with the Strasser faction in an attempt to split the Nazi movement. He offered Strasser the twin posts of Vice-Chancellor and Prussian Prime Minister, but the negotiations crumbled when Hitler stripped Strasser of his party offices and ousted him from the NSDAP. In the end, despite these dramatic plans, Schleicher formed a cabinet containing, with only two exceptions, the same conservative ministers who had served under Papen. The new cabinet composition antagonized the SPD and other democratic parties, and offered fresh hope to the Nazis that power might soon be in their grasp.

Once in office, the new Chancellor established further contact with the trade unions, ostensibly in order to obtain their full support or to include them in a major reorganization of the government.[47] In late December, in New Year's greetings to the workers, Leipart assailed those who were accusing the ADGB of compromising itself by associating with reactionary groups. The ADGB, he asserted, must improve the lot of the workers within the current economic and political circumstances and strive simultaneously for socialism. It knows Schleicher does not want socialism, yet it cannot oppose his plans merely because of his political philosophy.[48] At an ADGB meeting in January 1933, Leipart averred that the unions were not a political party and that they had no authority, and not even the means, to overthrow the government; there could thus be no talk of

[72]

toleration. Unions, he insisted, must discuss their demands with each minister of labor and his experts, or with the chancellor regardless of party membership. But they will never bind themselves to any government, even when the chancellor and the minister of labor are socialists.[49] Under the veneer of these union statements lay a mixture of opportunism, nationalism, and conservatism designed to stave off National Socialism.

The SPD viewed Leipart's increasingly nonpolitical stand and his willingness to accept Schleicher's plans as damaging to the union-party links. It maintained a negative attitude toward Schleicher throughout his short reign, even though he tried to gain its favor too. In mid-December he submitted to the SPD Executive a plan calling for the party and a consolidated labor federation to join the cabinet, for the NSDAP to be banned, for the dissolution of Parliament, and for a postponement of elections. The SPD rejected the plan because it did not want to join a government under a man who had been involved in a host of intrigues and in the Papen coup. In January 1933, Breitscheid dissuaded Leipart from supporting or seeing the Chancellor any more, especially when the latter had fired many pro-SPD school administrators.[50]

The denouement to the Schleicher drama came swiftly in late January. After the Chancellor's failure to drive a wedge into the NSDAP, he offered a cabinet post to the ADGB. But labor leaders who were sympathetic could not receive clearance from the SPD. Without a firm popular base for his government, Schleicher engaged in more intrigues behind the scenes to shore up his government, and asked the President to proclaim a state of emergency. But it was to no avail: Hindenburg was satiated with palace intrigues, and turned to Adolf Hitler to solve Germany's problems. As Hitler began preliminary negotiations to form a cabinet, Schleicher attempted once again to involve the unions in a final effort to stop Hitler's appointment. He tried to intimidate the President by telegraphically summoning top labor leaders to an immediate conference in the War Ministry. Government chiefs wondered whether this move might be the prelude to a general strike, but it came to nought.[51]

In retrospect, the strains and stresses between ADGB and SPD during the Schleicher era reflected the turbulent political atmosphere. Both organizations supported the policy of tolerating the Brüning government, but the SPD shifted its position during the

because of the unreliability of the Chancellor. Political
... Karl Dietrich Bracher criticizes the SPD for having pursued
.. policy of toleration only when the government "corresponded to its
image of democracy." It should have realized that Schleicher once in
power was attempting to keep the Nazis out of power.[52] On the other
hand, there remains the question whether SPD and ADGB toleration
of Schleicher would have been enough to keep him in office. Only
their participation in the government might have prevented a Nazi
assumption of power. If the SPD and ADGB had known what the
future portended, perhaps they would have taken that step.

THE DEATH OF THE UNIONS

The trauma-laden Weimar Republic expired in 1933. On January
28, President Hindenburg, responding to Papen's backstage intrigues
and pressures, ousted Schleicher. Two days later, the President
administered the oath of office to the new Chancellor, Adolf Hitler,
who, ironically enough, promised to uphold the Constitution. January 30 was the beginning of a fateful period for the democratic
organizations that had remained alive but not well since the birth of
the Republic.

Whether the unions would undertake any last minute action to
rescue the nation from political extremism, as during the Kapp
Putsch, or remain passive, as during the Papen coup, could not be
predicted immediately. They had been as surprised as others in
Germany about Hitler's assumption of power and were not sure how
to respond. They knew that Hitler was a danger to them, but they did
not know its magnitude. They felt that Hitler's writings about them
were ambivalent, although a close reading would have shown his
determination to destroy them. In one section of *Mein Kampf* he
characterized them as the "ram of the SPD for the destruction of the
national economy," and in another he asserted that no unions other
than national socialist ones would be allowed in his new order,
although he admitted that unions were one of the most important
institutions in the national economic sphere.[53] When a Berlin labor
leader called Leipart's attention to these passages and urged him to
read the book, the ADGB chief replied that the workers' movement
had been powerful in the Weimar era, and that Germany was not
Italy.[54]

Leipart also believed that Nazi attempts to capture the workers' support by emphasizing the "pro-labor" and "socialist" character of the Nazi party and by creating a Nazi cell movement in the shops (National Socialist Works Organization, NSBO) had fizzled. This assessment was exaggerated: the NSBO, founded in 1929, did make inroads into some ADGB bastions and by January 1933 captured the support of 300,000-400,000 workers.[55] At the same time, Hitler courted the business community, whose financial support he needed. Thus a duality in Nazi propaganda and ideology appeared, often contradictory but understandable in terms of the pragmatic and opportunistic nature of Hitler's program.

Although union leaders were unsure about the new Nazi government, the instinctive reaction of many in the rank and file was to protest on the streets. On January 30, workers in a number of cities spontaneously staged mass demonstrations, while Iron Front and Reichsbanner members made feverish preparations for a strike. The KPD called on the SPD, ADGB, and AfA to declare a general strike. On January 31, delegates from a number of large factories arrived in Berlin to ask Leipart whether directives for a general strike were going to be issued. He replied, "Not yet, but get everything ready, we will call you."[56] Reportedly, labor leaders also bought guns for the protection of various trade union headquarters.

In the night of January 30-31, union, SPD, Reichsbanner, and Iron Front officials met in emergency session to discuss policy alternatives. One SPD official is said to have asked Grassmann, "What do the unions intend to do; do they intend to just accept the takeover?" to which the ADGB leader replied, "We have prepared everything and are not ready to sacrifice the gains of half a century." Hans Jahn, head of the Railroad Workers Union, assured the participants that in case of a general strike not one locomotive would move on the tracks. SPD Chairman Wels said, "Everything is ready for action," while SPD Deputy Chairman Hans Vogel asserted, "A signal will be given."[57] With these expressions of assurance, most of the participants left the session with the impression that the leadership had decided on a centrally coordinated national action and was waiting only for the most propitious moment.

To the leadership, the moment never came, even though the impression of impending action was reinforced at a SPD Executive session on February 5, at which Leipart and Grassmann were present.

The latter reportedly stated that we need merely to give the signal, and all will stand still.[58] One week later, Grassmann told a cheering audience at a rally of the Iron Front in Berlin that organized labor would successfully stop Hitler. During February, Wels also sent Vogel on a mission throughout Germany to win over the unions for the general strike proposal. Although Vogel was still optimistic that "if we press the button, then all will start," others in the party high command were less optimistic, such as one official who commented, "Vogel could have pressed the button, but the wire was missing."[59] At an ADGB Board session in mid-February, some speakers still were reported to be preparing a general strike, including sabotage in the chemical and other industries.

A general strike never was called. Top labor leaders began to have second thoughts about precipitating any rash action for the same reasons as after the Papen coup. For instance, when in mid-February Wels asked Leipart whether it would not be best to offer resistance to the Nazis if they were to outlaw the SPD and ADGB, Leipart replied "that he could not bring himself to the point of pressing the button and thereby giving the signal for a civil war," especially since the outcome was certain.[60]

Militant union cadres and workers who were willing to go out on strike regardless of the consequences felt betrayed by their leaders. They did not readily accept statements of Leipart and associates made then and later that the Chancellor had assumed power legitimately; that the unions could not yet discern the totalitarian character of the fascist movement and believed Hitler would not remain long in power; that the unions could hope to save themselves by becoming nonpartisan (in effect disassociating from the SPD); and that the odds were against the Left in any uprising, especially since the Reichswehr would intervene, and since there were 5 to 6 million unemployed workers who were ready to back any regime promising them work.

There were of course other and more fundamental reasons than those expressed for the lack of a union strike initiative: the leadership lacked the will to deal with the deteriorating situation, it had fallen into a dangerously passive mood which had a contagious effect on much of the rank and file, and it had failed to present a positive alternative program to the Nazi realities.

The ADGB leaders, tacitly disapproving of a general strike,

retreated into the safer routine of using traditional pressure group tactics. As early as January 30 and 31, they issued only mildly critical public declarations after having put pressure on the President not to appoint a Nazi-led government and after unsuccessful attempts to have an audience with him. In their joint declarations with the SPD and Iron Front, they characteristically requested the workers to remain calm and to follow the slogan of the hour, "Organization, not demonstration." Still optimistic about the future, they predicted that the new government, to which they would present labor's demands, would not be able to overpower the workers and their organizations.[61]

Hitler's assumption of power, however, prompted a belated drive for united action among Left forces. Militant union spokesmen told SPD and KPD workers to bury their differences and unite. In Berlin, Clothing, Transportation, and Lithography Workers Unions urged the ADGB to promote a united front accord between the SPD and KPD. But the ADGB took no action, for it had already decided a year earlier that it would not put its weight behind a unity campaign then demanded by the KPD until the KPD had stopped attacking it and the SPD. It was especially furious about KPD statements to ADGB members that their leaders had sold them out to the Nazis.[62] Although the ADGB reacted negatively, unofficial contacts between the two Left parties may have taken place.[63] Indeed, on February 1, Hitler feared the formation of a Left political and labor bloc against his government, but his fear was unrealistic given the improbability of two parties, whose bitter feud had played into the hands of the Nazis, suddenly burying the hatchet.

In early 1933, a number of labor leaders sought a different kind of unity. They resuscitated a plan, not seriously discussed since 1931, to merge the socialist, Christian, and liberal labor federations as a major counterforce to the Nazi government. A committee of top leaders from the federations met secretly to work out a basic statement of their common position on the questions of party neutrality, religious tolerance, and renunciation of revolution and class struggle. The statement, finally agreed on in April, was never published because of the politically precarious situation and expected Nazi opposition to it. Needless to say, a merger never took place, and Wels' fears that such a merger would cause the union deputies in the SPD Fraktion to desert the party were assuaged.[64]

On another political front, Leipart met twice in late February with Schleicher, then out of the government but still with considerable influence on the Reichswehr. Not having abandoned the art of intrigue, the former chancellor was ready to organize a coup with Reichswehr and union support against Hitler that was expected to lead to the latter's arrest and shooting. The coup would be preceded by a general strike, would entail the ouster of Hindenburg, and was expected to lead to the formation of a government to include SPD and union leaders. Leipart replied that a general strike could not be called before a coup, but that the unions would cooperate with Schleicher if the constitution were not to be violated. The grandiose secret plan failed when the Nazis heard of it. It was followed by the Reichstag fire, which in turn unleashed a reign of terror against Nazi opponents.[65]

Attempts to unite the Left or the union federations, and to carry out a coup against the Chancellor, had no perceptible influence on Hitler's strategy of eliminating his opponents. In a get-tough policy, he initiated a campaign of terror against the unions and other democratic groups. On March 8, members of the paramilitary SA assaulted the ADGB training school in Bernau. Other Nazi and police attacks on union property occurred. In many German states, Nazi officials issued decrees that no labor leader could hold a party office or agitate against the government. Public authorities also periodically confiscated and suppressed some union newspapers, with predictable effects on the others, and dismissed ADGB members in works councils.[66] The ADGB responded to these moves with protests to the President and the ministers. Not receiving any satisfaction, they belatedly realized that protests were futile.

ADGB ranks were split on what policy to pursue as a result of the illegal Nazi acts. For instance, at the ADGB training school in Bernau, its head, Hermann Seelbach, a secret Nazi Party member, revealed that among his students, mostly minor union functionaries, a small group advocated illegal anti-Nazi action, while a larger group favored a "let us wait and see" policy, although a still larger group would have yielded to the Nazis (an attitude prompted by Seelbach himself.)[67]

A number of senior leaders, increasingly on the defensive and ready to accommodate themselves to the new power configuration, began to advocate a disassociation of unions from party politics in order to preserve their organization.[68]

On March 21, Leipart transmitted to Hitler an ADGB Executive statement affirming the union's independence from political parties and employers, its noninterference in politics, its right to seek fulfillment of social goals no matter what government is in power, and the government's right to intervene in the establishment of wage accords and arbitration awards.[69]

The lack of a positive response from the Chancellor to this veiled declaration of loyalty produced another communication to Hitler on March 29. In a desperate effort to keep the unions afloat, the labor chief offered to have the unions sever all ties to the SPD and to collaborate with the employers for a solution of pressing social problems. On April 9, the ADGB Executive issued still another declaration in which it agreed to subordinate the unions' freedom of movement to the "higher right of the state to act as representative of the national community," and to the creation of a corporative order and a unitary trade union movement supervised by the Reich.[70]

A clear indication of the misreading of Nazi intentions is contained in a letter sent by Leipart in early March to his old SPD friend, Wilhelm Keil. After admitting that many mistakes had been made, Leipart wrote "I have no intention of increasing my political visibility, since I do not consider it wise. . . . My concern in the first instance must be a dedication to the unions which perhaps are benefiting now from my constant efforts to hold back slightly from party politics."[71]

The Nazis were not appeased by these declarations of nonpartisanship. Whether they would have accepted the existence of free unions in a corporate state or whether they wanted to eliminate them was not entirely clear in this turbulent period, not even to Hitler. On March 17, the Christian unions declared themselves nonpolitical and tried, with the liberal unions, to discuss with Goebbels their participation in the new state. On March 28, AfA President Aufhäuser resigned, and the Executive evolved reorganization plans for the organization. On April 6, the General Federation of German Civil Servants (the socialist federation) disbanded in anticipation of some government move against it. The ADGB Executive decided to maintain its precarious existence under the leadership of politically neutral members, while leaders once active in the SPD or in the international labor movement were resigning.[72] Union weeklies urged their readers not to voice political opinions but to strengthen the unions and devote themselves to economic matters.

The union appeasement policy contributed to an estrangement with SPD officials who were aware of the policy shift, but not of its extent. Apparently without communications from the ADGB leaders, they may not have known of direct and secret talks between ADGB and Nazi officials begun during this time on the position of unions within the Nazi state.

For instance, at the request of the ADGB, Professor Ernst R. Huber, a constitutional law advisor to Hitler, drafted a document on the legal position of the unions in the new state, which recommended their transformation into public legal bodies and their coordination (Zuordnung) with the Third Reich.[73] Union leaders discussed these recommendations or other ways to save the unions with conservative and moderate Nazi cabinet members and minor Nazi chieftains.[74]

On April 13, ADGB Executive members Leipart, Grassmann, Eggert, and Wilhelm Leuschner met with NSBO Reich Commissioner Ludwig Brucker and other leaders. The latter revealed that they intended to form a unitary labor organization, incorporating the free unions. The organization, to be headed by NSBO leader Walter Schumann, would regulate wages and prices. Swift approval by the free unions was necessary because the pressure to destroy them was growing in Nazi ranks. Leipart and his associates retorted that the unions had fought a valiant struggle in the past to obtain their gains, and that they would not agree to the appointment of a new leader.[75]

The meeting may have misled the ADGB leaders into believing that their federation could survive if only some of them were to resign. They were unaware of the fact that at the time Robert Ley (future Labor Front chief), Goebbels, and other right-wing NSDAP leaders were counseling Hitler to crush the movement in order to prevent a power struggle between a unitary labor organization and the NSDAP. Goebbels discussed the details with Hitler who, worried about possible protest strikes, had been undecided on a course of action until then. The Chancellor consented to the plan, although Goebbels foresaw possibly a few days of struggle. By May 1, Goebbels had changed his mind: "Resistance is nowhere to be expected."[76] He would have concurred with a Nazi apologist who wrote, "The seemingly invincible Marxist colossus in reality was just an air balloon, which on the first powerful thrust on our part would lose air, and voluntarily vacate all positions which it held."[77]

In the meantime, on April 15, the ADGB Executive, without

notifying the SPD, welcomed the government's publicized decision to sponsor May Day rallies, even though they were intended to preempt the ADGB's traditional Left holiday. The ADGB left the question of participation in the marches up to the members. Since the workers did not know how to respond, and other trade union federations put pressure on the ADGB, the ADGB Board four days later requested the members to participate " . . . for the honor of creative labor, for the complete incorporation of the working masses into the state."[78] The request represented a clear-cut capitulation to the regime; the SPD headquarters, incensed, sent a memorandum to its affiliates: "No Social Democrat will voluntarily participate in the demonstrations."[79]

The ADGB appeasement policy included an endorsement, in the last issue of its journal, of the "socialist" principles embodied in National Socialism:

> We certainly need not strike our colors in order to recognize that the victory of National Socialism, though won in the struggle against a party which we used to consider as the embodiment of the idea of socialism (SPD), is our victory as well; because today the socialist task is put to the whole nation.[80]

This last desperate effort to save the ADGB failed. Leipart, by then an emotionally broken man, saw no other way out but to yield to the Nazis in the hope that they would allow the ADGB to survive under a commissioner who would espouse the union cause. As scheduled, the Nazis sponsored mass demonstrations on May Day. Many trade unionists even marched—some voluntarily, some not—behind Nazi banners (while many others stayed home).[81] The purpose of the demonstrations was to legitimize the Nazi program and to rally the workers to the state.

Also as scheduled , on May 2, at 10 A.M., the Nazis launched their last assault on the free labor movement. SA and SS units arrested ADGB leaders and staff officials, threw them into detention centers, and occupied all union buildings in a lightning thirty-minute national action. On May 13, the Nazis confiscated, without legal sanction, all union property and funds. The free unions had become the first victims of the Nazi "Gleichschaltung" campaign in which all democratic organizations were to be "coordinated" with the state, but in reality dissolved. In later weeks and months, the Nazis suppressed the Christian and Hirsch-Duncker labor federations and then all political parties other than their own.[82]

Before the ADGB capitulation, IFTU leaders had offered the unions financial and military aid to combat the Nazis. But, as IFTU Secretary General Walther Schevenels notes, the ADGB was convinced until the last moment that it could win the struggle without outside support, and that if it were to accept aid its existence would be threatened. Thus, in February 1933 ADGB leaders did not even participate in a special Zurich session of the IFTU Council. There, after Schevenels reported on talks he had held with Leipart and colleagues, leaders from Switzerland and several other countries favored an immediate general boycott of German goods. But they could not receive backing from the Council majority which feared a Nazi annihilation of the German socialist unions. (International trade secretariats did organize boycotts soon thereafter.) The Council decided, however, that it could not remain silent on developments in Germany, and issued a statement denouncing the Hitler regime. Although the statement was moderate in tone in order to protect the ADGB, it marked a break with Leipart who had pleaded with the IFTU to refrain from any move. As the political situation deteriorated, the IFTU decided to move its headquarters from Berlin to Paris on April 30, unaware that the Nazis planned to occupy the premises on May 2.[83]

Although the international community and the German democratic community slowly woke up to the real nature and goals of the Nazi regime, one must still pose the haunting question, why did a number of leading German labor leaders, among other leaders equally committed to a democratic political system, attempt to compromise with the Nazis during this period? There is no facile answer. Certainly the labor leaders, bound up in their dogmatic anti-Communist position, failed to foresee the ruthlessness of the Nazi policy, its drive to totally eliminate the Weimar institutions and organizations, and its crushing opposition to any non-National Socialist ideas. In making opportunistic appeasement moves, which had no chance of success, they mistakenly expected the Nazis to spare their organizations from the totalitarian web.[84]

The tragic end of the free labor movement stands in sharp

contrast to its action during the Kapp Putsch when it took the initiative to protect the Republic against an internal threat. During the declining Weimar years, however, the conservative governments and the Depression had sapped the vitality of the union movement and other democratic institutions. When the Nazis were given political power and moved relentlessly against their foes, the labor movement had lost its strength of will to resist.

Part Two

THE ADGB, TARGETS, AND IMPACT

IV

THE SOCIALIST UNIONS

Organization and Politics

BIG AND COMPLEX organizations are characteristic phenomena of the twentieth century. Their hierarchical, bureaucratic structure aims to maximize their size, power, and chances for survival. Their membership is separated from the top decision makers by layers of intermediate decision makers. In Weimar Germany, the structures of unions and employer associations fit this universal model. Yet each organization had its specific structural and decision-making characteristics influenced by its own history, traditions, and environmental pressures. The ADGB had to grapple, for instance, with the problems of craft versus industrial unionism and political factionalism which other German union federations did not have to face to the same extent.

In 1891, the General Commission unions numbered sixty-two, but as a result of continuing concentration among smaller national unions, the ADGB began with fifty-two and ended with twenty-nine constitutent unions. Yet even in the final Weimar period, giant, medium, and small national unions were well balanced numerically. In 1928, a typical year, the ADGB membership was 4,653,000. The six giant unions, which made up more than 50 percent of this membership, were the Metal Workers (884,000 members), Factory Workers (458,000), Construction Workers (435,000), Transportation Workers (368,000), Wood Workers (307,000), and Textile Workers (306,000). The medium-sized unions were the Municipal and State Employees

(244,000), Railroad Workers (241,000), Mine Workers (196,000), Food and Beverage Workers (160,000), Agricultural Workers (151,000), and Carpenters (107,000). The small unions ranged from Printers and Shoe Makers to Chimney Sweeps and Film Workers, the last being the smallest with 1,300 members.[1]

Membership figures varied from year to year. In 1918, the ADGB unions had close to 5.5 million members; in 1920 and 1922, they reached a peak of 7.9 million, declining to between 4 and 5 million from 1924 on.[2] As noted earlier, the phenomenal membership rise after the 1919 Revolution was caused by employer recognition of the unions, state protection, the demobilization of soldiers and their joining the ranks of industrial labor, and socialist idealism. But this peak could not be maintained long with the swift onset of inflation, unemployment, and disillusionment with the leaders' political course. Thereafter membership figures stagnated: the industrial unions, stymied partly by the power of the craft unions, could not attract enough support among industrial workers.

The proportion of female members in the ADGB unions sank from a high of 21.8 percent in 1919 (1.2 million to nearly 5.5 million members) to 14.7 percent in 1929 (723,000 to 4.9 million). Although the ratio was low in 1929, it represented close to one-third of the total female labor force.[3] Age distribution among male and female members corresponded approximately to that of the entire labor force. In 1929, 6 percent of the ADGB members were under 18 years old. In the Metal Workers Union, the highest percent of members (18 percent) were from 21 to 25 and three out of four members were below 40 years old.[4]

A survey of the hierarchical structure of the ADGB reveals that it differed little from that of any other major union federation in Germany or elsewhere. The pyramid-shaped organization was broad based locally, narrowing to a peak nationally with its decision makers concentrated at the top and transmitting decisions downward, although permitting a measure of internal democracy and national union autonomy (see figure 1). The relationship between the ADGB and its constituent unions normally was close, even though political dissension, as discussed below, occurred frequently, leading in a few instances to the expulsion of communist-controlled local councils.

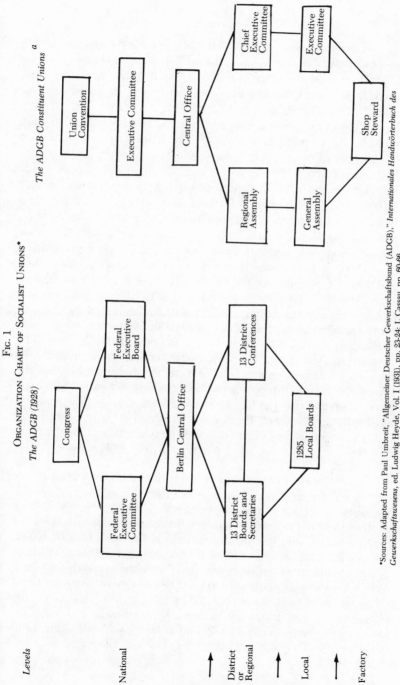

Fig. 1

ORGANIZATION CHART OF SOCIALIST UNIONS*

The ADGB (1928)

The ADGB Constituent Unions [a]

*Sources: Adapted from Paul Umbreit, "Allgemeiner Deutscher Gewerkschaftsbund (ADGB)," Internationales Handwörterbuch des Gewerkschaftswesens, ed. Ludwig Heyde, Vol. I (1931), pp. 23-24; J. Cassau, pp. 60-66.

[a] A number of unions also had Executive Boards.

At the peak level, the ADGB Congress constituted the parliament of delegates representing the affiliated national unions. Meeting infrequently and large in membership, it could not be involved directly in the day-to-day decisions that count so heavily in any organization. Therefore, it stood at the periphery of decision making. Each union delegation consisted primarily of officials rather than rank and file workers. Since the size of each delegation depended on the number of members in the union, the numerically larger unions had a sizable bloc of votes and could influence general policy. For instance, at the 1919 Congress, 645 delegates represented nearly 5,500,000 union members, of whom almost twenty percent were from the giant Metal Workers Union. On occasion, friction developed between the large and the small unions, with the latter worried that their interests would not be adequately represented.

A typical congress agenda was replete with speeches by leading politicians, especially invited for the occasion, and by a number of high union officials. Certain government officials, such as a minister of labor, usually accepted invitations automatically, but the chancellor did not. In one instance, union leaders sought to have Chancellor Brüning appear at the 1932 Special Congress so that he would be exposed to a discussion of an emergency employment program. At an earlier cabinet session, the Minister of Labor counseled the Chancellor not to appear for political reasons. When ADGB chiefs gave assurance that the Congress would not engage in a vendetta against the government, the Chancellor promised to appear. But at the last minute he had to participate in an international meeting and sent the Minister of Labor as his deputy. ADGB leaders were not pleased.[5]

Speeches and discussions at a congress centered on a few major topics, which normally did not provoke fiery discussion, because the speakers were carefully chosen by the ADGB high command. On a controversial topic, such as an ADGB reorganization, speakers for the affirmative and the negative provided the basis for discussion, but skillful parliamentary maneuvering assured a compromise or postponement of a decision whenever factions were deadlocked. ADGB leaders also made sure to keep to a minimum the number of controversial resolutions introduced by local organs.[6] Therefore, the congresses served primarily as formal debating assemblies, as a publicity medium for the ADGB, and as framework for airing long-range policy. They did not affect the rank and file directly.

[90]

Since the congresses normally met only every third year, smaller bodies had to supply policy guidance in the interval. The most important was the Federal Executive Committee (Bundesvorstand), with fifteen members, of whom seven were paid functionaries elected by Congress delegates. The seven were the ADGB president, two vice-presidents, the journal editor, the treasurer, and two secretaries. The other members, selected at meetings of the Federal Executive Board (Bundesausschuss) and approved at the congresses, were the presidents of eight constituent unions.

The Executive Committee was a collective decision-making unit, although the ADGB president stood *primus inter pares*, comparable to the British prime minister and his cabinet. The Executive was powerful, yet it operated under the broad constraints of not only the public, the employers, the political parties, and public bodies, but also the union rank and file and those presidents of affiliated unions who had not been selected as Executive members. The latter, who held membership on the Board, were not remiss in defending their interests. (Thus the Executive could not have ordered the mine workers in the Ruhr to go out on strike; such a decision was the workers' to make in a membership vote.)

The Executive had to convene meetings of the Congress and the Board, and carry out their resolutions; coordinate union activity in the economic, social, women's, young people's, educational, and international spheres; support strikes; collect statistics; issue propaganda materials and the union journal; and provide reports to the central executive bodies of the affiliated unions and the ADGB Congress. For this purpose, the Berlin central office, with Board approval, hired a staff of professional specialists, set up standing committees, and with the SPD maintained a joint research institute.

The Board was another important policy-making body. Membership consisted of the president of each affiliated union; larger unions were entitled to an additional seat for every 300,000-500,000 members.[7] ADGB Executive members had to attend all meetings in order to provide policy coordination and to report on their own work, but had no voting rights. The Board met normally twice a year to discuss measures to carry out Congress resolutions, to supervise the work of the Executive and the treasurer, to hire professional staff (Sachreferenten) for the ADGB headquarters, and to decide on policy recommendations. Immediately binding Board resolutions had to be adopted unanimously, providing a veto power for each union. Other resolutions could be accepted by majority vote and were binding within one month if no union objected. In either case, the resolutions could deal only with matters outside the internal jurisdiction of the unions. On financial questions, each Board member received one vote, granting the larger unions greater influence. Yet, in the case of the Metal Workers Union the influence was not enough to put the ADGB on a political Left course—thus producing frustration among the radical leaders who were unable to whittle down the power of the conservative craft union bloc in the top ADGB councils. Although the Board did not carry the weight of the Executive, it was an important agent in decision making because its members carried the greatest authority in their national unions.[8]

At the regional level, the ADGB formed District Boards (Bezirksausschüsse) whose task was to coordinate the work of the local boards, to promote education and propaganda, and to ensure adequate representation of union interests in the Länder (state) parliaments and governments. In 1928, there were thirteen District Boards for the country, each consisting of five to seven members elected by a district conference. ADGB headquarters selected the district secretary, who also served as Board chairman, and who provided a link from Berlin to all districts.

At the local level, Local Boards (Ortsausschüsse) serviced the ADGB in cities and towns. Board members were the local representatives of affiliated national unions who were responsible to a yearly assembly attended by delegates from the unions. In turn, the Boards sent delegates to attend the district conferences. By 1930, the ADGB had formed close to 1,300 local units, of which twenty-six had a membership surpassing 25,000.[9]

To finance the work of the ADGB, the federation assessed each affiliated national union a monthly sum based on the number of its members.[10] These dues amounted to about one-third of the yearly income, which was supplemented by revenue-producing holdings in banks and other properties. In 1925, for instance, revenue amounted to a total of nearly 4 million Reichsmark (RM), or $1 million. Expenditures flowed into staff salaries, the ADGB journal, educational and research institutes, and propaganda. In addition, the District Boards received subsidies from national headquarters, although most of their operating expenses came from the Local

Boards. These, in turn, were subsidized primarily by the local branches of the national unions. The Local Boards spent their income on the maintenance of the secretariats and information centers, and on administration, education, and propaganda.

The ADGB balance sheet showed fairly modest sums, but total yearly income and expenditures of the affiliated unions in the late twenties was at a magnitude of 250 million RM, or about twenty-three times the income of the SPD. More than 6,500 employees had to be paid, workers on strike had to be aided, and high expenses were incurred for administration, organization, propaganda, press, and education (the unions sponsored many evening and weekend courses for workers). The unions financed these expenditures through dues and income from sizable capital investments, union-owned office buildings, people's houses, insurance companies, banks, credit institutions, publishing houses, and firms making office supplies and other products bought primarily by them.[11]

The ADGB-affiliated unions guarded jealously not only the right to maintain their own budgets, but also the right to shape collective bargaining accords and to call strikes. Therefore they acted as a counterweight to the centralized ADGB structure and produced a confederal system with its normal strains and stresses. Their own organizations were centralized and bureaucratic, partly as a counterweight to the centralization of industry and employer associations and partly out of long tradition.

The organizational pattern of the national unions, nearly all of which were formed during the Imperial era, showed a striking uniformity among them. At the factory level, a shop steward (and often the works councils) represented the interests of the union. At the local level of town or city associations (Ortsvereine), a general assembly of workers elected—usually for one year—a small executive committee, which then hired a paid staff and received policy directives from the monthly workers' meeting. This measure of internal democracy had to be limited where the membership was too large. Then executive committees and district assemblies, which met several times a year, had more autonomy to shape organization campaigns or the improvement of job conditions. Provisions for referenda, primarily on local issues, were written into union constitutions and bylaws, but were used sparingly; hence, as direct democracy diminished in importance, the representative system became more widespread.

At the regional level (Gau), an assembly of delegates from the local constituencies met yearly to determine wage policy and the budget. Its guidelines were executed by regional leaders appointed by the chief executive committee (Hauptvorstand). At the national level, a union convention (Verbandstag) was in theory the chief policy-making unit, but in practice the executive committee made policy. The latter consisted of paid functionaries, each responsible for one union activity, and a number of unpaid functionaries, selected to keep tabs on the first group.[12]

This examination of the constitutions, structures, and finances of the ADGB and its constituent unions has provided only some clues to their ways of operating; an examination of their political dynamics, that is, their decision making, their recruitment and circulation of leaders, their measure of internal democracy, and their organizational and political problems is as important.

THE DECISION-MAKING PROCESS

In the formulation of decisions at the ADGB national level, no blanket answer can be given as to who was responsible for any given decision. Obviously none was made in the abstract, but by a number of leaders and staff specialists in the key policy-making units of the ADGB and the constituent unions. The latter often recommended a course of action to the ADGB or on occasion vetoed a decision of the ADGB chiefs. As a consequence, Leipart and associates acted more within a system in which power is shared with the constitutent units than one in which power resides primarily in the center. The ADGB staff at national headquarters also fed ideas and proposals to the "inner core." Once a decision was made, they worked on its details and implementation.[13]

The typical union chiefs in the founding decades of the nineteenth century rose from the rank and file. Imbued with a vision of a brighter socialist future, when faced by untold hardships at the hands of hostile governments and employers, they put in extra unpaid time as union organizers and built up a strong union movement. They related well to the workers, having shared the same experiences and limited education.

Typical of these leaders was Carl Legien, who headed the

movement until his death in 1920. Rising to power because of his relentless drive for work and determination to build up the unions, he was the undisputed leader among the seven General Commission members. Critics accused him of having a despotic character; Lenin, in an article entitled, "What one should not imitate about the German trade unions," disliked his opportunism.[14] But such negative comments could not hide his considerable achievements.

After Legien's death, the ADGB executive organs had to choose his successor, and immediately faced a mixture of constitutional and political problems. On the Board, a procedural dispute erupted as to who had the right to replace Legien in the Executive. The four radical members, including Robert Dissmann, President of the Metal Workers Union, invoked the ADGB statute to argue that only the Congress had this right. They urged a postponement of the election until the next Congress would meet more than a year hence, because they hoped that the Congress, with a strong radical minority, might select a president with more radical views than those of Legien. Nine Board members, who opposed the suggestion, argued that the Board had the right to proceed to an immediate election. Since the Executive had already forwarded to the Board the name of Theodor Leipart, he was nominated and elected, with the radical members voting in the negative.[15]

Leipart was chosen not only because his views coincided with those of the majority of members of the two executive bodies, but because, in contrast to most other leaders, his concern with union matters ranged beyond the confines of his own union, the Wood Workers Union, which he had headed. Compared to his predecessor who was adept at grand organizational design, Leipart was more of a specialist with a knack for working out details, and a pragmatist skillful in organizing team work and a smooth running bureaucracy. But he lacked charisma, was not a great orator or ideologue, and had little political talent. A former labor leader recalls his patriarchical manner and snobbishness, and one writer pictures him as "lean, tall, slightly stooped, grey, with a pointed beard, well groomed, resembling a British lord of the Victorian era."[16] Although some personal characteristics obviously did not endear him to colleagues and staff, his administrative talents were strong enough to ensure his repeated reelection until the destruction of the ADGB in 1933.

Leipart surrounded himself with a loyal team of administrators, specialists, and theoreticians who received the continuing support of a majority of the two executive bodies. Among the paid members on the Executive for the entire period, or most of it, were vice-presidents Peter Grassmann and Hermann Müller, treasurer Hermann Kube, editor Paul Umbreit, and secretaries Alexander Knoll and Wilhelm Eggert. Lothar Erdmann served as theoretician of the movement and speech writer for Leipart. The career of Vice-President Grassmann typified the upward mobility of ADGB staff officials. He was born in 1873, became a printer's apprentice, wandered through Europe for three years, and at the age of 20 became active in the printers union and in the SPD. Ten years later (1903), he became a regional head of the union. At 35, he rose to union vice-president, and soon thereafter became a member of the IFTU and ADGB Executive. In 1924, he also won election to the Reichstag as SPD deputy.

The majority of Executive members were heads of the constituent unions. Although some of them served continuously from 1919 to 1933, others retired or died, producing a limited circulation of elites.[17] It must be noted that none of the ADGB leaders were women, even though female union members constituted a sizable minority of the total ADGB membership. Rather, men born between 1870 and 1885 constituted the second generation of labor leaders. They were schooled by Legien and other elders who had to make the most sacrifices for the movement. Despite having to encounter fewer obstacles, they were still not educated enough to match the top leaders and bureaucrats in industry and government. They rose in union ranks through modest leadership abilities, often being co-opted by their elders into positions of responsibility. During the Weimar period a network of educational centers was established to train promising union members, who constituted the third generation of leaders, most of them born between 1885 and 1900. The war had interrupted their education and they were eager to move up from the rank and file. The most talented members, however, chose to satisfy their political aspirations by switching to party work. As a result, in each national union only one or two individuals stood out as prominent and skilled leaders. They were underpaid for their work, but the members did not want to see a big gap in income between themselves and their leaders.[18]

Fritz Tarnow, head of the Wood Workers Union and member of the ADGB Executive until 1933, was typical of a prominent constituent union leader. He was born in 1880, became a carpenter's apprentice, and in 1906 was appointed secretary in his union. In 1920, he rose to union presidency and ADGB Executive membership. Among other prominent Executive members who served for various terms were presidents Alfred Janschek (Mine Workers Union), Nikolaus Bernhard (Construction Workers Union), and Hermann Jäckel (Textile Workers Union).[19]

Characteristic of nearly all Executive members was their political allegiance to the right wing of the SPD. At the 1919 ADGB Congress, when SPD and USPD were rivals, the union radicals put up a slate of candidates, including Jäckel, for the top three ADGB positions, but the slate lost.[20] At later congresses, no rival candidates ran for office. Although the radical wing was underrepresented on the Executive, this was less true of the Board, on which several members of radical unions had seats. Among them was Robert Dissmann, a President of the Metal Workers Union. Born in 1878, in the same period as Grassmann and Tarnow, his early career hardly differed from theirs, except that he was an opponent of reconciliation between social classes. In 1917, he was one of the founders of the USPD, became a district secretary, headed the radical opposition in his union, and in 1919, along with Alwin Brandes, another left-wing leader in the ADGB, captured control of the union from the conservative leadership.

Despite the presence of a left-wing bloc, Leipart's rule as president was never challenged successfully. He always had the support of a majority of Congress delegates or Executive and Board members. Yet discords on substantive issues did not disappear. If the issues were political or economic, Dissmann, Brandes, Jäckel, and a few left-wing colleagues challenged Leipart, Grassmann, Tarnow, and the majority. Dissmann, the spokesman of the Left, inevitably lost these skirmishes: for instance, on the extent of socialization or the powers of the works councils. But that made him the more eager to remain the gadfly to the ADGB establishment. He and his radical colleagues at the 1919 Congress also challenged the draft of the ADGB organization statute. To enhance internal democracy, they suggested that meetings of the Congress be held every two rather than three years. Grassmann, representing the statute commission, opposed the proposal on the basis of high costs and added preparatory time. It was defeated. (Communist delegates at the next Congress urged, unsuccessfully, that the Congress meet every year.)[21]

On a few nonpolitical substantive issues, other divisions within the Executive surfaced. Among the most controversial was that of craft versus industrial unionism (to be discussed below), which demonstrated the power of the craft union leadership in the ADGB, attained on the basis of seniority in the labor movement. On most issues, however, after an exchange of views on the Executive or Board, a consensus developed that cut across divergent ideological or other viewpoints.

The picture of an entrenched, occasionally feuding leadership, which emerges in a study of the ADGB, is somewhat akin to that described around the turn of the century by Robert Michels in his famous "iron law of oligarchy," for which the SPD (and to a lesser extent the socialist unions) served as a model. The union leaders were able to govern without a serious challenge to their rule from the rank and file. They wielded power for a lengthy period because they possessed expertise and had built up a sizable, efficient, and loyal bureaucratic machine.[22]

As a by-product of this accretion of power, they acquired status, prestige, and privileges—important elements in any social system. It would have been difficult to dislodge them unless they had proved to be totally incompetent and unresponsive to rank and file aspirations. Since this was not the case—a measure of internal democracy did prevail—the disciplined and loyal members respected them, and had confidence that their interests were being well represented. As a result, the members tended to become passive and to have less influence over policy formation, although they were still dreaming of moving into a higher social status. But to be a blue-collar worker meant to be at the bottom of the ladder, with little chance for the children to move up one rung. A mood of apathy led many members to quit the union movement. They were joined by still others who failed to see any benefits in continuing to pay dues, or who left for other reasons. As a consequence, the turnover in membership may have run as high as 30 percent in a number of unions.[23] For those who remained in a union, it provided them with a familiar shelter and a community of shared interests.

The pattern of an entrenched managerial and oligarchical elite supported by a lethargic rank and file was and is typical of trade union movements in other countries. It matches the one-faction or one-party model of American union governments in which unanimity is the goal, and factionalism and dissent are viewed as inimical to the good cause.[24] Although in Germany this pattern prevailed in normal times, strains between leaders and the rank and file arose during periods of economic and political crises. Then workers went out on wildcat strikes or looked for extremist political solutions to their desperate problems. They put the blame not only on government officials and employers but on their own leaders as well. In turn the union leaders became more mistrustful of the radicalized workers' spontaneous initiatives for fear that the gains achieved over decades might be suddenly lost. The leaders sought to preserve and to perpetuate their vested interests, causing new cleavages within the ADGB.[25]

The Great Depression especially reflected this malaise. When union members demanded action and denounced the labor "bosses," often at the behest of radical leaders, the ADGB elite, on the defensive, issued a pamphlet entitled "Fight the Bosses!" According to its author, the members certainly have the right to criticize their leaders, but they must do so on objective grounds. The workers should not accuse a union boss of becoming a highly-paid bourgeois official since he is a product of the working class. He has not betrayed his former occupation as long as he represents the masses. The author admitted that the gap between the rank and file and top ADGB officials had widened, but argued that it could be bridged by union functionaries at the local and district levels who heavily populated the national congresses. He concluded with a plea for the establishment of a humanitarian bureaucracy.[26]

Although the erosion of internal democracy was not restricted to the ADGB in the Weimar period and has become a universal characteristic of large-scale organizations, in the instance of Weimar Germany the consequence was more disastrous. Extremist groups exploited the rift—real and alleged—within the trade unions, weakening their fiber at a crucial time in German history.

Craft versus Industrial Unionism

The ADGB had to grapple not only with the problem of bureaucracy, but also with the controversial question of the basic structure of its constituent unions. As in other countries, the intense debate centered on the question of whether the craft or the industrial union should be the prototype. The feud within the ADGB had its antecedents in the pre-World War I era when vertical concentration started in industry, producing an amalgamation of craft and unskilled workers in the same factory. The horizontally structured craft unions, proud of their tradition of skilled work in a medieval setting, found it difficult to adapt to the new industrial era.

At first, these unions balked at uniting into larger unions that would correspond more closely with the industrial age. Their leaders feared losing rank and status in any reorganization; their workers considered themselves the aristocracy of the labor force and looked down on the unskilled workers—or they feared a loss of pay or of strike benefits if an amalgamation took place. After the turn of the century, however, the leaders reluctantly assented to a merger of related craft unions into national ones, although they continued to reject the alternative of creating industrial unions.[27]

During and after World War I, heavy industry expanded, causing renewed discussion among labor officials. Those favoring industrial unions were motivated by pragmatic and ideological considerations. They viewed craft unions as organizations eager to feather their own nest; hence willing to come to terms with the capitalist system and to gain benefits at the expense of unskilled workers. Those favoring craft unions denied these allegations. In any case, the number of industrial unions with a predominance of radical and class-conscious workers mushroomed. By the early 1920s 85 percent of all ADGB members belonged to the 15 industrial unions, unlike 1891 when the industrial workers constituted only 20 percent of the total General Commission affiliated union membership.[28]

As a consequence, Robert Dissmann introduced a resolution at the 1922 ADGB Congress calling on the ADGB to reorganize on the basis of industrial unions. He advanced new arguments: industrial unions could bargain more effectively with employers on an industry-wide scale and were a more rational basis for organizing factories employing workers with many different skills. Fritz Tarnow led the opposition to the resolution. He feared that the craft union would perish, thereby endangering the very existence of the ADGB. His views did not prevail; the delegates, including a number of craft union delegates who had been convinced of the need for a major reorganization, supported the Dissmann resolution by a vote of 465 to 163.[29]

The 1922 Congress set up a commission to work out a plan for reorganization, and requested it to transmit its proposal to all affiliated unions for discussion and action prior to submission to the 1925 Congress. The commission ran into a number of roadblocks. Inflation soon hit the country, and the unions were too busy fighting its effects to worry about reorganization. By 1924, the Executive had repeatedly warned commission members to reconvene; when they did they had to contend with the die-hard opposition of eighteen craft unions that threatened to quit the ADGB if industrial unionism were to become the base. Finally, the 1925 Breslau Congress, over the objection of the Metal Workers Union, approved a compromise plan worked out by the commission. It reaffirmed the principle of industrial unionism, but allowed the craft unions to maintain their existence subject to a continued concentration process among them.[30] The small craft unions supported the proposal since they had already amalgamated into federations before World War I in order to maximize their strength.

Therefore, before the demise of the ADGB in 1933 no reorganization took place other than the already cited continuing concentration. This process, accompanied by a shift from craft to industrial unions, and occurring in other industrial countries as well, was a necessary adaptation to new economic and technological conditions in which giant industries dominated the market.

POLITICAL FACTIONALISM

In its brief lifetime the ADGB faced serious political schisms that multiplied its internal problems and robbed it of some cohesion. Its lack of political homogeneity led to the creation of three rival wings reflecting the historic propensity toward sectarianism on the political Left, in this instance accentuated by the Russian Revolution. Foremost among the factions was the majority bloc, otherwise known as the "Right" or "reformist" wing, headed by Leipart and Grassmann. This bloc, assessed earlier in this chapter, set ADGB policy and controlled much of its machine. It endorsed the cooperative relationship with the SPD, and received the unstinted support of most theoreticians and publicists of the labor movement.[31] It was challenged by two rival factions—the communists and the radicals.

The Communist Faction

The communist bloc never assumed enough power to seriously influence the top ADGB reformist decision makers, even though it had pockets of strength and became important during periods of crisis and unemployment when it received the support of a sizable number of workers desperate for a solution to their problems and alienated from the system. At the height of the inflation in 1923 the bloc showed the greatest numerical power, claiming that one-third of the socialist union members (or about 2.5 million) were in sympathy with it.[32] Although this claim seems exaggerated on the basis of other studies, there was considerable communist strength in the Metal and Textile Workers Unions, and in thousands of trade union district and works councils, especially in the Ruhr and Upper Silesia.

By late 1925, during a period of relative economic and political stability, communist strength in the free unions had declined to approximately 10 percent, and in the Metal Workers Union to 16 percent.[33] The bloc registered a similar decline in the number of delegates at ADGB congresses. At the 1922 Congress, Communist Party (KPD) strength shrank precipitously because of attrition in communist influence within the rank and file.[34]

Yet the Communists were able to exploit legitimate workers' grievances in a period of prosperity as well. One graphic account by a Communist worker in a machine factory illustrates the tensions that arose at times between socialist leaders and the rank and file. One day in 1928 the factory workers read a notice buried in the press that their union (Metal Workers) had concluded an agreement with the Metal Employers' Association extending the existing wage levels. The workers were furious at not having been consulted by their union leaders before the agreement. One worker exclaimed, "I can find no word for the behavior of the union leaders," while another yelled, "They are corrupt scoundrels—employer agents." The workers, including those loyal to the SPD, voted to go out on a wildcat strike. Management immediately locked them out.[35]

Not only did the national business cycle and the occasional insensitivities of labor leaders to the rank and file feelings have an effect on communist strength within the ADGB, but the top leadership of the KPD, at the behest of Communist International (Comintern) and Red Trade Union International directives, changed tactics at a dizzy pace, which caused confusion among KPD workers with marginal loyalty to the cause. At different times, KPD leaders advocated either destroying the free unions or capturing them by boring from within, or establishing rival unions.

In early 1919, they considered unions superfluous in the revolutionary struggle, and urged that workers' councils replace them. Then, at the end of 1919, they demanded the revolutionizing of existing unions through the organization of communist cells and the ouster of SPD officials. In 1920, they accepted the Red Trade Union International twenty-one point program, of which one point read that Communists had the duty to wage a struggle within the socialist unions against the socialist IFTU.[36]

In pursuit of this aim, KPD leaders in November 1923 organized a Weimar Conference, attended by delegates of the communist-captured ADGB district councils, ostensibly to create unity within the ADGB but in reality to create a central opposition to the reformist bloc. The ADGB, hardening in its anticommunist stance, denounced the conference and expelled local councils refusing to follow its policy directives.[37] Thereupon the KPD urged members dismissed from the unions for engaging in communist activity and the unorganized workers to join newly created (but short-lived) opposition trade unions. ADGB constituent unions similarly expelled KPD members; the Construction Workers Union, for instance, revoked the membership of 4,000 unionists.[38]

At the 1924 KPD Convention, the line veered again as the Russian-born KPD chief Arkadij Maslow, supported by a letter from Stalin, urged the delegates to attack the free unions from within. The Soviet leader's interest and intervention in German labor affairs had an impact on KPD policy, which toed the Moscow line faithfully.[39]

Since the KPD had failed to steer the free unions on a leftward course, in 1929-1930 it decided at the behest of the Red Trade Union International to form communist unions outside the ADGB framework. The new organization, the Revolutionary Trade Union Opposition (RGO), attracted the core of communist workers and a number of unemployed, but its membership in 1932 did not surpass 312,000.[40] It remained in existence until 1933, although it faced a host of difficulties: a rigid, oligarchic leadership not willing to permit any internal democracy; employer resistance; weak financial support to workers on strike (the legendary Moscow gold was not flowing in); and the predicament of weakening the workers' revolutionary fervor by establishing unions to better their conditions.

Plagued by these problems, the KPD did not entirely abandon its policy of working within the ADGB, but again scored little success. It captured control of less than 2 percent of the ADGB local councils, and in July 1932 and January 1933 failed in its appeals for a general strike. When it denounced the ADGB bosses as "the vanguard of social-fascist (SPD) leadership," and attempted to drive a wedge between them and the rank and file, the effort did not have much effect.[41]

The noncommunist rank and file viewed the communist denunciations of its reformist officials as attacks on itself, and as a ploy to smash its unions. Therefore the denunciations had the opposite effect from the one intended, for they reinforced rank and file loyalty to the leaders. In turn, ADGB leaders exaggerated the communist threat in order to hide their own failures and to justify refraining from making policy changes advocated by militant workers.

The Non-Communist Radical Faction

The reformist majority bloc had to contend also with the rivalry of a strong radical faction, pursuing a policy of loyal opposition rather than the more antagonistic communist policy. As noted, the radical faction emerged during World War I and supported the USPD. After the war, the young radical, unskilled workers who streamed into industry also streamed into the free unions. Their exposure to radicalism came through membership in leftist youth organizations or through association with seasoned radical workers in the mammoth factories. Many of them had been unable to obtain jobs during the war and were dissatisfied with the system or they had become radical as a result of idealism. No matter what their motivation, their joining the unions produced a damaging factionalism within the movement, mirroring the fratricidal warfare between the USPD and the SPD at the political level. At the 1919 ADGB Congress, the strength of the USPD was respectable; it represented about one-third of the organized workers.[42] As a consequence, the USPD bloc in the ADGB was successful in forcing the conservative union officers to abandon their policy of supporting the SPD only and to accept a resolution on political neutrality.

The sectarianism within the unions had another result. When both factions realized that the political Left was being weakened by the continuing feud between SPD and USPD, the 1922 ADGB Congress approved a resolution calling on the two political parties to collaborate with one another in the Reichstag and support the demands of the workers. The resolution helped to seal the merger of SPD and the right wing of the USPD later that year. But the move, while applauded by the noncommunist Left, did not heal the ideological fissures, which no institutional shake-up could end. Indeed, it created a new cleavage within the SPD, as the USPD adherents formed a left wing in the reorganized party.

The radical faction within the free unions maintained its existence because of continued dissatisfaction with the reformist majority policy. Led by Dissmann, Brandes, and AfA head Siegfried Aufhäuser, it received strong support from the Metal and Textile Workers Unions and a minority of members in the other free unions. In the early twenties, it held strength especially in Saxony and Thuringia, although even there the union leadership rested in reformist hands. In the executive organs and at conventions of the constituent unions, the radical faction year after year challenged the views of the reformist bloc. The challenge produced politicization and polarization within the unions.

For instance, at the 1919 convention of the Construction Workers Union KPD and USPD delegates attempted to oust the President, Friedrich Paplow, but they failed. Yet they succeeded in having their views on controversial topics given equal time with those of the majority: two keynote speakers, pro and con, addressed conventions held thereafter. (A similar procedure was instituted in the ADGB and other constituent unions.) As a consequence, a spokesman for the reformist majority in the Construction Workers Union voiced sorrow that since 1919 the union conventions resembled party rather than union meetings.[43]

Despite its minority status, the loosely organized radical faction had a chance to affect political and economic goals in the ADGB and SPD to a limited extent because its leaders were members of their policy-making councils, and because at SPD conventions its supporters numbered up to one-third of the delegates.[44] But the limited representation meant that in political controversies the reformist majority bloc had no difficulty in remaining in the saddle in the SPD and ADGB. Having the power to determine national policies, it tolerated the opposition of the radical faction, especially as the area of discord between them was often narrow.

Therefore, in retrospect, it is evident that the majority wing exercised substantial control over ADGB affairs. Only in the early and final years of the Republic was its authority precarious when postwar chaos and economic turmoil produced a strong KPD and radical opposition. Stability in the intervening years made it more difficult for the opposition groups to gain ground, and they had to be satisfied with pursuing their role as minority factions. Their relative weakness made it easier for the majority blocs in the ADGB and SPD to govern, for the blocs could not have been interlinked as effectively if the opposition had been more powerful.

OTHER LABOR FEDERATIONS

The AfA

The ADGB, it must be recalled, was but one of three socialist union federations in existence during the Weimar years. While it represented millions of blue-collar workers, two other federations organized the salaried employees and civil servants.

The General Free Federation of Salaried Employees (AfA), founded in October 1921, was the successor to a number of prewar organizations established to support improved rights and social welfare schemes for white-collar workers. The AfA initially had a membership of over 650,000, the largest organized group of salaried employees. It harbored a number of unions ranging from the Central Association of Salaried Employees to sea captains, artists, and bank employees, and organized a majority of technicians and foremen. Despite this auspicious beginning, total membership declined soon thereafter, reaching a low of fewer than 400,000 by 1927, and rising only slowly thereafter. Whereas the AfA was the largest organized salaried employees federation in the early twenties, by 1927 it had been eclipsed by the Christian labor federation. The shift toward more conservative unions was caused primarily by the nation's political instability and inflation that ruined the savings of many employees, as well as by the "radical" stance the AfA took on a number of occasions. Not only did it have to cope with declining membership but also with its inability to organize the great percentage of salaried employees remaining outside the unions.[45]

The AfA established the normal hierarchical superstructure to provide for coordination and central leadership over the affiliated, but primarily autonomous, national unions. In theory, AfA's highest decision-making organ was the Congress or Parliament of Employees, composed of delegates from the affiliated unions. Meeting more frequently was the Federal Board (Bundesausschuss), composed of national union leaders, which had a supervisory function over the central secretariat. The Federal Executive Committee (Bundesvorstand), elected by the Congress, was responsible to Congress and Board, but not directly to the affiliated unions. The latter had jurisdiction over social and economic problems facing employees and dealt with salaries. The central secretariat, with the help of a number of specialized committees on which sat experts from the unions, prepared position papers on government drafts of bills and participated in negotiations with government officials and Reichstag deputies.

The AfA rejected the prewar attitude of most economists and employee federations that the white-collar workers were a new middle class located in a buffer position between employers and blue-collar workers. Rather, it viewed the employee class working for the private sector as a segment of the working class, equally exploited by the capitalist owners of production. Thus, it characterized socialism as the higher form of economic organization, not, according to President Aufhäuser, as "a party dogma, but as economic cognition."[46] Although more AfA leaders, including its President, were in the radical faction than their ADGB brethren, the two federations maintained an amicable relationship throughout the Weimar era.

The ADB

The third pillar of the socialist federations was the General Federation of German Civil Servants (ADB). It had its antecedents as a faction within the politically neutral and numerically powerful German Federation of Civil Servants (Deutscher Beamtenbund, DBB). In the immediate postwar era, faction members supported the freedom of civil servants to organize and to strike if necessary. This emphasis on union objectives evoked opposition within the DBB, especially from the more professionally oriented south German associations, which in 1922 did not support a strike of railroad civil servant personnel. As a consequence, the dissident faction withdrew from the DBB that year. At first, ADGB and AfA tried to bring the faction members into their union affiliates by creating civil servant sections for them. But in June 1922 the dissidents insisted on creating their own federation, to be recognized by the ADGB and AfA on a parity basis.

The ADB began with a membership of 420,000, of whom 200,000 were organized in the Railroad Civil Servants Union, and the rest in such fields as post and telegraph, justice, education, national and local government, fire and police. Until 1925, the two civil service federations made attempts to amalgamate, but failed because of conflicts over jurisdictional questions and over the close ties the ADB was establishing with the other socialist federations. Not only were ADB attempts to raid the DBB ranks for new members unsuccessful, but the ADB membership declined by 1928 to 173,000, primarily because of the disaffiliation of several unions. To compound the ADB difficulties, its links to the SPD became strained when the party also maintained its support of socialist members in the DBB. The ADB's organizational structure mirrored those of the other socialist federations.[47]

Federation Links

A measure of cooperation marked the activities of the three socialist federations in the political, economic, and social realms. In March 1923, they concluded an organization pact. It provided for continued autonomy for each federation, but cooperation whenever necessary in the defense of the Republic; the espousal of a socialist economic system; and the support of the IFTU. In practice the ADGB, AfA and ADB executive bodies met jointly on a number of occasions, especially in periods of national crises, to map out strategy. Moreover, each federation sent a representative for observation and liaison to the executive meetings of the other socialist federations.[48] In addition, the leaders drafted joint memoranda to government and parliament, negotiated with public officials, and organized mass rallies and demonstrations. Obviously when three federations with a combined membership of 8 million in 1920 (but less later) acted together, they could expect to influence national policy. Yet countervailing forces, ranging from employer associations and nonsocialist political parties to conservative governments, blunted their power.

If the free union and nonsocialist federations had been able to cooperate more closely with one another and frame common objectives, then their impact on public policy undoubtedly would have been greater, but historic schisms and competition to unionize the same major social groups (the manual workers, salaried employees, and civil servants) led to only occasional joint actions. To understand this limited cooperation, a brief survey of the Christian and liberal union federations during the Weimar era is necessary.

Christian Unions

In November 1918, the Christian and liberal federations formed a united movement, but the effort was short-lived as differences between them multiplied. In 1919, the liberal federation split off, and the Christian unions formed a peak organization, the German Trade Union Federation (Deutscher Gewerkschaftsbund, DGB). The DGB served as a coordinating body for the three main affiliated Christian federations of blue-collar workers, salaried employees, and civil servants. In 1922, it claimed 1.7 million members, but by 1931 it only had about 700,000.[49]

The federation of manual workers was strongest in the Catholic areas of southern and western Germany, and allied itself primarily with the Catholic-dominated Center Party through which it exerted power in the national arena. The salaried employees and civil servant federations, having more Protestant members, maintained links not only to the Center Party, but also to the more conservative parties. Affiliated to the salaried employees federation was the ultraconservative, nationalist, and antisemitic German Union of Commercial Employees (Deutschnationaler Handlungsgehilfen Verband).[50] The German Union had close ties to the German National People's Party and later to the Nazi Party. It had one-third representation in the DGB Reichstag bloc, the vice-chairmanship in the DGB, and 80 percent of the members in the salaried employees federation. Given this power, its occasional threat to leave the Christian movement if there were an opening to the Left had an effect on the other DGB decision makers, whose difficulties were compounded by ideological schisms and programmatic differences among the nonsocialist political parties, which they were supporting on an individual union or federation basis.

To ease these tensions, DGB chairman Adam Stegerwald, former Prussian Minister of the Interior, in 1922 attempted once more to merge the nonsocialist union federations and to create a nonsocialist, Christian and national labor party. When he failed in both attempts, he opted for a coalition of the Center Party with the right-wing parties. An official coalition never materialized, although united positions on issues were taken more frequently as the Center Party became increasingly conservative. Stegerwald also had to face a challenge to his leadership by the more radical head of the Mine Workers Union, Heinrich Imbusch, who was critical of the way Stegerwald had accentuated the political tasks of the unions. In 1929, when reconciliation of views proved impossible, Imbusch replaced Stegerwald as head of the DGB.[51]

Notwithstanding differences within the Christian movement, an accord on some basic union issues emerged. The DGB supported the Weimar Republic, but with reservations. It welcomed the government's social policy, including state arbitration, but also favored maximum self-administration in employer-employee bargaining efforts. In cooperating with the ADGB, especially during the Depression, it called for an improvement in wages and working conditions for the workers.

DGB influence on government and parliament was not as minimal as might be suspected from the relatively low membership figures. It faced bourgeois and not socialist coalition governments during most of the Weimar years, and could count on the sympathetic support of Labor Ministers Heinrich Brauns and Stegerwald, who held office from 1920 to 1928 and 1930 to 1932 respectively. But since conservative employer associations also wielded influence on the bourgeois governments, economic and social policies reflected the tug of war between rival interest groups.

Paradoxically, while bourgeois governments were in power, Christian unions were not necessarily favored over the socialist unions. For instance, in 1931, in a dispatch to the Chancellery, the DGB complained about the practice of ministries forwarding written communications to the ADGB, as the largest union federation, with the request that the ADGB then transmit the news to the other labor federations. Such a practice is an embarrassment to us, wrote the DGB, especially when in some areas of Germany the ADGB was not the largest organization. The DGB urged that communications be sent promptly and directly to its national headquarters in Berlin.[52]

Relations with public authorities produced difficulties between the Christian and socialist unions, but the religious issue was the source of deep-seated tensions between them. When DGB theoretician Theodor Brauer spoke of Christianity as a principle of freedom which must counter the "dark, ungodly and unchristian coercion of socialism,"[53] he must have become *persona non grata* at ADGB headquarters. One DGB brochure accused the free trade unions of anti-Christian activities, such as promoting secular schools and appealing to union members to leave the Church.[54] The ADGB refuted these accusations, but did not convince the DGB.

On a number of occasions the Church became directly involved in the interunion conflict. For instance, in the early twenties, a regional bishops' conference adopted a resolution opposing the membership of Catholic employees in AfA. The AfA retorted that it had maintained a religiously neutral line, that there was a League of Religious Socialists, and that no contradiction between economic socialism and religion existed.[55] In 1928, in Trier, the ADGB complained to the local bishop that tensions had arisen between Catholic members of the ADGB and some priests who had said publicly that they would not give communion and last rites to ADGB members. The bishop replied that the priests had acted correctly since any worker can join the Catholic trade unions.[56] While such Church interference in union matters caused consternation and anger in socialist ranks, it reflected the Church view that secular matters are closely intertwined with its own religious mission. But the result was the creation of a seemingly unbridgeable gulf between the Christian and the socialist federations. It made amalgamation seem a utopian prospect during the years of the Republic.

Hirsch-Duncker Unions

The Hirsch-Duncker liberal unions might have been more amenable to amalgamation with the free unions because religious cleavages did not plague their relationship. Indeed, they worked closely with the free unions on a number of economic and social issues, but their basically antisocialist economic position, the ideological conservatism of most of their white-collar employees, and their insistence that each member vow not to join the SPD precluded a close fraternal link.

The unions, maintaining their anti-SPD stance, supported the

German Democratic Party, even though their chief, Anton Erkelenz, defected in 1930 from the party, of which he had once been chairman, and joined the SPD. In 1930, Erkelenz pleaded for an amalgamation of all union federations, but the Christian unions especially remained hostile.

Since their founding days, the liberal unions had based their ideology on a theory of liberalism and on the harmony of interests between capital and labor, production and consumption. But they had to make ideological compromises in the face of increasing state intervention and regulation of the economy. Not willing to call strikes during labor disputes, they had to accept the formerly disliked principle of arbitration.

With this kind of ideological underpinning, the liberal unions could hardly expect to attract millions of workers in a country prone to class conflicts and to little social mobility. Hence, their strength lay among the salaried employees and railroad workers, who were classified as civil servants, rather than among blue-collar workers. Organized in the Trade Union Ring of German Associations of Workers, Employees, and Civil Servants, the peak federation had a tripartite structure encompassing each major social group, comparable to the Christian DGB. In 1922, when other union federations had their peak membership, the Trade Union Ring had 230,000 workers, 350,000 salaried employees, and 65,000 civil servants as members.[57] In the late Weimar years, membership plummeted as unemployment skyrocketed.

In addition to the three major union federations (socialist, Christian, and liberal), the spectrum of unions and workers' groups included numerous independent unions, the weak syndicalist German Free Labor Union, communist unions, and the Nazi-organized shop council movement. As a gauge of their respective strength, the elections to shop councils in 1931, in which the unions and groups put up separate slates, can be cited as a barometer of workers' ideological preferences. The socialist unions, even during the dark Depression days, had a commanding lead over all rivals with 116,000 representatives; the Christian unions 11,000; the Communists 4,700; the liberals 1,500; and the Nazi groups 700.[58]

In short, while the free unions were by far the most powerful, they were faced by internal factionalism and external competition from other unions and groups. These sapped the entire labor movement and weakened it vis-à-vis government and party officials. The recurring political and economic crises racking Germany, however, produced ad hoc alliances among the federations that strengthened, albeit briefly, their bargaining power on the national scene.

V

THE SOCIAL DEMOCRATIC PARTY

Links to the Political Ally

INTEREST GROUPS must seek access to the decision makers in the political parties and the government in order to achieve their goals. Pressures must be applied on the multiple targets but in different time sequences and with varying intensity depending on the locus of decision making and the importance of the decision maker. One important target is the political party, whose representatives may become the spokesmen of interest group views in the appropriate governmental decision-making units.

In Weimar Germany, interest groups had no difficulty in approaching the spectrum of parties, each tending to represent one ideological direction. For the socialist unions, the SPD was the natural target as well as the natural political ally. Although a spirit of fraternal cooperation existed between them, the leadership, especially of the unions, discouraged any move toward closer integration comparable to the relationship between the British Labour Party and the Trades Union Congress. The insistence of the German organization on maintaining a greater degree of autonomy than the British can be largely explained by their different historical development and organizational form. The British Labour Party was an outgrowth of the trade unions and therefore accorded them a direct voice in its executive organs. On the other hand, the German socialist unions and the SPD had been rivals in their formative years, and consequently were eager to maintain the hard-won status of equality

[114]

and autonomy. As Legien stated in 1919, the unions must not be strictly social democratic organizations if they are to fulfill their tasks. Yet their leaders also had the duty to instil a class consciousness in the worker that would lead him to the SPD as "the party representing the worker as a class."[1]

Although the institutional linkage between the free unions and the SPD was limited, a spirit of friendship cemented their bonds, arising not only from programmatic accords, but from overlapping membership, and union electoral and financial support for the party.

Social Composition of the SPD

Overlapping membership could be one indicator of linkage. Not surprisingly, a high proportion of SPD members were simultaneously union members, a characteristic common to the labor movements in other countries. This overlap ranged from the national party elite to the rank and file. Many of the top party leaders who were no longer actively associated with the unions had started their careers as apprentices in skilled trades, risen in the trade union movement, and then switched to party work in later life. They retained their nominal union membership and regarded the union movement as a vital ally of the party. Among prominent SPD leaders who followed this path were Friedrich Ebert, Reich President, who originally learned the saddle trade and became a union secretary in 1899; Philip Scheidemann, Reich Chancellor in 1919, and Otto Braun, Prussian Prime Minister, who started their careers in the printing trades; and Carl Severing, Prussian Minister of the Interior, who had once been a business agent of the Metal Workers Union.

At other levels of the SPD, the integration was just as effective. The economist Eugen Varga estimated that in 1924-1925 the party numbered approximately 3,000 top leaders and 50,000 officials employed in state and workers' organizations, of whom most were union members. The party rank and file had about 500,000 workers, 100,000 salaried employees, 70,000 civil servants, 100,000 small shopkeepers and housewives, and 30,000 professionals.[2] This estimate shows that the majority of the 853,000 members were in strongly unionized occupations (workers, salaried employees, and civil servants).

From 1924 to 1926 the SPD conducted three regional surveys of its membership and then made a national projection of the social composition of its male members (see table 1). It estimated that of the 658,000 male members, 84 percent were in the strongly unionized occupations. If the female members are added to this total, and those members who did not join a union are subtracted, then a rough estimate is that approximately 530,000 members, or two-thirds of the entire membership were unionists.[3] In 1930, the SPD surveyed 400 districts comprising almost 120,000 members. The result indicated that as party membership had increased so had the numbers of members in occupations prone to unionization, producing an estimated total of 700,000 unionists or 66 percent in the party.[4] Although the union members were not organized in a cohesive bloc within the party, their leaders had an opportunity to influence policy decisions and to block those inimical to their interests. The consequence was that the SPD was tagged as a workers' party and had difficulty broadening its constituency base.

SPD Penetration of the Unions

As a consequence of the interpenetration, the union members within the SPD also constituted the SPD group within the unions. There they tended to be the activists, rising to major and minor posts,

TABLE 1
Social Group Classification of SPD Male Members*
1924-1926 Surveys

Social Group	Average three areas a (in percentage)	Total of SPD male members (projection)
Workers	73.1	481,282
Salaried employees & civil servants	11.0	72,580
Self-employed	4.6	30,401
Professionals b	2.0	13,424
No response	9.2	60,341
Total	100.0 c	658,028

* Source: SPD, *Jahrbuch der deutschen Sozialdemokratie für das Jahr 1926* (Berlin: Dietz, 1926), p. 23 (hereafter referred to as SPD, *Jahrbuch, year*).
a Bremen (two surveys) 1924, 1925; Hamburg, 1925; Hannover, 1926.
b The category includes "free trades" and "intellectuals."
c Rounded off.

not because of the party membership but because of their union activity. If they were high union officers then they were usually only nominal party members because of limitations of time or the need to have a separation of office-holders between the two organizations. If they were middle-level union officers then chances were high that they would spread the party gospel at union meetings where they were the most assiduous in attendance and did most of the work. According to Varga's estimate, 95 percent of these minor officials and secretaries were concomitantly SPD members or officials.[5]

Despite the high SPD membership in the top and middle union echelons, the actual percentage of party members among the union rank and file was low. If, as was estimated, 530,000 to 700,000 SPD members were union members from 1924 to 1930, then conversely only one out of every seven or eight unionists (12 to 14 percent) was an SPD member.[6] The great majority of the other unionists, however, were socialist sympathizers and, as noted below, voted for the party at election time.

Another classificatory scheme to estimate dual membership is to compare SPD and ADGB membership by states (see table 2). While

TABLE 2
SPD and ADGB Membership by States, 1930*

States [a]	SPD membership (in 000's)	ADGB membership	Ratio SPD members to ADGB members (in percentage)
(1) Saxony	170	664	25.6
(2) Berlin-Brandenburg	116	557	20.8
(3) Rhineland-Westphalia	110	491	22.4
(4) Thuringia	116	424	27.3
(5) Hamburg	129	372	34.6
(6) Bavaria	84	341	24.6
(7) Hanover, Braunschweig	75	293	25.6
(8) Wuerttemberg, Baden	71	251	28.2
(9) Silesia	50	274	18.2
(10) Hesse	64	261	24.5
(11) East Prussia	15	94	16.0
(12) Pomerania, Mecklenburg	41	79	51.9
Total	1,041	4,101	25.4

* Sources: SPD, *Jahrbuch 1930*, p. 201; ADGB, *Jahrbuch 1930* (Berlin: Verlagsgesellschaft des ADGB, 1930), pp. 376-377.

[a] The state lines are those of the ADGB districts.

the unadjusted ratio of one out of four is high, the adjusted ratio would be closer to the above-cited one out of seven or eight.[7] Not surprisingly, party and union strength was concentrated, with few exceptions, in states with a high urban rather than a conservative rural population.

Confirmation of the ratio in membership strength may be obtained by comparing the occupational classification of SPD and union members (see table 3). Significantly, more skilled workers, such as the graphic and leather workers, both craftsmen with a long socialist tradition, held dual membership in party and union than did unskilled workers.

TABLE 3
OCCUPATIONS OF SPD AND UNION MEMBERS, 1930-1931*

Occupation	SPD Members (national projection)	Union Members [a]	Number of SPD Members for every 100 Union Members
Construction	79,720	462,428	17
Mining	19,080	190,855	10
Textile	48,930	276,574	18
Graphic	33,470	38,985	86
Hotel & Restaurant	5,130	30,290	17
Wood	54,460	299,924	18
Land & Agriculture	12,500	165,505	8
Leather	21,460	34,236	63
Painter	11,870	57,894	21
Metal	182,790	940,578	19
Music	2,320	19,265	12
Food & Beverage	23,970	174,469	14
Stone	5,240	56,635	9
Tobacco	3,660	72,543	5
Communications	41,480	913,785	5
Unskilled workers	63,370	441,292	14
Salaried employees	117,660	462,263	26
Total	727,110	4,637,521	16

* Sources: SPD, *Jahrbuch 1930*, p. 194; ADGB, *Jahrbuch 1931*, pp. 300-301; Bergmann, Schleiter, Wickel, p. 29, for AfA total. To project the regional SPD figures to a national total, all SPD figures were multiplied by ten, which may introduce some distortion, but which makes a comparison with national union figures possible. In the 1930 survey, members were classified into 28 occupations. For the purpose of this analysis, 17 occupations having corresponding unions were selected.

a All figures refer to ADGB membership, except for the salaried employees who were AfA members.

The Vote for the SPD

The interrelationship of the two organizations can also be demonstrated by studying the voting pattern of free union members.[8] Perhaps 65 percent of them voted for the SPD in most elections, the rest voting for other parties, especially the KPD, or not voting at all because of lack of interest, their nonvoting age, and other reasons.[9] In the representative election of 1928, this proportion would have meant that more than 3 million ADGB members cast their ballots for the SPD, totaling 33 percent of the nearly 9,150,000 SPD votes (table 4). Perhaps another 5 percent came from AfA and ADB members, and the remainder from housewives (including wives of union

TABLE 4

COMPARISON OF ADGB MEMBERSHIP AND SPD VOTE, 1928*

States [a]	ADGB Membership Actual (000's)	Adjusted [b] (000's)	Estimated number ADGB voters for SPD [c] (000's)	SPD vote (000's)	Estimated percentage ADGB voters for SPD
(1) Saxony	635	734	477	1000	48
(2) Berlin-Brandenburg	549	635	413	1320	31
(3) Rhineland-Westphalia	488	565	367	1245	30
(4) Thuringia	396	458	298	932	32
(5) Hamburg	352	407	264	724	36
(6) Bavaria	343	397	258	706	37
(7) Hanover, Braunschweig	277	320	208	852	24
(8) Wuerttemberg, Baden	290	335	218	596	37
(9) Silesia	266	308	200	668	30
(10) Hesse	262	303	197	569	35
(11) East Prussia	90	104	68	264	26
(12) Pomerania, Mecklenberg	75	87	56	271	21
Total	4023	4653	3024	9147	33

* ADGB, *Jahrbuch 1928*, pp. 294, 308-309 for actual ADGB membership; Cuno Horkenbach (ed.), *Das Deutsche Reich von 1918 bis Heute* (Berlin: Verlag für Presse, Wirtschaft und Politik, 1930), pp. 456-470, for vote by states.

[a] State lines represent the twelve ADGB districts (Saar excluded). The SPD vote in each state represents the total of various election districts, of which there were thirty-five throughout Germany. No. 1 ADGB district=election districts nos. 28-30; 2=2-5; 3=17-18, 20-23; 4=10-12; 5=13, 34-35; 6=24-26; 7=14-16; 8=27, 31-32; 9=7-9; 10=19, 33; 11=1; 12=6.

[b] In 1928, 630,000 members were not allocated to or reported by individual districts. The author has distributed them proportionately among the twelve districts in order to make a more valid comparison with the SPD vote.

[c] Based on an estimated 65 percent vote for the party.

members), small shopkeepers, nonunionized workers, and professionals. Since every third SPD voter was an ADGB member, the latter constituted the largest bloc of votes within the SPD total vote.

Table 4 indicates that the proportion of union votes varied from state to state. The party received much support from union members in industrial states and less support in nonindustrial states. On the other hand, in some Catholic industrial areas, such as the Ruhr and Silesia, many workers voted for the KPD, or joined Christian trade unions and voted for nonsocialist parties.

To sum up, the membership and voter linkages can only provide clues to the substantial influence which the free unions and the SPD exerted upon each other. In the SPD an estimated two-thirds of all members were simultaneously free union members. A number of them rose to prominent positions in the union movement, and were especially active in mobilizing support among the union rank and file for the party, especially at election time. The union vote, constituting more than one-third of the total vote for the party, was larger than any other pro-SPD group vote; it was bound to have an effect on SPD policies.

Other Links

Mutual accords and customs further cemented the bonds between the ADGB and the SPD. In the latter Weimar years, each organization sent an official observer to some executive and board meetings of the other. Both benefited from this custom as they were able to discuss mutual problems and to iron out difficulties that arose between them. In addition, private meetings and unofficial consultations took place. The two executive committees also held occasional joint conferences to discuss political or parliamentary problems significant to them.[10] On a more ceremonial basis, it was the custom to invite SPD Chairman Otto Wels as a guest to ADGB congresses and Leipart to SPD conventions. One historian notes, "Direct trade-union influence came, not up from below but across, as it were, from one oligarchy to the other."[11]

These ties did not constitute an attempt at amalgamation, but rather indicated the close liaison between the organizations. At the same time, each maintained a maximum degree of autonomy. The well-defined delineation of function and personnel was nowhere more evident than at the highest party councils and conventions. On the nineteen-member SPD Executive and the forty-two-member Board not a single union leader had a seat. At party conventions, a few national and middle-level union officials were present. The majority of delegates were nominal union members, but devoted most of their time to party affairs.[12]

For instance, at the 1927 SPD Convention, only ten national union leaders were among the 415 delegates, but they were activists in the party, all being Reichstag members and serving on SPD committees.[13] At the convention, they spoke on topics of interest to both organizations. Although their participation was motivated as much by political ambition as by involvement in the unions, they nevertheless could not disassociate one activity from the other, and were instrumental in presenting the union point of view to the party delegates and the party point of view to delegates at the union congresses. The free unions also made their views known at SPD conventions by having SPD district councils from strongly unionized areas introduce resolutions reflecting the economic and social problems of organized labor.

Union Views on Links to the SPD

Union newspapers and congresses provided labor leaders and members with opportunities for voicing their views on the kind of relationship to be established with the SPD. As expected, most were in accord on the need for close links, but not on the details.

The union press proved an important medium for communication of views and for encouraging members to vote for the SPD. Most of the eighty-four organs appeared only once a week, but their circulation in the mid-twenties amounted to an impressive six million copies. Many unionists also read faithfully one of the 196 SPD dailies, whose editors usually stemmed from the union movement, but whose circulation reached only one million copies. Thus, to the chagrin of labor leaders who dreamed of every union member becoming a subscriber to a socialist newpaper, millions of unionists who voted for the SPD still read the bourgeois non-SPD press, in which they could not obtain much SPD and union news, or did not read any newspaper.[14]

Union support for the SPD in the labor press or at its congresses was delayed in the early Weimar years because of the split in the socialist movement and factionalism within the ADGB. Not until the

Reichstag election slated for December 1924 did the ADGB Executive issue its first postwar appeal to members to vote for the SPD. It characterized the party as the only one truly representing the workers' interests.[15] The election resulted in a larger vote for the SPD than one held earlier that year, but whether the more intensive support the unions provided was the crucial variable is difficult to determine.

From then on, the ADGB reaffirmed its support for the SPD during the numerous election campaigns.[16] In the 1928 Reichstag election, the union press was filled with articles extolling the party "that does not manipulate the unions, but stands at their service."[17] Typical of the far from subliminal message was one from a local ADGB branch, "Workers . . . No vote for the bourgeois parties, no vote for the communists! Whoever votes bourgeois or communist, commits treason to his own class! Therefore on May 20 each one vote for List 1 of the SPD."[18] In 1928 labor appeals constituted only one of many techniques in the wide-ranging electoral campaign to maximize the SPD vote. Mass rallies, parades, leafletting, and propaganda films were also scheduled. Nor was the new medium of the phonograph forgotten. Buyers of records featuring socialist songs and the voices of socialist and union leaders were reminded that the records could be put to good use at assemblies and meetings.[19] After the election, in which the party made significant gains and in which a socialist became chancellor, the union press hailed the results and hoped that the SPD would energetically proceed with a policy supportive of the workers.

In the national elections of 1930, 1932, and 1933, the ADGB maintained its unqualified support for the party, despite some policy differences. Concerned with unfavorable economic and political developments, it sought to rally not only the organized but also the unorganized workers to the SPD banner.[20] Yet some national unions withheld their unqualified endorsement or made support conditional on the SPD's agreeing to certain demands. In 1930, for instance, the Construction Workers Union journal said that full support from its union would be forthcoming only if the SPD selected one of its leaders as a Reichstag candidate. The SPD acceded to the request.[21] Left-leaning unions, such as the Metal Workers Union, had doubts about the degree of liaison necessary with the SPD and about the advisability of engaging too intensely in parliamentary action at the expense of nonparliamentary action. Among the metal workers, the decision to provide official support to the SPD was made only after intensive discussions at various levels of the union hierarchy, reflecting a measure of intragroup democracy.[22]

Union-Party Discords

Two major fraternal organizations are bound to disagree in the face of recurrent political and economic crises, and occasional personality clashes. But more important, the discords between SPD and ADGB had their origin in the problem of jurisdiction caused by accretion in union power, in ideological and tactical conflicts, and in class disparities.

The organizations had to be careful in delimiting their respective fields of action; there were issues in which both seemed to have jurisdiction. Joint consultation and action could not always successfully bridge the gap between them, as, for instance, in the degree of political activity the unions could safely engage in without encroaching on party prerogatives, and the kinds of economic policy declarations the party could properly issue.

The ADGB not only seized the initiative in economic affairs of direct import to itself, but also framed the economic clauses of the revised SPD program presented to the 1925 Heidelberg Convention.[23] The party made no objection, but bristled when the ADGB sought to dictate the important clauses on party ideology, a realm considered by the party as its own; hence not subject to ADGB approval. Leipart, who had received a copy of the program only at a very late stage, wrote a lengthy letter to Hermann Müller, SPD Chairman, suggesting specific changes in it. He noted the union's conviction that the party should adhere to reformist principles and not propagate the outdated class struggle tenets. He objected particularly to paragraph 9 of the draft: "The struggle of the working class against capitalist exploitation is of necessity a political fight."[24] This struggle, according to Leipart, was in the first instance an economic one waged by the unions to achieve a new distribution of power in the economy.

Leipart futhermore demurred at paragraph 11: "The struggle for liberation of the working class is the task of the SPD; the party shapes the political struggles as well as the struggles of the unions and cooperatives into a conscious and unitary whole and shows to them the common goal."[25] The ADGB President was none too pleased by this imperial declaration. He retorted that the party was neither in a position to direct union activities, nor in a position to claim it had waged the economic struggles. The program reminded him of the past when the SPD felt itself to be the trustee of the unions, and denied them independence and autonomy. The unions had always taken issue with the party when it suggested to them in what direction they should move and what goals they should pursue. The unions now insisted on their full independence.

Leipart asserted bluntly, "The claim of the SPD for the ideological leadership of the unions can be as little recognized as the leadership claim of the Communist International, which has been vainly attempting for years to force its goals and its tactics on the unions."[26] The party, the unions, and the cooperatives all advocate the basic transformation of the capitalist economy, are equally entitled to be recognized as the bearers of the socialist idea, and can establish a united program for the movement solely on the basis of joint consultation. The only appropriate task for the SPD Convention, he concluded, is to frame the political program of the movement, giving consideration to the programs of the unions and the cooperatives.[27]

Party leaders, aware that they had blundered but perhaps not expecting such an onslaught, swiftly yielded to Leipart's lengthy objections and incorporated his proposals in the draft program. The revised paragraph 9 stated:

> The fight of the working class against capitalist exploitation is not only an economic one, but also of necessity a political fight. The working class cannot wage its economic struggle and develop fully its economic organization without political rights.[28]

Thus, the SPD put the economic aspects of the struggle on a par with the political aspects. The revised paragraph 11 again alluded to the SPD liberation of the working class, but declared that the party "still seeks its ultimate goal through constant struggle and effort in the political, economic, social, and cultural fields."[29] Reference to the primacy of political activity in the struggle of the working class was omitted in both paragraphs. In justification of these changes, SPD leader Rudolf Hilferding asserted at the Convention that the party would be the last one to desire tactical difficulties with the ADGB, and that it was in accord with the ADGB recommendations.

The controversy was symptomatic of the ease with which a seemingly innocuous wording of a party platform could explode into a momentary power struggle. The SPD could not easily have pushed the ADGB into a corner; by then the union federation was too powerful and was intent on asserting its rights, even if the consequence was an invasion of the SPD domain. In this instance, the SPD openly yielded to the ADGB. Although no undue loss of prestige or fundamental principles were at stake, a feeling of tension developed underneath the more amicable surface.

Not surprisingly in view of the controversy, it was the ADGB that at its 1925 Congress reaffirmed the principle that the leadership of the working class must rest with it in all economic questions.[30] The party never refuted this sweeping declaration, especially since it collaborated without friction with the ADGB on those economic issues, such as taxation, finance, tariffs, and employment, that transcended immediate union demands. True, during the Depression union and party experts failed to concur over proposals to combat it, but then their discord crossed rather than paralleled organization lines.

In comparison with the relatively conflict-free economic sphere, political questions were bound to lead to collisions in view of the rapid expansion of union interests and the increasing role of the government in economic affairs. As noted already, ADGB and SPD were at odds on a number of major political issues (Kapp Putsch, Müller crisis, etc.). These occurred especially when union interests clashed with broader SPD interests. Each organization raided the sphere of the other, with the unions unquestionably more guilty than the party for pushing into the political arena and taking the initiative in some political crises.

A tactical dispute with political overtones caused another squabble between the SPD and the free unions. At issue was the party's refusal to extend its unequivocal support of the ADGB and AfA to the socialist civil service federation (ADB). The party always took an ambiguous stand on this matter because many of its members were enrolled in the DBB, the more conservative civil service federation and rival of the ADB. The thorny issue was debated at several party conventions and never resolved during the Weimar period (nor at present). At the 1925 SPD Convention, Hermann Müller won approval for a policy of neutrality toward both ADB and DBB. At the 1927 Convention, party leaders requested that the policy be continued because the socialist members in the DBB could effectively block that federation's support of bourgeois parties in the Reichstag. In reply, AfA President Aufhäuser tagged the DBB a reactionary organization, urged the SPD to support only the ADB, and introduced a resolution affirming the duty of each Social Democrat to belong to a free union. A majority of the delegates passed an amended resolution omitting the word "duty," but requesting party organizations and press to support free union activities.[31] Despite the resolution, the SPD maintained its equivocal stand. It could not overcome the dilemma of conflicting pressures from its clienteles, and in turn could not provide support to one federation for fear of losing significant electoral support from the other.

Another area of friction between the unions and the SPD stemmed from disparities in class and membership profile. Leaders of each union federation had to concentrate only on a narrow range of interests to satisfy their single-class constituency, but party leaders had to mediate occasionally conflicting interests from a sociologically diverse constituency, which included not only the unionized groups but small businessmen, artisans, housewives, and professionals.[32]

In sum, a review of major schisms shows that many were caused by the self-interest of each organization, and in the Heidelberg controversy by a shift in power from the SPD to the ADGB. In this shift, the ADGB wielded a strong, conservative influence on a party still using Marxist slogans or, more rarely, taking radical actions. One historian notes, "The ADGB leaders displayed far more zeal in preserving the independence of the unions from political influence than they did in preserving the independence of the SPD from union influence."[33]

In cataloguing the discords one should not lose sight of the fact that the alliance rested on a firm historical foundation in which both organizations shared the same *Weltanschauung* and reinforced each other in an often hostile political and economic environment. The unions needed the SPD as a conduit for their legislative program while the SPD needed the unions for membership, voter, and financial support. This type of relationship differed little from that of interest groups and political parties in other Western political systems; indeed, it served as a model for other continental labor movements.

Financial Support

If interest groups are to be politically significant, they must have strong financial and/or organizational resources. Without these, their appeals would be ignored by government leaders swamped by requests from a multitude of groups for executive and legislative action. Money talks, a membership of millions talks—and the socialist unions had both. With this kind of a base, the unions used their links to the SPD to good advantage as an entry vehicle into the executive and legislative spheres in which the SPD had a limited degree of power.

The unions provided financial support to the party partly in order to receive immediate dividends through their leaders' nomination for Reichstag seats on the SPD ticket, and partly in order to ensure the survival of the SPD as a political ally on the national scene. To this end, they fully supported the party during the numerous election campaigns. While the contributions constituted a tangible but little publicized link between the two organizations, their magnitude was shrouded in some secrecy (union donations were not identified separately in union or SPD balance sheets).[34]

Yet, rough estimates may be made of the degree of union financial support based on the party's balance sheets and discussions at ADGB Board meetings. The bulk of party administrative and electoral funds was derived from membership dues and special assessments. Since a large proportion of party members were also union members, their contributions were important to total income.

The party also received contributions from allied organizations, which included the national unions. As a peak organization, the ADGB apparently did not make any direct contribution because of its desire to maintain tactical independence from the party and to avoid criticism from antiunion circles. It did support the SPD indirectly by inserting advertisements in the party press and by placing at its disposal the facilities of the union-sponsored bank (Bank der Arbeiter, Angestellten und Beamten).[35]

Some of the funds from allied organizations came rather from national unions and regional union bodies and were then disbursed to the SPD through ADGB headquarters or directly to SPD regional and local organizations. As a way of ensuring an equitable assessment, the ADGB Executive met with national union leaders before national election campaigns in order to set a minimum figure for each union calculated on a per capita basis.[36]

This simple procedure caused occasional complications, as revealed at ADGB Board meetings. At one such meeting in 1930, a Metal Workers Union official (Schäfer) stated that in addition to the national union allocation to the SPD, local union treasuries had funneled money directly to SPD district treasuries. He believed that the SPD Executive should have told its district headquarters not to accept such additional funds, because inquiries by his union had shown that as a result of the local fund-raising the union's total disbursement to the SPD had exceeded its original quota. He argued that if funds are given the SPD then the unions must also have a say in their use to avoid the impression that the party did not disburse them responsibly. A SPD spokesman (Vogel) present at the meeting assured him that the party would account for its fund distribution, including money raised from the unions. Other union leaders told their colleagues at the meeting of the resistance encountered from their communist and radical-controlled locals to the disbursement of funds to the SPD. In some instances, the locals, dissatisfied with union support of SPD policy, raised money instead for the KPD.[37]

Opposition groups circulated a number of rumors or made claims about big slush funds, because the exact amount of union funds given the SPD was never revealed publicly. The only clue the public had was that one-eighth to one-fourth of party revenue came from allied organizations, of which the unions provided an unspecified share.[38] One communist union local, for instance, claimed that the ADGB unions had given 1 million Reich Marks (RM) to the SPD for the September 1930 Reichstag election campaign. But, according to one ADGB Executive member, the claim was false. The national unions would have had to assess each member more than 20 pfennig (pf.), too high a sum given the massive unemployment and under-employment rate.[39]

If the claims were exaggerated, what was the magnitude of union funds to the party? Only a partial answer can be given because of the scarcity of information. For the July 1932 election, an SPD spokesman (Sigmund Crummenerl) told ADGB Board members, the party had disbursed 2.8 million RM and the districts almost 3 million RM. He revealed that in the first ten months of 1932 the party had received about 384,000 RM from the unions. His figure would indicate that nearly 7 percent of the party's total election expenditure came from the unions, assuming funds had been channeled to the party's national and district treasuries, or 14 percent if the funds had been channeled only into the national treasury.[40]

The SPD spokesman also asserted that in the coming election of November 1932, more financial support from the unions would be necessary in view of slumping party income caused by the Depression. A union speaker apprised him of similar financial difficulties the unions were encountering, and insisted that the SPD Executive should be satisfied if the individual national unions donated the maximum amount of money possible. Leipart, with the approval of other Board members, concluded that the Board would raise again 10 pf. (or 5 pf. in some instances) from each union member for the next election.[41] Such an assessment would have netted the party about 400,000 RM.

Whether the ADGB contributed a greater percentage of party revenue in earlier golden years could not be ascertained. But it was common knowledge that the unions, in addition to contributions to the SPD, also made donations to party-allied organizations, such as the Republican defense groups, Reichsbanner and Iron Front.

At an ADGB Board meeting in September 1930, for instance, an official revealed that the Reichsbanner had requested the ADGB to provide additional funds for members injured in fights with political extremists during the campaign. The ADGB Executive had authorized an initial payment of 10,000 RM, and urged the national unions to provide more. A representative of the Metal Workers Union replied that, on the basis of his union's lack of extra funds, union-sponsored institutions should dig into their reserve funds for support. But the Board sustained the proposal to aid the Reichsbanner.[42]

These isolated examples of union financial support to the SPD and some of its allied organizations represent but a glimpse of the intricate web spun between them. Without the support of millions of union members, the party would have been strapped for money incurred in costly election campaigns and high administrative all-year expenses. As indicated, the unions expected some dividends from their largesse, one of which was the nomination of their candidates for positions on the SPD tickets to the Reichstag.

Conclusion

To gain its objectives in the political sphere, the ADGB had to focus its attention on selected major targets: the SPD was a crucial one. Any private associational group must establish a liaison with one or more parties since the latter are able not only to wield additional political influence but also able to act at the core of the decision-making process. After all, it is the party and not the interest group that can nominate candidates for public office, capture control of the government, and thereby determine the direction of public policy.

Hence, the ADGB exerted influence on the SPD to pursue policies favorable to the unions, especially when the party was a member of a governing coalition. The institutional and unofficial links between the two organizations facilitated this process. Both benefited from the links: the SPD in the form of an influx of members, increased voter support, and heavy doses of financial aid; the ADGB in the form of access to the decision makers—the legislature and the executive branch—through the channel of a political party. By such a route the ADGB gained a degree of legitimacy in the political process not made possible by the normal direct lobbying activities—which it did not abandon either.

VI

THE REICHSTAG

Representation and Influence

INTEREST GROUPS seek access not only to political parties but also to all important public decision-making bodies that determine the welfare of their members. In Weimar Germany, the national legislature was one such body, although it was usually overshadowed by the executive. As they turned their attention to the legislature, the union federations did not seek equal access to the upper and lower houses, but focused primarily on the latter, the Reichstag, as the more powerful in the legislative process. Not that they neglected entirely the upper house, the Reichsrat, which represented the states. They did seek to influence the Länder executive officers who had the authority to select members to the Reichsrat and give them voting instructions.

The labor federations' financial and electoral support for their allied political parties was expected to produce the immediate payoff of gaining maximum representation in the Reichstag. Labor leaders had the advantage, unlike their United States colleagues, of being elected as legislators and operating from within the chamber. Many were successful in this effort, as several parties included a significant number of them on their tickets. Needless to say, the conservative parties included a number of businessmen on their slates.[1]

Nominating Process

The socialist unions turned to the SPD for representation. But they (and other interest associations) operated under the constraints of the proportional representation system, in which the parties prepared national and district lists, the latter including from ten to sixteen candidates. Given the number of competing parties, only candidates placed high on the list had a chance of winning a Reichstag seat. Hence parties aggregating a number of diverse interests had to balance their tickets in order to get maximum voter support.[2] In the SPD, the unions were but one of several groups vying for the top places on the lists; thus they could not expect to receive from the SPD high command as much representation as they desired.

In theory, according to its organizational statute, the nominating process of the SPD was as follows: members of district party organs were to recommend candidates for the Reichstag. These recommendations were to be assembled into a list by the regional leaders (Bezirksleitung), and then agreed on by a regional convention. The Board and Executive were to nominate candidates only for the national list, although they could give advice to the regional bodies. The Executive would settle any dispute between organizations on nominations.[3]

In practice, however, the SPD Executive often did meddle in the nominating process for the district lists. It would make a preliminary survey of the available candidates in the districts by consulting various organizations, including the unions, in order to come up with slates representing a balance of forces within the party, and reflecting its geographic, social, and economic interests. The slates would then be presented to the regional conventions, which in most cases automatically ratified them. To give a semblance of intraparty democracy, votes were taken to determine the order of the candidates on the lists, but only occasionally did the conventions recommend changes.[4]

Although the unions acted under constraints within the nominating process of the SPD, both organizations benefited from the proportional representation system since they were able to win seats in areas where under the prewar system they had not scored any success.[5] The unions also had a chance to send to the Reichstag via the national list top leaders who could not have won election in districts because they lacked the time or the oratorical skills necessary for direct campaigning. If a union leader was the top candidate on the district ticket, he was expected to carry the burden of active campaigning for the party in that constituency.[6]

As a matter of fact, some union leaders were not reluctant to devote most of their time to party work. Legien had entered party activity at an early period, and his Reichstag mandate was more important to him than his work at union headquarters. On the other hand, Leipart never ran for the Reichstag because he wanted to devote most of his time to union affairs. Nor was he eager to have the ADGB central office staff become immersed in politics, as evidenced by the rule that ADGB Board approval, or in an urgent case that of the Executive, was necessary for any staff member to run for public office.[7]

An analysis of the SPD nominations indicates that those high-ranking union executives who were interested in legislative service were usually inscribed at the top of district and national lists in order to assure their election to the Reichstag. On the other hand, the names of minor union officials were scattered throughout the ticket; some were elected, some were not. In districts where the industrial population and the number of union workers were especially large, many labor leaders received top candidacies.[8] Thus, the strongest slate appeared in the two industrial Westphalian districts because of the concentrated and intensely unionized mining and metal industries in the area.[9] The SPD could not help giving the unions a prominent position in regions with such a potential vote. On the other hand, in East Prussia, Baden, Bavaria, and other areas where comparatively few union members resided, the SPD failed to nominate a single union leader.

The unions were usually satisfied with their representation in a majority of districts, but in others points of friction inevitably developed concerning the number and ranking on the SPD lists. In 1924, labor leaders pointed out that the unions because of their number of members and their power should receive more slots on the lists so that they could exert more pressure on the SPD Reichstag parliamentary group (Fraktion) for favorable legislation and could weaken the SPD radical minority. They stated that union-party accord should be reached on the local level since any attempt by national ADGB and SPD officials to influence the party district councils in their selection of candidates would meet with resentment and resistance.[10]

But on a number of occasions, such accords failed. For instance, after the death of Legien in 1920, a successor to his seat had to be nominated. The Kiel union district council wanted a union candidate to head the slate again, and suggested Tarnow for the post. The party objected to Tarnow's candidacy because he contended that he had no time for campaigning. When a nonunion substitute candidate was nominated, the union council protested on the ground that campaigning was of secondary importance. In the end, the SPD compromised by keeping its own candidate on the district list and according Tarnow one of the top places on the national list for which no excessive campaigning was necessary.[11]

In October 1932, Leipart bluntly told Crummenerl, the SPD observer at the ADGB Board meeting, that the unions did not see why they should make financial contributions to the party for election campaigns unless they received a greater share of seats. As a typical instance, he mentioned the case of ADGB Vice-President Grassmann who had represented the Hamburg election district since 1924, but who had not been renominated. The Hamburg union headquarters, having trusted that the SPD would place him on the list, had not even been informed of the negative decision. Crummenerl replied that the SPD Executive Committee had only heard about the Grassmann incident when the local SPD had already nominated another candidate. The Executive told the SPD Hamburg affiliate that its action would directly affect union-party relationships at the national level, but such pressure had no immediate impact on SPD Hamburg (a victory for intraparty democracy, the SPD observer might have added). He hoped that a future party convention would grant the Executive more power in the nomination process. "We will not let our party-union relationship be muddied by any party secretary," he concluded.[12] Soon after this ADGB meeting, the SPD Hamburg local changed its mind, and put Grassmann's name high on the district list to assure his reelection to the Reichstag. At the meeting, Crummenerl also said that top party organs will have to be more responsive to union sentiments, but that the unions had already a sizable number of their representatives on the lists, including four out of eight candidates on the national list.

The incident had a sequel reflecting the importance, but also the limitation, of personal links between the ADGB President and the SPD Chairman. In 1932, Leipart wrote two letters to Otto Wels requesting party support for the candidacy of Anton Erkelenz for the Prussian state diet (Landtag). Erkelenz, head of the Hirsch-Duncker unions, had been chairman of the German Democratic Party, but in 1930 had switched to the SPD. Leipart, in his personal capacity, urged the SPD to make an exception for tactical reasons to the rule that individuals switching parties not immediately assume responsible posts. Wels refused to make such an exception.

Erkelenz that year also sought nomination on an SPD Reichstag list. Wels wrote to him that the national list had already been completed, and a change could only be made on pressing grounds. Since a top ADGB leader in 1932 had been put high on the national list, it was impossible to put him in a similar position. According to Wels, "To put you lower down did not seem fair to you, whose esteem we praise. We hope that you have understanding for our predicament."[13]

Despite the continuing outbursts of dissatisfaction in union circles, the ADGB could not dictate policy to the SPD in the politically sensitive matter of nominations. Since the ADGB had some influence on the make-up of the election lists, it was not as dissatisfied as might appear. After all, it never requested a specific number or proportion of places on the lists, but merely wanted more representation in specific instances. It was well aware of the constraints put on the party by its multi-interest constituency.

Critics outside the labor movement joined the debate about the Reichstag numbers game, which had broader implications of interest representation in a legislative body. They argued that the views of union deputies were too narrow and could not possibly represent those of a majority in the district. The unions retorted that their candidates were SPD members, and therefore once elected would not merely express their special interests in the Reichstag, but would be guided by party policy and by the voters whom they represented. Such debates, as is usual, proved inconclusive.

REPRESENTATION

Union pressure on the SPD to nominate many labor leaders on the Reichstag slates, and the union support given the party during the election campaigns had their payoff. Of all parties, the SPD had the largest proportion of union leaders in its Reichstag Fraktion, and the Center Party, numbering a contingent of Christian unionists, the second largest. Not surprisingly, the more conservative parties were less generous in providing labor with much representation.[14] There was no cohesive organized interparty union bloc in the Reichstag, but there were enough unofficial links between deputies from the rival union federations to make some impact on legislation of concern to them.

Although union members formed the largest group within the SPD rank and file, their deputies did not constitute the largest bloc within the SPD Fraktion, since the party had no desire to apportion its Reichstag seats according to the proportion of its members or voters from each occupational segment. The union bloc in such a case would have been the strongest within the Fraktion. Foremost a political organization, the party reasoned that its own leaders should have the majority of seats as a reward for their loyalty and as being the most capable party spokesmen in the Reichstag.

Despite this constraint, the number of union deputies in the SPD Fraktionen was considerable. It varied from a high of nearly 28 percent in the National Assembly (1919-1920) to a low of nearly 17 percent in March 1933, with an average of close to 20 percent for the Weimar era (see table 5).[15] In this calculation, only union leaders and employees are included, and not the majority of SPD deputies who were also nominal card-carrying union members, but whose primary activity was in the party. Workers, of whom there were precious few (ranging from 3 to 10 percent), are also excluded, since they did not serve directly as union representatives. Indeed, SPD (and union) reluctance to put more workers on its ticket, unlike the KPD with its 50 percent worker representation, demonstrated a reward system for its own cadres and a trend toward political professionalism in the Fraktion.[16] SPD and free unions, in justification of their stand, argued that their deputies had originally come from the ranks of the workers and were familiar with the workers' problems. Critics contended that the officials had left the workbench a long time ago and could not possibly be as sensitive to the problems as was claimed. Most workers, aware that the unions had selected capable spokesmen for the Reichstag to represent their interests, did not appear to be dissatisfied with the trend toward professionalism.

TABLE 5
UNION REPRESENTATIVES IN THE SPD FRAKTIONEN*

	National Assembly [a]	Reichstag Sessions			
		1920-1924a	May-Aug. 1924	1925-1928	1928-1930
Union representatives (No.)	51	34	19	23	28
SPD Fraktion members (No.)	187	194	100	131	152
Percentage of total	27.3	17.5	19.0	17.6	18.4

	Reichstag Sessions			
	1930-1932	Aug.-Sept. 1932	Dec. 1932	1933
Union representatives (No.)	28	28	22	20
SPD Fraktion members (No.)	143	133	121	120
Percentage of total	19.6	21.1	18.2	16.7

*Sources: Horkenbach, all eds; Reichsamt des Innern, *Handbuch für das Deutsche Reich, 1922* (Berlin: Reichsamt des Innern, 1922); RT, *Reichstagshandbuch, 1924, 1928, 1930, 1932, 1933.* For a list of union representatives, see Appendix C.
[a] Includes USPD.

In the 435-member National Assembly, of the 51 free unionists who held seats, 20 held positions at the national union level (5 General Commission members, 9 presidents and 6 executives and journal editors of national unions), and 31 at the district and local levels. The Christian unions were represented by 20 deputies, and the Hirsch-Duncker unions by 4 deputies.[17]

The 1920 election witnessed a sharp rise in votes for the USPD and a decline for the SPD. The USPD increased the number of its union representatives from one out of twenty-two members in the National Assembly to eleven out of eighty-one in the first Reichstag period (1920-1924). The number of unionists in the SPD Fraktion simultaneously dropped from 50 to 23 (out of 165 and 113 members respectively).[18] The drop was caused chiefly by the SPD's ability in 1920 to draw more experienced party politicians to its slate, and to scuttle numerous minor union officials and workers' secretaries who had played a role in the revolutionary period.

From the 1924 to the 1933 elections, the percentage of union members in the SPD Fraktion remained relatively stable. Even when, as in the 1928 election, the SPD received an avalanche of votes (more than 9 million), the union representation remained proportionately the same, although it increased numerically. Five members (Grassmann, H. Müller, G. Schmidt, Janschek, Tarnow) of the 15-member ADGB Executive then held Reichstag seats. Although this ratio was high and symbolic of top union leaders' political involvement, Leipart would have preferred their devoting full time to the movement. But he realized that there were payoffs in such representation.[19]

The last free Reichstag elections witnessed relatively few changes in the SPD Fraktion. The steady decline in the number of union leaders in the Fraktion corresponded to an almost equal decline in SPD power. This would seem to suggest that the free unions tacitly accepted a not too flexible number of slots in the Fraktion.

A study of the list of union deputies demonstrates a low circulation of elites, not peculiar to labor officialdom. Many veteran labor leaders who had risen in the movement to the top executive organs were eventually rewarded with a Reichstag seat on the basis of their prestige and their service to the cause. This reward system caused stagnation in leadership, but to the Reichstag it had the advantage of providing substantive and parliamentary expertise.[20] Although only three veteran union chiefs (Alfred Janschek, Robert Schmidt, and Rudolf Wissell) held seats in all legislative sessions, eight out of nineteen who were elected in May 1924 still were in the Reichstag in 1933.

As a result, the average age of the union deputies was relatively high (fifty to fifty-five), about five years above that of all Reichstag members.[21] In turn, this meant that younger members in the SPD Fraktion came preponderantly from party rather than ADGB ranks. Of the forty-three SPD deputies under forty-five years of age in the 1928-1930 session, only three were union leaders.[22] Needless to say, the ADGB policy of rewarding seniority in its elite caused dissatisfaction among younger, politically-aspiring leaders who found their way barred to important legislative bodies.

There was also dissatisfaction among small unions about the pattern of distribution of Reichstag seats. Reflecting the power constellation among the free labor federations, all national unions with a sizable membership were represented in the Reichstag by their presidents or other executive committee members. Smaller unions, on the other hand, received only occasional representation, although the party preferred that two members of a national union executive should not simultaneously sit in the Reichstag in order to grant other unions an opportunity to be represented.[23]

Certain salient features emerge from this inquiry into union representation in the Reichstag. Not only did the SPD Fraktion contain more union members than that of any other Fraktion, but the veteran union members constituted one of the largest blocs within the SPD Fraktion. Since the SPD granted a sizable representation to the unions as a *quid pro quo* for membership, voter and financial support, it obviously had to expect the union bloc in the Fraktion to make policy demands.

INFLUENCE IN THE REICHSTAG

The free unions could press their demands in a number of ways ranging from meetings of the SPD parliamentary group to the Reichstag plenary sessions. An important target was the nerve center of the party in the legislature, the Fraktion, in which every SPD deputy had a seat.The Fraktion or its thirteen-member executive committee, in which a few union leaders sat, met frequently to decide on such important matters as the Reichstag committee assignment for each member, what policies and tactics to pursue in the deliberations and votes in the plenum, and which members would speak on proposed new legislation. The Fraktion had its own specialized committees, such as labor and foreign affairs, which discussed proposed bills in their fields, and advised the Fraktion executive on what action the party should take on each bill.

Union members did not form their own caucus within the Fraktion, primarily because they were split into ideological factions paralleling those of the SPD. They voted according to their convictions; left-wing union members supported the Left bloc within the Fraktion, and the more numerous right-wing union members supported the majority bloc. On most questions the two wings reached an acceptable working compromise which, coupled with parliamentary discipline, resulted in a united front and a common policy in the legislature.[24] Regardless of ideological conviction, the mission of the union deputies necessarily had to be a dual one, for the members represented both union and party. Rare were the instances in which this created a potential conflict since the two organizations seldom clashed on policy.

Union policy makers who petitioned the Fraktion leaders to introduce bills important to them generally received positive responses, and in turn exerted pressure to amend or squash unfavorable proposals or bills. As evidence of positive responses, there is the catalog of bills on social affairs offered by the Fraktion to the Reichstag. As evidence of an SPD-inspired proposal squashed by the ADGB, there is a resolution carried at the 1929 SPD Convention urging the lowering of compulsory retirement from sixty-five to sixty years. The Fraktion could not adopt it: there was substantial union opposition and it would have boosted government expenditures.[25]

The efforts of unionists in the Fraktion were supplemented by their activity in the Reichstag itself. They made ample use of the several opportunities to influence the legislature. It was standard operating procedure for SPD members to represent the party in the Reichstag according to their field of interest and qualification. Except for certain experts in the unions who were assigned broad economic subjects, union deputies spoke in the plenum on economic, social, and budgetary matters that affected their individual union specifically. To cite but one example, Otto Hue and Janschek, heads of the Mine Workers Union, discussed the harsh working conditions in the mines, the high rate of accidents, and the political power of the mine owners.[26]

Parliamentary resolutions and the question hour gave the unions other pressure points. Union deputies in the SPD drafted resolutions and questions designed to move the government into a policy direction supportive of their goals, such as a resolution on the unjustified dismissal of workers in industry.[27] But the Reichstag committees were the most strategic location for influencing bills. Union members sat on those of particular interest to them. In the twenty-eight member Committee for Economic Affairs, from 1928 to 1930 six out of nine SPD members were national union leaders, including committee chairman Josef Simon, president of the Shoemakers Union.[28] The other union leaders were Bergmann (Food and Beverage Workers Union), Brandes (Metal), Limbertz (editor, Mine

Workers Union journal), R. Schmidt (former General Commission member), and Tarnow (Wood). Union deputies also held a considerable number of seats in the Committees for Social Affairs, Civil Servant Affairs, and Labor. In these committees, they could support bills, and challenge, amend, and defeat others.

In sum, labor influence in the Fraktion and in the Reichstag was at least proportionate to its representation in these bodies. Union members contributed their expertise in specialized areas by publicizing their positions in the appropriate legislative committees and the plenum. Their success on the legislative scoreboard depended on the power constellation of interest groups and party blocs, the national economic welfare, and the attitude of the public and the government.

VII

THE EXECUTIVE

Pressure on Cabinets and Ministries

IN THE TWENTIETH CENTURY, a universal phenomenon of politics has been the accretion of power to the executive branch of government. In Weimar Germany, the Constitution granted the chancellor and his ministers a range of powers surpassing those of executives in many other parliamentary systems at the time. As a consequence, the German interest groups turned toward the executive for support of their demands, requesting action on legislation and executive orders.

Although the Weimar executive branch gave the unions a sense of legitimacy and official sanction for their activities, they still had to mount strong campaigns to gain their objectives, especially during periods of economic crises. In addition, the increasing involvement of the government in economic and social questions made union action imperative. The unions could not ignore matters of foreign and domestic trade, taxes, cartels and agrarian policies, or the more traditional issues of wages, hours, and working conditions.

The Constitution

The initial impetus strengthening the organized labor movement was the downfall of the oppressive Imperial government; the birth of a democratic Republic; and the enactment in August 1919 of a liberal Constitution, whose provisions in the economic and social spheres were among the most progressive of any constitution existent at the time. The new Constitution was drafted by Hugo Preuss, a constitutional law expert, and subsequently modified by a Constitutional Commission and the National Assembly meeting in Weimar. Preuss, lacking interest in provisions dealing with economic and social questions, omitted them in the original draft. But as a result of pressures on their colleagues by the strong union and socialist contingent in the National Assembly, and the constitutional drafters' fears of radical uprisings in various parts of Germany, these path-breaking provisions were included. The Constitution recognized unions as legitimate economic organizations with clearly delineated functions in the state. Article 154 provided that they be placed under the special protection of the government, and Article 159 guaranteed them freedom of association, with any limitation on this right deemed illegal. Article 123 affirmed their right to hold public meetings and distribute leaflets (the latter was an implied right). Article 124 guaranteed them the right of association "without limitation by preventive measures," and precluded their dissolution by emergency decree.[1]

Some provisions attempted to meet the demand of workers for economic security. Article 161 affirmed the government's intention to adopt a comprehensive social insurance system in whose management the insured would predominate. Article 162 committed the government to support the international regulation of the legal status of workers. Article 163 guaranteed every German an opportunity to gain a living by productive work, and minimum maintenance if suitable employment could not be procured for him. Article 165 provided for a system of works councils and district and national economic councils, and granted the worker an equal voice with the employer in the regulation of salaries, working conditions, and economic development.[2]

The constitutional drafters, who represented the spectrum of democratic political parties, sought an equilibrium of the economic forces. Recognition of the unions and their activities guaranteed them a chance to participate in the state machinery on a more equal footing with rival economic groups than had previously been the case. The Constitution also envisaged the government acting as a neutral arbiter in settling disputes between capital and labor. Yet in practice the government maintained a position of neutrality with difficulty, usually supporting one side or the other in a dispute. The problem was compounded in those instances in which it took on the role of an employer operating numerous transport industries and utilities. This led to confrontations with its workers over working conditions and other labor questions.[3]

The President

The targets of union pressure in this new constitutional setting ranged widely within the executive branch. The unions mobilized their resources to influence the government through orthodox lobbying techniques—conferences, communications, pressures via the SPD—and through membership in some decision-making units.

The German president was the top figure in the executive branch. As chief of state he had only limited political powers, although one famous constitutional provision, Article 48, granted him emergency powers. The unions were not reluctant to send him telegrams and letters or to request a meeting when crucial economic and social problems were as stake. These efforts were often effective when Friedrich Ebert (SPD), who had once been active in the labor movement, was president (1919-1925). But they became more symbolic toward the end of the Republic when Ebert's successor, the politically conservative President von Hindenburg, intervened frequently in public affairs.[4]

The Chancellor

More effective at times were the links established with the chief policy maker, the chancellor. He formed the cabinet, made political appointments, and set broad public policy. If the chancellor was a socialist, as happened in the periods from 1919 to 1920 and from 1928 to 1930, then the unions could expect to meet little resistance to their demands. And if from 1919 to 1920 the socialist chancellor was also a former labor leader, as was true of Gustav Bauer, once a Vice-President of the General Commission, then the unions could expect significant support, assuming the coalition partners gave their blessing. That Bauer could have been appointed chancellor without holding a leading position in the SPD reflected the degree of union political power at the time.[5] Even when the chancellor was a conservative, he had to maintain a linkage to the unions and be subject to many pressures from them. In some instances, ADGB leaders attempted to see the chancellor, but were shunted instead to the minister of labor. In other instances, the Chancellor's Office would dispatch incoming written communications to the ministries for a response.[6] This "passing of the buck" led to procrastination and bureaucratic delays.

The Cabinet

The next top-level target of union pressure was the cabinet. The unions were interested in direct representation in it in order to help shape government policy. Nonsocialist chancellors-designate, even though they rarely gave the free unions any cabinet posts, on occasion solicited union views concerning specific future government policies or were the recipients of such union advice. Socialist chancellors-designate consulted union leaders not only on the government program, but on the composition of the cabinet. For instance, after the 1928 election, Leipart told the ADGB Board that in talks with high SPD officials he raised no objections to two former conservative cabinet ministers, who had been sympathetic to labor's cause, retaining their economic affairs and labor posts in the new SPD-led cabinet. If they did not want to stay on in the cabinet, then the SPD should take over the posts. He asserted that "the trade unions do not have the intention to tell the Fraktion what position it should take, but since the opinion of the ADGB Executive had been sought, we must declare that the influence of the workers' movement in the pending coalition government must be vigorously brought to bear on the appointment of strong personalities."[7]

The ADGB attempt to colonize cabinets with its own leaders met with success when the SPD formed a cabinet or was requested to participate in one as a coalition partner. To illustrate, in February 1919, Philip Scheidemann, SPD, chose three national union leaders out of seven SPD appointees in his sixteen-member coalition cabinet.[8] In cabinets headed by an SPD chancellor, the unions invariably received the posts of minister of labor and of economic affairs. Despite the number of cabinet upheavals, the turnover among socialist union leaders was small; four repeatedly held a number of posts in various cabinets.[9] They had the opportunity to channel union views to the other cabinet members without intermediaries, and to influence directly the drafting of bills, administrative orders and regulations.

When cabinets were bourgeois dominated, socialist labor leaders did not necessarily face an uphill struggle in receiving a favorable hearing if stable economic conditions permitted the cabinets to make concessions to them. In addition, the cabinets were under pressure from Christian and liberal trade union federations, which had influence in the governing bourgeois parties, to blunt antiunion proposals emerging from some ministries. When Heinrich Brauns, a Center Party leader sympathetic to union aspirations, headed the Ministry of Labor from 1920 to 1928, all union federations could expect to receive some support from him.[10]

Even when the socialist unions were represented in the cabinets, they knew that because of the coalitional nature of cabinets and the multigroup constituency of the SPD their program would not be implemented automatically. Thus, in 1928, when the socialist-led cabinet was formed, Leipart pledged labor's support, but warned the SPD that the ADGB did not consider itself bound in any manner to the coalition; it would present its legitimate demands to the cabinet, and would criticize the cabinet if necessary in order to protect labor's interests. The ADGB journal added that only if the new cabinet were to adopt labor's planks in the social field could a spirit of confidence be established between them.[11]

This tough policy toward socialist-led governments was designed more as a warning to the SPD that the ADGB meant to maintain its independence and freedom of action, while still expecting to reap legislative dividends, than as a declaration of war against its political ally. In this sense, the ADGB position hardly differed from that of the British TUC vis-à-vis the Labour governments in the post-1945 period. The ADGB attitude, understandable from its point of view, increased the strain with the SPD, which expected greater understanding from the unions for its broader commitments. But the ADGB justified its position of detachment toward all cabinets, no matter what their political coloration, by arguing that the test of support of a government would be its specific policies in spheres affecting labor's interests.

The Ministries

Another target of union pressure was the ministries. When civil servants meticulously prepared drafts of bills subject to cabinet and parliamentary approval, they were liable to the cross-pressures of unions and other interest groups. Unions showered the civil servants and ministers with memoranda, telegrams, letters, and petitions signed at mass meetings, or requested meetings with ministers handling social and economic legislation.

One labor official asserted that he met with civil servants in the Ministry of Labor on the average of three times a week concerning bills of interest to his union. He maintained close links with them regardless of the party affiliation of the minister in charge.[12] But other union lobbyists believed that their advice often was not sought, primarily because employer influence was strong or because the upper civil service ranks still contained many adherents of the Imperial regime with an antiunion bias. Lateral entrance of union specialists into civil service ranks was difficult because the civil service required legal training as a prerequisite for a professional career.

At times, the unions sought to have government representatives come to their own meetings. Such a tactic led to complications, as in October, 1923 when the ADGB requested Minister of Labor Brauns to appear at a public conference in order to "cross-examine" him. The Minister, in relating this request to the cabinet, viewed it as a bad precedent which would be followed by other organizations. He deemed it sufficient to send his state secretary who would then report to him. But Chancellor Stresemann did consent to receive a delegation from the conference.[13]

In their attempts to influence the policy makers, the unions could not ignore the countervailing pressure from the business community, especially from the powerful National Association of German Industry (RDI, Reichsverband der deutschen Industrie), claiming 78,000 member firms in 61 affiliated associations. The employer pressure on proposed legislation led to sustained struggles with the unions. If a ministry and the cabinet accepted the employer draft of a bill, the unions registered strong protest, and vice versa. As a result, government officials attempted to frame compromise proposals more acceptable to both parties.

No doubt the business community could expect to receive a more favorable hearing for its demands when a succession of conservative cabinets, with employer representation, ruled the nation. Labor repeatedly denounced this employer influence, and charged that the industrialist bloc had unduly increased its power in the nation, without any effort on the part of the government to combat it or to consult labor. But, as noted, labor did score gains when economic conditions were favorable or when the minister of labor triumphed over the more conservative ministers of economic affairs and finance.

Administrative Agencies

While the chancellors and ministers mapped out general policy, and civil servants prepared the bills or decrees designed to implement that policy, a number of administrative agencies were established in the initial Weimar years in order to manage or regulate the economy. Such organs as the cartel and finance courts; the ministerial advisory councils; the National Economic Council; the Employment Service and Insurance Agency; and boards to supervise social security, the Reichsbank, the Post Office, electricity, and national and state railroads performed a host of administrative, regulatory, or advisory functions. Other agencies had limited control over coal, potash, and iron and steel industries.

In most of these agencies, the government allocated seats on their governing boards to its own representatives and to the major interests—usually the unions, business, and consumer organizations. Union representation ranged from a low of one member out of twelve on the Post Office Board to a high of five out of twenty on the National Railroad Board.[14] As agencies mushroomed, the unions faced the problem of staffing the available posts with experienced personnel to match the more skilled employer representatives. The unions instituted special courses to provide the necessary economic and technical skills to its personnel, but it took a number of years before the problem could be remedied.

National Economic Council

One of the pioneering developments in this administrative structure was the establishment of economic councils at the shop level and the Reich level (pursuant to Article 165 of the Constitution). The unions had mixed feelings about the shop councils (see Chapter VIII below), but lobbied hard for the creation of a national economic council that could be expected to provide them with another outlet for policy advising.

A permanent national council and district councils were never established during the Weimar period owing to political opposition, but a decree of May 4, 1920 created a provisional National Economic Council. Its powers were limited: it could assume only an advisory role to Parliament on bills pertaining to economic matters routed to it prior to legislative consideration. It had 326 members, approximately one-third of whom represented labor, one-third employers, and one-third government and the public. In this tripartite arrangement, labor and employers could often be expected to vote on opposite sides. Consequently, as in other agencies, the burden of the final decision was carried by the government and public members. But the labor bloc, representing all trade union federations, did not always maintain internal cohesion. Then the dividing line in the Council became more blurred, as socialist union members supported by some members of the government and public bloc voted against a conservative coalition of employer, nonsocialist union and other group representatives. Socialist members of the Council held caucuses to map strategy. There the union representatives, holding a majority, substantially influenced the other socialist members, unlike the SPD Reichstag Fraktion where, in the minority, they could not influence that group as effectively.[15]

The Council was handicapped in its functions not only by the divergent economic interests of its members, but by its mere advisory role in the legislative process. Therefore, the busy labor leaders, such as Leipart, Aufhäuser, Schmidt, Umbreit and Wissell, who held many other positions, missed a number of committee meetings in which most business was transacted. In the course of time they realized that more could be accomplished by presenting union demands through the traditional ministry and Reichstag channels, despite pleas by the Council Executive to them to use its machinery to the full in order to lighten the burden on the policy makers.[16]

Cognizant of Council weaknesses, the unions nevertheless remained one of its defenders because they did derive a number of advantages from it. They gained a more comprehensive knowledge of economic and social problems facing Germany through receipt of information compiled by government and other agencies. They made use of the Council as an additional organ in which to present their legislative package and influence bills emanating from the government. Most labor leaders were satisfied with a Council having these limited advantages but some doubted its usefulness, while a few sought to broaden its powers and form it into a veritable economic parliament on the corporate model.[17]

The Weimar Council idea has not passed into oblivion. Other states, democratic and fascist, have made use of economic and social chambers to provide economic groups with an organ for articulating their interests. In some instances, such chambers, as in Fascist Italy, became the legislative one; in others, they have replaced the upper house, as in Bavaria at present; and in still others, as in France, they are as weak as was the Weimar Council.

Conciliation and Arbitration System

At a time when the unions participated in the administrative machinery of the government, the latter invaded the unions' primary sphere of activity, but with their open or tacit consent. The government set up a number of control organs in the labor-management field, especially in the conciliation, arbitration, and labor court systems.

A decree of December 23, 1918, recognized the validity of collective agreements (Tarifverträge) concluded between unions and employer associations on a regional or national basis, rather than on a local basis as was true before the war. The industry-wide contract aided workers in factories where employer influence was exceptionally strong, but, on the other hand, it froze wages for a period of time when negotiations for their revision could not be undertaken. Consequently, in some years wages were lower than if more frequent bargaining had been possible.[18]

In order to settle disputes arising from collective agreements, a state-nominated chairman was empowered to set up joint conciliation boards on a provisional basis. The boards' decisions could not be legally enforced unless recognized by both parties. By 1920, labor leaders, after some discussion, favored granting boards the power to make binding awards. They viewed compulsory arbitration as a way of politicizing wages, as a way of avoiding strikes, and as a useful tool of a socially-oriented state. The weaker partner in collective bargaining, the unions could expect to gain more often than lose at the hands of arbitrators sympathetic to their goals of creating a social and economic democracy. The employers, on the other hand, opted for nonbinding awards which would give them the freedom to reject any wage boosts ordered by the boards.

In 1920, Chancellor Bauer (SPD), in sympathy with the union position, urged legislative action to set up a permanent compulsory arbitration system. The Labor Ministry introduced a draft proposal to this effect, but because of employer pressure appended a clause limiting strikes. When the unions rejected the draft, the Ministry formed a committee with experts from labor, employers, and other interested parties to frame recommendations for a more satisfactory bill. In 1921, the Ministry prepared a bill based on the committee's proposals and sent it to the National Economic Council for comment. In March 1922, it finally reached the Reichstag, but domestic crises led to no legislative action.

In October 1923, the Stresemann government promulgated by official decree a conciliation and arbitration system. The decree created boards to be headed by government appointed arbitration officials and to consist of an equal number of assessors from union and employer ranks. The Ministry of Labor was assured of a decisive influence in labor disputes, receiving the right to formulate general principles for arbitration officials to follow. The jurisdiction of the boards extended to disputes arising from individual shop to national collective agreements. If the parties could not reach an accord, then the arbitrator would act as a voluntary mediator. If he failed he could declare the board's award binding upon an entire trade or industry, even if one party did not accept the decision.

Arbitrators were busy; in 1929, for example, 52 percent of all collective agreements were concluded on the basis of awards, although not all of these were binding.[19]

When the SPD governed, or when the minister of labor was favorably inclined to labor (as was true until 1930), then the unions could expect to receive a modicum of support in their conflicts with management. But there were exceptions, as in the case of the "Ruhr iron dispute" which erupted in October 1928. In a joint action, the metal workers unions of the three labor federations demanded a 15 pfennig per hour wage increase (later reduced to 12 pf.), which the employer association rejected. When the unions in turn rejected a counteroffer by the employer association, an arbitrator awarded 6 pf. per hour to several categories of workers. The unions, accepting the award reluctantly, requested that it be made binding. Minister of Labor Wissell met the request, but the employer association questioned its legality, contended that the industry could not absorb such a wage hike, and on November 1 locked out more than 250,000 metal workers, pursuant to an earlier threat. Then the association launched appeals through the hierarchy of labor courts. It lost an appeal at the Land level, but in January 1929 the Reich Labor Court sustained its objections. The Court contended that the award encroached on the existing collective agreement. The decision was a severe setback for the unions.

The cabinet sought to end the injurious lockout by proposing to both sides that Minister of the Interior Severing be made special arbitrator and that his award be accepted in advance. Both sides gave their consent. On December 3, the employers ended their lockout; less than three weeks later Severing made an award giving workers a wage boost of 1 to 6 pf. In this battle between the economic giants there were no victors or losers. The unions could not claim success when confronted with the minimal wage boost and with the Labor Court's weakening of the principle of binding awards.[20]

Until 1930, the ministers of labor attempted to peg wages to the prevailing price structure, but with the advent of the Great Depression the conservative governments through emergency decrees or awards repeatedly ordered wage cuts and longer working hours. Where formerly a friendly minister of labor had permitted discussions of his policy, a hostile minister now merely heard the unions' requests. He was aware that the labor movement was financially weak and unable to assume the offensive to combat the wage cuts and the lower standard of living.

By 1930, employer associations and unions both shifted their positions on the issue of binding awards. The employers who in the past had favored nonbinding awards suddenly reversed themselves when the government's deflationary policy could be expected to lead to a policy of cutting wages. At the same time, the unions, in a volte-face, opted for nonbinding awards in the hope of stemming dangerous wage cuts.

In October 1930, these shifts in position were dramatically illustrated in the famous case of the Berlin metal workers. When an arbitrator ordered their wages cut by 6 to 8 percent, they went on strike. In turn, the employers threatened to lock them out unless the award was declared binding. But the unions and the Social Democrats, with the aid of Communists and National Socialists (all vying for the workers' electoral support), persuaded the Reichstag to adopt a resolution ordering the minister of labor not to declare the award binding. Though this resolution carried no legal weight and ran counter to the guaranteed independence of the arbitrator, the political pressure caused the minister to establish a board to consider the case anew. The board decided that the original award was just; the unions yielded.[21]

From the unions' point of view, government intervention during the Weimar era had positive and negative effects. As a weaker force in the bargaining process, they welcomed the assistance that the government had rendered them in raising the wage level before the Depression. When they belatedly realized that the power of the government could also be wielded against them, it was too late to change the damaging policy.[22]

Labor Courts

After 1919, the unions put pressure on the government for a reform of the court system handling labor disputes between individual workers and management. Wary of the conservative judges and the ordinary courts lacking a uniformity of law, they rejected a Labor Ministry bill that would have incorporated the labor courts into the regular court system, and demanded instead a separate system of labor courts. After their pressure killed the first bill, the government finally introduced in June 1925 a new bill, more satisfactory to the unions, which was enacted into law in December 1926.[23]

A separate system was set up to adjudicate conflicts between employers and employees, including claims arising out of collective agreements. Each court was composed of a judge, appointed by the government to serve as independent chairman, and two assessors, one nominated by the unions and the other by employer associations. The assessors were to represent community interests, but in practice they felt responsible to the organizations that had nominated and furnished them with the necessary training. Their number reflected the size of the system; in 1931, the ADGB alone delegated 10,000 personnel to the courts.[24]

The system was divided into three court levels. On the local level, the courts of the first instance, only union officials were allowed to represent the workers, thereby adding to the union power in the system. In the courts of the second instance (district level), a union official or a lawyer could represent the workers, but in the court of the third instance (Federal Labor Court), only lawyers could do so. The courts had to reconcile the clashing views of management and labor, with the result that one side or the other often criticized their decisions. The employers before the Depression believed that the courts were too social minded to apply justice while the unions during the Depression criticized negative decisions made by conservative judges. Despite these misgivings, the unions were satisfied with the labor court system, and their deputies in the Reichstag quashed all attempts to revise it.[25]

Conclusion

When crucial decisions are made in the executive branch, interest groups must use an array of lobbying techniques to gain their objectives. The unions articulated their demands in meetings with top-level and low-level executive officials, and could expect more favorable hearings when the SPD headed a governing coalition. They gained political leverage and an inside track position when they occupied the chancellorship, or posts in cabinets, ministries and administrative agencies. But the increased intervention of the state in the economic realm, especially during the Depression years, and labor participation in public administrative bodies, accentuated the problems faced by the unions in their relationship to the state. As a result, the unions increasingly lost their independence of action and their militancy. Ironically, this trend occurred after the unions had openly or tacitly welcomed government intervention in the labor field as a means of improving their own position.

Since the survival of democracy in Germany depended on the strength of organizations committed to its defense, the position of the trade unions vis-à-vis the state was of crucial importance. If a proper balance in their relationship to it had been established, such as less reliance upon its services, then they would have enjoyed more autonomy and freedom of action. This might have resulted in a greater degree of militancy against the fascist menace.

VIII

ECONOMIC POLICY

From the Eight-Hour Day to Socialism

DURING THE FREQUENT crises of the Weimar years, the unions (as detailed in Chapters II and III) used their influence upon public policy makers to support the Republic and to thwart attempts to wreck their organization. At all times, they used their influence to shape the content of industrial relations and economic affairs legislation. These actions, typical of trade unions anywhere, were crucial because the welfare of their membership was at stake. To evaluate their measure of influence, their degree of success, and the types of techniques used, it is important to assess their actions on selected key economic issues—the eight-hour day, unemployment insurance, reparations, socialization, and works councils—and then their views on two-long range policies—economic democracy, and socialism.

Eight-Hour Day

Evidence of strong union pressure, and countervailing employer pressure, upon the government policy makers may be found in the legislative chronicle of the eight-hour day, an explosive issue symbolic of the tense conflicts between the two antagonistic economic groups and symbolic of the workers' struggle for improvement in their life. One 13-year-old worker's apprentice noted, "At that time (1924) one still worked ten hours a day. To the construction site one did not go by trolley car, but on foot, even if it was more than an hour away. In the evening, once again home on foot, tired from the many loads which I carried up the ladder each day. When I sank into the sofa, I felt as if I had been beaten with a heavy club."[1]

In the struggle for the eight-hour day, unions were able to get the support of the SPD, but they scored only limited success because of strong opposition from political and economic groups. In the immediate postwar era, as noted earlier, unions and employer associations reached an accord on a maximum work period of eight hours per day, and incorporated it into the November 15, 1918 Agreement. This union victory was promptly legalized by the government's three provisional decrees establishing the eight-hour day for the demobilization period.[2] The employer associations accepted the decrees most reluctantly and soon wanted them rescinded, claiming that increased production could be achieved only through longer hours. In reply, the unions argued that higher productivity would be gained by more mechanization and not by the scrapping of the eight-hour day. The latter had historic significance to them: each May Day before World War I they had demanded "eight hours work, eight hours free time, and eight hours sleep." The eight-hour day had also become to them a symbol of the Revolution.

In July 1921, in an effort to provide permanent legislation, Chancellor Wirth (Center) presented a controversial bill to the National Economic Council and Parliament for their deliberation. The bill had no chance of becoming law: the union leaders took a negative stand because of its loopholes; the employers opposed its regulatory features; and a cataclysmic inflation hit Germany in mid-1922, which made all talk of limiting hours academic. As a result the unions, on the defensive, attempted to maintain the life of the provisional decrees. Industrialists August Thyssen and Hugo Stinnes started a counteroffensive designed to extend working hours to ten a day without overtime compensation, but they failed—the decrees were not amended. In practice, however, on the basis of collective agreements, workers and salaried employees in many industries and trades worked overtime, with or without extra compensation. For instance, in the metal and textile industries, the workers were kept on a minimum fifty-four hour a week shift, with 20 percent of them working even longer.[3]

In December 1922, the dispute intensified when union delegates withdrew from participation in the National Economic Council after having been outvoted on a revised eight-hour day proposal. At the end of 1923, Chancellor Wilhelm Marx (Center) replaced the provisional decrees with a new decree containing a number of escape clauses.

From 1923 to 1925, the unions embarked on a campaign to win back the eight-hour day through international regulation. They sought government ratification of a convention adopted at the International Labor Conference in Washington (October 1919-January 1920) that limited hours of work in industrial firms to eight a day and forty-eight a week. By 1924, the British, French and Belgian governments were ready to submit the convention for ratification to their parliaments. But the German government, reiterating employer views, refused, arguing that production had to be boosted by a longer workweek.[4]

In 1925, the Textile Workers Union and others requested the ADGB Board to press the cabinet to hold a national popular referendum on the reinstatement of the maximum hour ruling. This constitutional tool of direct democracy, used on a number of occasions in Weimar Germany, seemed a perfect solution to labor's woes, but it also held dangers. ADGB Board leaders feared that if only SPD voters supported their position then a defeat in the referendum would set back their movement for years to come. They were willing, however, to support a referendum if union members were willing to make a special assessment for the expensive campaign. Such was not the case, and the request was dropped.[5]

Instead, as the economy finally stabilized, the ADGB sought to gain its goal through collective bargaining. Soon workers in half of the industries won contracts limiting their workday to eight hours. But the unions resumed the fight for new legislation as the other half of the labor force still put in more than eight hours a day. Finally, in April 1927, the Reichstag passed a law but with a number of loopholes in it. The union search for more satisfactory legislation led to a resumption of the cycle of pressure, followed by employer counterpressure, on the executive. As productivity increased, the 1928 ADGB Congress even sought to reduce the working day to less than eight hours, but the bourgeois coalition parties in majority in the SPD-led government stymied that proposal. When the Depression struck, union hopes to maintain the eight-hour day faded. In 1930, the ADGB Board urged workers to refuse to work overtime so as to give unemployed workers a chance. The appeal failed; workers grasped at every opportunity to boost their meager earnings by overtime. During the next two years the ADGB sought to spread the gospel of the forty-hour week, but its efforts were in vain.[6]

The eight-hour day controversy underscores the limited influence of the unions on public policy in a sphere important to the workers. Faced by employer and bourgeois parties' hostility, and recurring economic crises, their goal could not be achieved fully on the political level.

Unemployment Insurance

The unions waged a protracted struggle in another sphere important to the workers—unemployment insurance. From 1919 on, a sympathetic Ministry of Labor had drafted several proposals for a uniform federal insurance scheme to replace existing local unemployment benefit schemes and a postwar provisional decree. But each proposal had to be substantially revised when the political parties and interest groups raised questions concerning the degree of coverage, the linking of the scheme to health insurance, and the distribution of risks. In July 1922, the Wirth cabinet agreed to a bill settling most of these questions, and forwarded the bill to the National Economic Council for its advice. In early 1923, union and employer representatives were in accord on the basic premises of the bill, including the coverage of farm and domestic workers. Then the cabinet introduced the bill into Parliament where it met an untimely death before discussion in committee, even though the two main economic contenders were supporting it. In this instance the foe was the suddenly rampant inflation which upset all carefully prepared financial aspects of the bill; the government would have been unable to meet its obligations to the workers under authorized expenditures.[7]

In 1924, the unions put on a new lobbying campaign for unemployment insurance. Minister of Labor Brauns (Center Party) responded favorably, and had his civil servants prepare a new bill not differing appreciably from the 1922 bill. Since the conservative parties and employer associations were not in fundamental disagreement with its basic aspects, but only with some of its provisions, and since the inflation had been overcome, Brauns had little difficulty convincing his more conservative colleagues in the cabinet to support it. Once again, the bill meandered its way leisurely through the

National Economic Council and the Reichsrat (Upper House) where a number of amendments were recommended. In February 1927, the Reichstag began its deliberations. At that stage the ADGB, recommending a major revision of the bill, suggested that the unemployment insurance scheme be administered by a Reich-supervised network of labor employment and unemployment insurance centers. Since the ADGB was able to receive the approval of the conservative parties (then in the majority), the employer associations, and the Ministry of Labor, partisan political controversy was nearly absent from the committee deliberations. But this time the opposition came from the local governments viewing with alarm the loss of their role in the new scheme. After minor concessions to them, the bill, known as the Law on Employment Service and Unemployment Insurance, finally passed the Reichstag in July 1927, and was promulgated on October 1.[8] Its arduous trip had come to a successful end.

The law granted unemployment benefits to any citizen who was uunemployed but willing and able to work, and created an insurance fund from a 3 percent tax on wages to which employers and workers would contribute an equal share. The fund was designed to grant support for a maximum of 1.1 million workers who would receive benefits for up to twenty-six weeks, and in exceptional circumstances for up to thirty-nine weeks.

In 1928, the unions sought changes in the insurance scheme. Although the SPD had become the governing party and Minister of Labor Wissell (SPD) was sympathetic, the more conservative coalition partners were unwilling to make new concessions. The union efforts failed. Indeed, as the Depression struck, the conservatives began a counterdrive for a reduction in unemployment benefits. At the 1929 SPD Convention, Chairman Wels reiterated the resolve of the party and the unions to uphold existing benefits. By 1930 the party was less resolute, but the unions, as noted, convinced the SPD ministers to resign from the coalition government (which brought its downfall) rather than yield to the mounting conservative pressure for a cut in benefits. The Depression and the opposition of other parties doomed efforts to maintain the level of insurance payments. In July 1930, Chancellor Brüning issued an emergency decree raising the insurance tax and cutting payments. During the Depression the governments repeatedly had to borrow money to pay benefits to the swollen ranks of the unemployed because the fund had been depleted. To the individual unemployed worker, the loss of pay was a blow that the meager insurance payment could not compensate for. A mason, who returned during the Depression from journeymen's work abroad, could not comprehend the lack of work for him. He wrote, "It can't be that there is no work. In the coal mines one is still digging up coal, streets and houses are still being built, perhaps somewhere one needs a driver. It's unimportant what it is. Only it's got to be work."[9] He was forced to go on the dole.

Reparations

ADGB influence on the government was not restricted to the bread-and-butter issues affecting union members directly, but included areas of seemingly less direct economic impact on their welfare, such as Allied reparations policy. In reality, the average worker was as much affected by reparations payments cutting into his living standard as he was by the government's income policy. No wonder then that top labor officials launched a decade-long crusade against the Versailles treaty and its reparations clauses, in the process capitalizing on the nationalist feelings among the population.[10]

These officials appealed for support from the "workers of the world" against a 1921 Paris Conference decision setting reparations at 226 billion RM to be paid by Germany over a period of forty-two years. They argued that the sum could not possibly be repaid and would introduce " slave labor by the international capitalist fraternity."[11] After further diplomatic negotiations in 1921, the German government reluctantly accepted a Reparations Commission proposal for a reduced debt settlement. The ADGB sent a telegram to the International Federation of Trade Unions urging it to appeal to the workers in the Allied nations to rescue the German workers from economic slavery. In response, the IFTU took a middle-of-the-road position. It acknowledged the need for German restitution and reconstruction of the devasted areas, but called for the establishment of a nonpartisan commission of inquiry to work out an accord, through arbitration if need be, on the amount of restitution to be paid by Germany.

At the 1922 ADGB Congress, Leipart asserted that the unions expected the government to fulfil its reparations obligations, but not at the expense of social gains. As the economic situation worsened, ADGB leaders called for restriction of reparations to Allied reconstruction needs and the cancellation of German war debts. A German default on coal and timber deliveries to France led to French occupation of the Ruhr area in January 1923—and to the already described passive resistance on the part of the unions.

By 1924, the German political and economic situation had stabilized, and the Allies were ready to make concessions on the reparations question. When they requested General Dawes of the United States to prepare a new plan, he consulted in Berlin, among others, ADGB Vice-President Grassmann to obtain the union point of view. Grassmann reminded Dawes that the unions had made proposals for the reconstruction of destroyed areas and were ready to support a reasonable proposal that would not enrich foreign capitalists at the expense of German workers. In September 1924, the Dawes Plan was issued, calling for specific yearly payments (2.5 billion RM) but not setting a total sum or an expiration date. The unions objected to this open-ended feature.

By 1928, the economic situation had improved sufficiently for the Allies, in consultation with German representatives, to draft a final reparations plan, known as the Young Plan. In 1929, the unions, fearful that some provisions might adversely affect German workers, protested to the SPD-led government about its failure to give them seats on the preparatory commission. In response, the cabinet requested Minister of Finance Hilferding (SPD) to inform two top ADGB leaders that they ought to make themselves available to provide specialized information to the government or the commission. But the ADGB leaders were never called.[12] In March 1929, the Young Plan was signed (with Reichstag approval one year later). While it represented a financial easement of 20 to 25 percent as compared to the Dawes Plan, it was predicated on the maintenance of economic stability, and not on the Great Depression. By October 1930, the ADGB Board demanded a cancellation of payments in order to ease the skyrocketing unemployment.[13]

It was not until June 1931 that President Hoover, realizing the futility of demanding adherence to the Young Plan in the face of the Depression, decreed a moratorium on inter-Allied debts and reparations payments. The moratorium meant the end of any future payments, but this was not yet evident. Thus, Leipart warned that the moratorium might be merely an interlude before new reparations negotiations began. He did not see how Germany could resume payments at the same level in a post-Depression period.[14]

As a by-product of the international dispute, the reparations problem also caused an interorganizational dispute between the ADGB and SPD. Top labor leaders looked at the problem from an economic and nationalist point of view, while most SPD leaders concentrated on its political and international dimensions. The dispute erupted into the open, but not into the press, on December 16, 1931, at a meeting of socialist organizations, when Leipart declared that "we *do not* want to pay reparations any longer." SPD leader Breitscheid argued that "we *cannot* pay reparations any longer." The latter, supported by a number of other SPD leaders, used the more moderate language in an attempt to improve relations with France. He deemed it inopportune for Leipart to take a tough stance. On the other hand, a minority of more conservative SPD leaders disapproved of the party's ignoring the views of the ADGB.[15] This discord may have taken on the dimensions of a tempest in a teapot, but ideological, political, and jurisdictional questions were at stake.

The eleven-year struggle of the ADGB for an end to reparations and war debts represented the views of a very large segment of the population, but did not significantly shape the course of German reparations policy. Rather, it exacerbated ADGB relations with the SPD, which was critical of Leipart's nationalist outbursts and his alleged exaggerated statements about the reparations' effects on the German economy.

Socialization

Whether industry should remain in private hands after World War I or be taken over by the state became the subject of an intense debate within socialist union and SPD circles. The union attitude was expected to affect the outcome of the debate and government policy decisions. The reformist labor leaders, while professing to be in favor of a socialist economy, viewed socialization (nationalization) of industry as too revolutionary under prevailing conditions. Yet they could not stand aloof from the clamor for socialization expressed by workers' and soldiers' councils, the USPD, and large numbers of organized and unorganized workers.[16]

In November 1918 the socialist-led government agreed in principle that socialization should be undertaken. Accordingly, an eleven-member Socialization Commission was set up to ascertain which industries might be taken over by the state. Although a few nonsocialists sat on the Commission, the majority were socialist economists, as well as two union representatives (Paul Umbreit, editor of the *Gewerkschafts-Zeitung*, and Otto Hue, leader of the Mine Workers Union).

Despite the establishment of the Commission, most union and socialist chiefs continued to pay only lip service to the concept of socialization. They were fearful lest any precipitate action destroy the possibility of stabilizing the economy, bring starvation to the country, make the right to strike more difficult, and create an excuse for the Allies not to negotiate with a socialist Germany and thereby cause its ruin. Hue declared:

> There are no differences of opinion as regards the necessity of socialising the mines and associated industries, so as to deprive capitalism of its strongest support. But today the question arises as to whether the time is ripe for the socialisation of our extraordinarily complicated industry.... This period is not the present. The socialisation of such powerfully developed undertakings as the mines and iron and steel industries cannot be carried out according to the dictates of the minority, but only at the right time and for the benefit of the community.[17]

The reaction of union newspapers typified the negative position of labor leaders. The General Commission journal supported socialization initially, but with little enthusiasm. Other journals doubted the wisdom of the proposal for their own industry, but claimed support in principle. Thus, the Metal Workers journal, not known as a bastion of conservatism, stressed the ease with which other industries, such as steel processing mills and mines, could be converted to public ownership, but warned that the metal industry should not be socialized in times of grave political upheavals.[18]

While the debate raged on, the Commission in December 1918 and January 1919 issued preliminary reports. It warned of any attempt to socialize all industries, including such ones as foreign trade and food supply, and advocated instead the conversion only of basic industries. In a report of the coal industry (February 1919), it proposed the nationalization of all coal deposits, and governmental control over the market, prices, and the opening of new mines.[19] The report caused a mixed reaction among union and socialist leaders, no immediate commitment from the government, and a series of strikes and armed clashes between troops and workers. Since the miners in the Ruhr clamored for public ownership of mines, 400,000 of them supported a strike called by the left-dominated workers' and soldiers' councils. The Mine Workers Union failed to endorse it because of its leftist origin. As a consequence, the strike collapsed swiftly, but was followed by numerous brutal armed clashes between the workers and government troops under the order of SPD War Minister Noske. This in turn triggered off a new strike in early April, with the Mine Workers Union again remaining on the sidelines.

In the meantime, in Berlin the USPD and other Left forces, backed by the left-controlled Berlin Trade Union Commission, called a general strike on March 4 to enforce demands for their program, including the socialization of the entire economy. Although the socialist-led cabinet assured a strike delegation that the socialization laws would shortly be submitted to the National Assembly, violence erupted in the capital. The cabinet, afraid of a revolutionary uprising, ordered the Reichswehr to quell the strike. The General Commission, in a statement reflective of its conservative dogma, denounced the Berlin Trade Union Commission for having endorsed a political strike damaging to the economy. Rather, socialization would best be achieved through the action of the responsible and elected national leaders.[20]

The cabinet assurance and the strike did have an impact on the National Assembly. It passed laws on March 13 and April 15 empowering the government to take over enterprises suitable for socialization such as the coal and potash industries, which were managed by commissions of owners, workers, and consumers. This legislative development and the Weimar Constitution's provision that the Reich was authorized to transfer to public ownership any "private economic enterprise suitable for socialization" (Article 156) legitimized the moves toward limited socialization, but no actual state ownership of the coal and potash industries resulted.

The government's failure to implement fully the recommendations of the Socialization Commission was a principal cause for the latter's sudden resignation in April. The Commission claimed that it was hindered in its work by the National Economic Council, for which it was merely acting as an advisory organ, and by the National

Assembly. To fill the void in the economic sphere left by the defunct Commission, Rudolf Wissell, ADGB leader and SPD Minister of Economic Affairs, called for a planned economy containing a mix of public and private sectors. Leipart and other ADGB leaders, however, rejected the plan because of its impracticality under the existing economic circumstances, its attempt to change the economic system from above, and its exaggerated goals. They also feared that in the socialized sector the unions would find it more difficult to strike against a state management. Despite their opposition, Wissell presented his plan in July to the SPD-led cabinet; but when its majority also rejected the plan for the same reasons he resigned.[21] The ADGB was pleased not only that the cabinet members, most of whom were Social Democrats, rejected such a visionary plan, but also that they selected Robert Schmidt, a former General Commission Executive member and an opponent of planned economy, to succeed Wissell as Minister of Economic Affairs. Schmidt drafted a plan granting the Reich the power to socialize only the electrical plants under proper compensation. In December, the legislature adopted the bill, but it was never implemented.[22] After the SPD-led government agreed to a socialization provision in the settlement ending the Kapp Putsch in 1920, the ADGB urged the reestablishment of a broader-based Socialization Commission. Its proposal was surprising on the basis of its previous lukewarm attitude, but tactically necessary to dampen the strong Left forces. Accordingly, a second Commission was formed with twenty-three members, and again included Umbreit and Hue, as well as Adolf Cohen and Wissell, ADGB; Heinrich Kaufmann and Georg Werner, AfA; and delegates from the Christian and Hirsch-Duncker federations.

The union representatives on the Commission, however, could not agree on any one plan. In the final report on the coal industry (July 1920), Cohen and Wissell sided with the conservative majority urging a gradual public take-over, while the other free union leaders this time backed the radical minority requesting an immediate take-over. The conservative cabinet led by Konstantin Fehrenbach (Center) did not act on the report. The Commission, beset by rifts between its members, was unable to agree on any further recommendations and soon ceased its work.[23]

The failure of the two Socialization Commissions may be attributed partly to union and SPD leaders who consistently opposed proposals for immediate socialization because they feared a further deterioration of the German economy and a Left minority take-over of the country. Whether their fears were exaggerated remains a matter of conjecture; their opposition to revolutionary dislocations, however, was common knowledge. The unions' failure to endorse Wissell's planned economy program was even more symptomatic of their negative attitude toward any proposal intended to radically change the economic system. Undoubtedly, their uncompromising stand precluded any move toward at least partial socialization during the Weimar period. As veteran socialists, their attitude was understandable only in the context of their conscious shedding of the Marxist ideology and program.

Works Councils

Labor movements are concerned not only with the ownership of industry, but with rules and conditions in shops in which workers spend half their waking hours. In recent years, workers, especially on assembly lines, have become increasingly alienated from their work situation because they are unable to share in the decision-making process affecting their daily tedious routine. A number of countries have experimented lately with schemes providing for more diffusion of power and industrial democracy at the shop and factory levels: labor-management controls and teamwork on automobile assembly lines in Scandinavia, the kibbutzim in Israel, self-management in Yugoslavia, and codetermination in West Germany.

Codetermination rests partially on the concept of works councils (Betriebsräte), proposed as early as the nineteenth century by the German socialist unions. The councils, performing functions somewhat similar to those of the shop stewards in the United States and Great Britain, were first permitted by law in 1891 in large shops, but their importance was limited during the Imperial era.

During the early Weimar period, the socialist unions maintained an ambivalent attitude toward the creation of a more widespread system of councils. On the one hand, the unions were worried about the tendency of the politically potent workers' and soldiers' councils, established during the Revolution, to meddle increasingly in shop questions; and, on the other hand, they were worried that the works councils in the shops would encroach on their own functions.[24] In order not to remain too negative, the leaders threw their weight behind the permanent reestablishment of works councils with purely economic functions, as long as the unions would be able to dominate them. Thus, when on February 25, 1919, Chancellor Scheidemann (SPD) said, "No member of the Cabinet contemplates the incorporation, in any form, of the Council system into the Constitution,"[25] the General Commission reacted negatively, even though the Chancellor may have had only the workers' and soldiers' councils in mind. When indignant workers responded with strikes, the cabinet yielded and promised to incorporate the idea of councils with economic, but not political, functions into the Constitution.

The provision appeared in Article 165, and then had to be fleshed out by further legislative action. A government decree of December 1918 had already provided for works councils, but only in establishments with twenty or more workers. In May 1919, the Ministry of Labor drafted a more comprehensive works council bill after repeated consultations with employer and labor representatives. The draft of the bill was withdrawn, however, when the employer associations and the SPD objected to many of its provisions.

Thereupon the Ministry of Labor immediately drafted a revised bill providing for the establishment of works councils in all shops with at least twenty workers, and the election of shop delegates in smaller shops. Its chief effect would be to give the workers' representatives—the works councilors (shop stewards)—a limited influence upon managerial decisions, granting them control functions in the observance of labor laws and authorizing them to represent the workers in all shop problems. The councils, in cooperation with the employers who had to pay their expenses, were to set up working rules, promote safety regulations, and aid in the administration of welfare schemes and the enforcement of collective agreements. They had the right to obtain information on those issues affecting labor, such as wage records; employment prospects; and, in the case of big business, balance sheets; and could appoint members to the board of directors. The unions were to receive an advisory voice in the councils by sending one of their representatives to attend its sessions if the shop was organized and if one-quarter of the councilors agreed.[26]

In August 1919, Chancellor Bauer's cabinet, consisting mostly of SPD and Center Party ministers, approved the draft, and sent it on its legislative journey. The bill received a thorough scrutiny in the

National Assembly's Social Affairs Committee where it was debated heatedly for seven weeks. Minister of Labor Schlicke (SPD), who had been chairman of the Metal Workers Union for a long time, spoke up as government representative on a number of occasions to defend it. A member of the ADGB Transport Workers Union Executive, who was also a member of the Social Affairs Committee, expressed ADGB support for it, but hoped that it would be amended to provide the unions with more representation in the councils and that council functions would not conflict with union functions. He could count on the backing of Schlicke who had kept in close touch with the unions during the drafting of the bill. The SPD also expressed its support (necessary for passage of the bill), but the salaried employees unions labeled the bill as too weak, and demanded more power for the councils. Radical workers, who considered the works councils as a poor substitute for workers' councils having political functions, demonstrated against the bill during the second reading in the plenum (resulting in fierce police reprisals). The National Association of German Industry again opposed the bill, but for other reasons than the Left: national industrial acitivity would decline, and council members would receive too many management prerogatives. Despite this array of critics, in January 1920 a majority of deputies (215-63) approved the bill; on February 4 it became law.

The Berlin and other left-controlled councils, however, were not yet reconciled to political powerlessness. To stymie them, ADGB and AfA sponsored in October 1920 a Congress of Works Councils. There they pushed through resolutions restricting the potential political power of councils by ensuring their existence only at the local and not at the central level, by prohibiting them from maintaining funds, and by insisting that in each district regional union offices control and guide them.[27]

The ADGB Board in 1920 and the ADGB Congress in 1922 adopted several measures intended to establish further free union supremacy over the councils. The federation decided that its local affiliates would aid in the preparation of shop elections, and that when an ADGB-affiliated union submitted a slate of candidates, all must be union members and none could be a candidate on a rival union slate. As a result of these initiatives, the free unions assured themselves direct control over the councils. In 1922, the ADGB noted that 75 to 80 percent of the 250,000 councilors were socialist union members.[28]

The record of the councils was mixed. In many cases the councils performed useful functions, but in others they failed to make gains, producing disillusionment among the workers. In instances of employer hostility, especially in small plants and during the Depression, workers were afraid of losing their jobs if they served as councilors. Nor did the councils cooperate with employers, as the latter had hoped, in increasing workers' productivity and efficiency or in introducing innovations. The councils viewed this as management's job and not theirs, especially since the results might be damaging to the workers. Employers also evaded some provisions of the law. They gave only scant information to the councils on the state of business and production. They circumvented the provision of councilors serving on the boards of directors by creating subcommittees without councilors or by transferring the effective and sensitive decision-making powers to the managers. In 1931, the ADGB won parliamentary approval for a law ensuring that all board members, including works councilors, receive all important company information. The law could not be tested adequately in view of the deteriorating political situation.[29]

Although the works councils did not meet all the expectations of their proponents, and certainly did not change the basic economic system of Weimar, they were instrumental in bringing a measure of democracy into the shops and firms. Yet radical workers distrusted the councils as organs upholding the capitalist system, unless they had captured control of the councils. Initially the ADGB (and its predecessor) had opposed them too, for different reasons, but later it viewed them as the first step on the road toward economic democracy, which was expected to tilt the system eventually toward more power for the workers.

Economic Democracy

In contemporary industrial systems, organized labor spokesmen are using the slogan "industrial democracy" more and more frequently. It has its antecedents in, among other countries, Weimar Germany, where a parallel slogan "economic democracy" was coined. During the course of Weimar, the free unions searched for a new ideal, a concrete program to replace the socialist dogma deemed to be too utopian. They gradually evolved a program of economic democracy consisting of immediate and long-range goals. This program became a cornerstone of the continuing ideological revision in socialist doctrine among labor leaders, and added substance to the evolutionary theories propounded by Eduard Bernstein at the turn of the century. Leftist critics, on the other hand, viewed the program as a sellout to the strongly-entrenched capitalist system.[30]

At the beginning of the Weimar era, the concept of economic democracy had not yet been formulated, but some steps, such as the creation of works councils and labor-management councils, reflected attempts to institutionalize a new power relationship in which labor would share increasingly in the decision-making process with employers. In 1924, the collapse of the labor-management councils created a void in union policies, and called for a new direction and programmatic goal. Therefore, labor leaders sought to promote a concept of increased workers' participation in the economy, or "economic democracy," as they put it, as a corollary to the SPD's program of political democracy.[31]

The 1925 ADGB Congress attempted to tackle the subject. But because of insufficient preparation, it became obvious that a definition of the concept, its basis, and its relation to socialism could not be framed during the proceedings, especially when speakers expressed different views. For instance, Professor Paul Hermberg equated economic democracy with a planned economy, since only planning can assure the democratic participation of the workers in the industrial life of the nation. The present system offered the workers merely an opportunity to develop the works council system on a local level. In the end, he argued, the new concept would be indistinguishable from a socialist economy. On the other hand, Leipart predicted that economic democracy could be achieved under capitalism by granting the workers a greater or equal share in the leadership of the national industrial sector. Tarnow concurred; he maintained that since the masses were no longer under the Marxist spell and since communist exploitation of this ideological vacuum required an effective antidote they needed more immediate spiritual satisfaction. He favored a pragmatic approach to economic democracy and implicity rejected the concept of a planned socialist economy for the near future. The Congress majority shared the views of Leipart and Tarnow.[32]

In the wake of the Congress, labor leaders attempted to formulate the concept more clearly. They commissioned Fritz Napthali, socialist economist, and others to draft a program acceptable to a majority of the labor community. Napthali sketched out the details at the 1928 ADGB Congress and in a published work. He envisioned economic democracy to consist, first, of a short-range program geared to a democratization of the economy, based on an expansion of the works councils, governmental self-governing bodies, trade union-sponsored enterprises, cooperatives, and public firms, which would give the workers more power at the expense of management. Second, economic democracy would consist of a long-range program geared to achieving a planned socialist economy. This could be done by breaking up the economic monopolies emerging in the late capitalist phase, and by introducing more political democracy in the state, which would create more freedom and democratization in the economic sphere. Hence, economic democracy would become a well-integrated complement to political democracy.[33]

The Congress accepted a resolution introduced by the ADGB executive organs embodying Napthali's short-range program, but significantly not emphasizing the long-range program. Although acceptance of the resolution did not signify any change in union policy, it did put the achievements of the unions in the Weimar era in a new framework, and reinforced the evolution of the ADGB as a carrier of programs separate from those formulated by the SPD. The initiative of the ADGB in repudiating Marxist dogma and espousing a reformist program of economic democracy, sustained by the SPD, was further proof of a shift in power from the SPD to the labor federation. As expected, it produced intra- and interorganizational strains, especially after charges by the radical factions that the ADGB had thereby abandoned its socialist principles. There was a measure of truth in their charges, as will be seen presently. But regardless of this controversy, the ADGB's formulation of a plan for economic democracy has become one of the bases upon which contemporary plans for industrial democracy are evolving in a number of countries.

Socialism

Most free union leaders and members perceived themselves as socialists. In their speeches the leaders paid lip service to the ultimate goal—a socialist polity in which the capitalist and private profit system would be eliminated; and a new society based on humanism, equality, and a classless society would be created. This vision of the future was part of Napthali's long-range program for an economic democracy; but during Weimar it remained a utopian dream, especially since the unions made no serious attempt to achieve it.

The dream had been nurtured during the formative decades of the unions. Then, and in the Weimar era too, unionists had been raised in a political subculture where Marx and Engels were revered names, where their votes were cast automatically for the SPD, and where their lives revolved around the party and its ancillary organizations. In short, they considered themselves part of a fraternal order with a messianic and a religious fervor. As a consequence, the right-wing labor leaders, constituting a majority in the ADGB, enunciated this faith in socialism on several occasions. At the 1919 ADGB Congress, the policy declaration stipulated that the unions consider socialism to be the highest form of national economic organization:

> The trade unions must not restrict themselves to the narrow, occupational representation of interests; they must rather become the focal points in the class aspirations of the proletariat, in order to help lead the fight for socialism to victory.[34]

In 1925, Leipart, in a letter to SPD chief Müller, insisted that the struggle of the working class against capitalism must be an economic as well as a political fight. In 1932, Leipart still asserted that the long-range task of the unions must be to struggle for socialism.[35]

Despite these professions of loyalty to ultimate socialism in which the unions would play a role equal to that of the SPD, the labor officials discreetly switched from an ideological to a pragmatic commitment. As they spoke up for moderation and realism in the tradition of Bernstein's evolutionary socialism, they began to reject the Marxian concept of class struggle still expounded in SPD statements and literature. They made the shift in order to gain maximum benefits for the workers under the entrenched capitalist system, but did little to weaken the system, as evident in their opposition to the socialization of industry. In pursuit of this pragmatic course, they were influential in swaying party leaders to take a more moderate ideological stance, reflected in turn in the party's political decisions.

Two examples follow. At the inception of the Depression, socialists and unionists had to resolve the dilemma whether to continue sustaining the crumbling capitalist economy in order to maintain the hard-earned benefits gained by the workers, or whether to use the opportunity to attempt its transformation into a socialist system. Symbolic of the rising labor influence in the SPD, the party invited Tarnow to give the keynote economic address to the 1931 SPD Convention. As expected, the ADGB leader rejected left-wing proposals to let the capitalist system crumble, and urged the SPD and the free unions to shore it up instead:

> Are we sitting at the sickbed of capitalism, not only as doctors who want to cure the patient, but as prospective heirs who cannot wait for the end and would like to hasten it by administering poison? We are condemned, I think, to be doctors who seriously wish to cure, and yet we have to maintain the feeling that we are heirs who wish to receive the entire legacy of the capitalist system today rather than tomorrow. This double role, doctor and heir, is a damned difficult task.[36]

Two left-wing members decried Tarnow's position, claiming that socialists cannot simultaneously cure capitalism and advocate socialism. Tarnow retorted that the economy and not capitalism had to be healed. Most convention delegates supported his views.

In another move to moderate the party's ideological tone, union officers repeatedly decried the influence of radical academic intellectuals who allegedly were strengthening their grip on the party, who paid little attention to the pragmatic day-to-day workers' problems, and who instead remained exponents of socialist dogma. As a result, the activities of intellectuals created uneasiness within the unions.[37] As an antidote, the ADGB officers called on members to increase their political activity, and to support the program of economic democracy which had more chance of achieving success than radical dreams.

Lothar Erdmann, a staff associate of Leipart and a theoretician of the labor movement, expressed these thoughts in a well-publicized article.[38] He maintained that organized labor's lack of a doctrinaire ideology gave it a chance to evolve an economic program based on attainable goals, such as economic democracy, for which the worker would show more understanding than for a revolutionary theory propounded by socialist intellectuals. The SPD could no longer be regarded as the leading representative of the workers' movement; the unions were demanding equality with the party in formulating a practical program for the movement.

Whether this alleged threat of the intellectuals to the unions was ever as serious as the ADGB implied is questionable. Rather, reflecting a tension between two disparate groups, common in other countries, the ADGB intended thereby to minimize the power of the Left in the SPD, and to produce a harmony of interests between the two organizations based on achieving immediate victories while professing to keep the faith in ultimate socialism.[39]

IX

THE POLITICAL POWER
OF THE SOCIALIST UNIONS

THE SOCIALIST UNIONS in the Weimar era were at times politically significant. In evaluating their role, it is necessary to distinguish between their two types of political activities: one, lobbying, ancillary to their function as an economic organization; and two, attempts to shape national political developments. They expected to pursue this dual role with some measure of success because the Weimar governments were assumed to be more favorably inclined to them than the Imperial governments, and because the 1919 Constitution gave them legal recognition, while granting the workers strong social guarantees and rights. When the unions also received representation on new governmental regulatory, administrative and advisory bodies, their expectation of becoming an important association in the body politic was enhanced.

This dream was not matched by reality. The functions of many new organs, especially the provisional National Economic Council, were limited to advice. The government was active in the arbitration and mediation machinery, and was the final arbiter. Union difficulties were compounded in the first and last Weimar years by a series of economic crises that included a devastating inflation and depression. The unions could not expect to make gains during such periods no matter what political parties were in power. Thus, when the SPD led a coalition cabinet in which the unions had direct representation, chances for a successful adoption of a prounion legislative package were dimmed when harsh economic realities produced a governmental austerity program (except for provisional decrees issued immediately after the trauma of the 1918 Revolution when the unions faced no appreciable opposition). Such was the case when the SPD and the socialist unions pushed hard for unemployment insurance, a mediation and arbitration system, and labor courts. These objectives had to be postponed in the founding years until economic circumstances improved after 1923. When such an improvement took place, nonsocialist cabinets, whose sympathies could be expected to lie more on the employer side, happened to be governing. Yet, paradoxically, these cabinets produced gains for the unions in the industrial relations sphere that had been blocked earlier. The explanation lay in their willingness to make some concessions to organized labor for political and economic reasons. Minister of Labor Brauns, a Center Party leader in office from 1920 to 1928, was able to persuade his more conservative colleagues to make these concessions because the governing parties needed the support of the nonsocialist workers and salaried employees and the times were ripe for the employer community to share its increasing prosperity with organized labor. The cabinet members were less prone to object to these arguments since public opinion was sympathetic to many union objectives, and the employers recognized their legitimacy.

In sum, from the point of view of the socialist labor federations, they could expect to make the greatest gains when socialists governed alone in a revolutionary era (1918-1919) or when the socialists were the leaders of a coalition during economically prosperous times (1928-1929). They could expect to make significant gains when bourgeois coalition parties governed in economically prosperous times (1924-1928). But they could expect few or no gains when socialist or nonsocialist chancellors governed during economically difficult times (1919-1923; 1930-1933).

Yet, whether the political and economic climate was favorable or not, and whether socialists or nonsocialists were the leading policy makers, did not affect union tactics and strategy. In any one of these situations, labor leaders sought to gain their objectives or to minimize potentially damaging legislation through an array of lobbying techniques common to interest groups everywhere. These consisted of conferences or communications with leading government officials, civil servants and deputies on administrative and legislative policies of direct concern to them. Or, in instances of political crises, they consisted of strikes, mass demonstrations, and public meetings to lend weight to union demands.

The free unions put considerable indirect pressure upon the government through their official and unofficial links to the Social Democratic Party. The major link binding the two organizations stemmed from the overlap of membership, which characterized the rank and file to a limited extent, but the leadership cadre to a sizable extent. Although only about 12 to 16 percent of the union members were simultaneously SPD members (in the late twenties), an esti-mated two-thirds of them cast their vote for the SPD, a reflection of the political subculture of socialism in which they lived. This vote constituted close to a majority of the total SPD vote, and had an effect on SPD policies.

The majority of decision makers in both organizations professed to pursue a moderate evolutionary socialist course, but in reality they did not challenge the basic tenets of the neocapitalist system—as for example, in their refusal to push hard for socialization of industry. Therefore they were challenged by a noncommunist left-wing mi-nority and, in the unions, by a communist minority as well. These minorities, though, had only a limited influence on party and union policies.

The fraternal links between free unions and party facilitated the nomination and election of union leaders to the Reichstag. In order to maximize their representation, the unions supported the SPD through intensive election propaganda campaigns and unofficial financial contributions, with the result that the general public vir-tually identified them with the party. The number of union leaders who were Reichstag deputies in each legislative period constituted on the average one-fifth of the SPD deputies. They played a vital role in the SPD Fraktion, the legislative committees, and the plenum by introducing or backing bills of special interest to their constituency.

Union political pressures on the executive and legislative branches directly or through the SPD were designed to evoke favorable responses from these organs to its economic and social demands. But in the formative and last Weimar years the unions realized that they could not avoid taking positions on political developments that were bound to affect their welfare and their very existence. Their support for a parliamentary democratic regime led to their mounting opposition to workers and soldiers councils, to their proclamation of a general strike during the Kapp Putsch, to their initiative for legislation to safeguard the nation from extremist forces, and to their relentless fight against Communists within and outside their ranks.

The unions wove nationalist fibers into the fabric of democracy, just as their counterparts did in other countries, thereby weakening international strands. They backed their government during World War I and in its opposition to reparations and the Versailles Treaty, and engaged in passive resistance during the Ruhr crisis. Such positions enhanced their legitimacy in the nation.

Union involvement in political affairs that had economic consequences was bound to produce friction with the SPD, which saw its prerogatives threatened—as in 1930 over the unemployment issue and in 1932 over the ADGB's flirtation with Chancellor Schleicher. These examples were the exception to their fraternal cooperation spanning the Weimar years when both were in accord on short-range goals, such as pragmatic reforms within the capitalist system, and on long-range goals, such as economic democracy.

During the crucial period of Hitler's consolidation of power, the unions abandoned their goals and fought for sheer survival. They lost this fight. Their capitulation seemed out of tune with earlier policies of shoring up the democratic system and assailing extremists forces; rather it represented the inability of weak and indecisive union leaders to mount a counteroffensive to stem the Nazi tide. Such a step would have been difficult under any circumstances; it was even more difficult in view of the depletion of union ranks by massive unemployment and the high risks of bloodshed and failure. Hence, the leaders took the road of least resistance and chose a strategy to save the movement at all costs. But Hitler's strategy would not allow such survival, and the movement came to a precipitate end in 1933.

The range of political activities of the unions during the Weimar period was wide; their degree of political power varied considerably, depending on a multitude of factors over which in some instances they had no control. Although in the early Weimar years they did not push hard for institutional and personnel reforms in the bureaucracy, the judiciary, and the armed forces; or for societal reforms; and although in the last Weimar years they could not block the rise of Nazism, they did exert enough influence on the SPD and the public authorities to achieve progress and to help maintain the democratic regime for a brief span in history. Therein lies their contribution: they promoted the gradual development of a democratic and social ethos in a nation not steeped in it historically.

The German unions made another contribution. In their pre-Weimar and Weimar developmental and organizational stage and in their partisan political position, they served as a prototype for other European union federations. Their contribution was not always positive, especially as bureaucracy and oligarchy, social stratification, and membership apathy seeped into their organization. Although these characteristics stem partly from a rigid status system, the difference from other labor movements was only one of degree. In most union movements, in practice, there existed (and exists) a limited internal democratic process. Most members directly affected accepted this limitation and did not participate greatly in union affairs. Seymour M. Lipset has argued that German workers tended to accept the permanent tenure of their leaders and hierarchical control more readily than workers in the United States.[1] On the basis of this German study, the difference in attitude between German and American workers was not significant, except for the rare union rank and file revolts in the United States.

The problem of membership apathy, already serious in Weimar, has been accentuated in the postwar period not only in West Germany, but in nearly all Western industrialized states. If the labor movements can foster more communication between leaders and members, and broaden the decision-making process, and if they can deal imaginatively with serious contemporary problems (inflationary pressures, technological changes, governmental incomes policies, social issues), then perhaps they may be able to solve some of their internal difficulties and come close to Harold Laski's prescription that "democracy means participation."[2]

The Weimar labor movement had to cope with another major difficulty. As in other Continental countries, deep ideological, political, and religious cleavages split the movement into competing socialist, Christian, and liberal federations. But even within the socialist federations, internal cleavages emerged as a result of additional schisms based on tactics and ideology, and of the necessity of taking a position on issues transcending the narrow bread-and-butter ones. Thus, Lipset would be correct in his argument that the more

[179]

politicized the European labor movements, the more cleavages appear—but only if he were to restrict himself to the Continent and exclude the politicized but unitary British and Scandinavian union movements. And yet a look at the present unitary and nonpartisan German Trade Union Federation (Deutscher Gewerkschaftsbund) shows that factionalism has not been avoided there either. The central Federation, created in 1949, is the successor organization to the competing Weimar labor federations. It now has a membership of about 7.5 million in 16 national industrial unions, with perhaps 80 percent of the members supporting the renascent SPD and 20 percent the Christian Democrats.[3] As a result of commitment to political action, the Federation has not been able to eschew ideological clashes between its politically moderate and radical members.

Federation leaders in the formative years of the Federal Republic knew that some factionalism was inevitable, but by creating a nonpartisan federation they hoped to avoid the extreme fractionization of the Weimar labor movement. They viewed the Weimar division as disastrous to the maintenance of the democratic system, and thus considered themselves—almost fanatically—as the major defense against any antidemocratic group that might threaten the Bonn Republic.[4] Most of them (the pragmatic majority) also reasoned, as they or their predecessors did in Weimar, that despite their professed sympathy for a socialist system they would have to work for incremental improvements within the framework of the entrenched neocapitalist system. This policy once again caused strains within the movement, with the left-wing minority attempting to achieve a restructuring of the economy.

Presently the activities of the majority hardly differ from those of the AFL-CIO establishment in the United States. Both are intent on maximizing their power vis-à-vis the capitalist elite. Only one important difference remains between them: the majority of American labor leaders are ideologically in tune with the ethos of the free enterprise system, while a majority of German and other European labor leaders still cling to their vision of socialism. But such ideological differences have little effect on the similarity of programmatic statements and pressures exerted on public decison makers on both sides of the Atlantic.

During the Weimar era, the ideological commitment of German labor leaders led to the linkage with political parties, unlike the AFL's policy of avoiding an entangling alliance with any one party. Para-doxically, in the post-World War II era, American unions have become more partisan, while the German labor federation has assumed, at least officially, a nonpartisan position. But in both countries, the labor federations are attempting to cope politically with issues arising from capitalist economic systems.

One such issue is codetermination, which has been resurrected from the Weimar Republic in modified form in West Germany, and has been accepted or rejected in a number of other countries. The recent emphasis on job enrichment and workers' participation in management affairs at the shop and company levels has its roots in the German works councils, the National Economic Council, and the concept of economic democracy. Whether codetermination will become one of the cornerstones of labor relations in industrial states and multinational companies remains to be seen, but the idea in various forms is gaining ground.

A comparison of Weimar socialist unions with labor in other countries elicits parallels or differences. There are strong parallels with other Continental socialist unions insofar as ideological cleav-ages with nonsocialist unions and an emphasis on pragmatic moder-ate reforms within the capitalist system are concerned, but the German model has served only as a limited prototype for the non-Western or Third World trade unions. Although there are a few parallels—the close ties to a political party (Empire and Weimar Germany) and the belief in socialism—the differences based on divergent cultural and historical factors between the nascent unions in Imperial Germany and those in the new non-Western nations of the twentieth century are much more significant. In the German in-stance, the state had been founded before the emergence of the modern labor movement and workers had to struggle for such basic political rights as the right to vote and to organize.

In the non-Western areas the development of the labor move-ment generally began during the colonial regimes and intensified during the period of political and economic nation-building when in a number of states party leaders established unions in order to use them as mobilizing agents for national independence.[5] An integral part of the nationalist movements, the unions became highly political in their twin struggle against colonialism and foreign corporations. After independence, their development was closely interwoven with the political fabric. In many countries, they had political influence through their close ties to the governing party and the new government. In other countries, their influence was small if they were put under state control. Then their primary task was to supervise and discipline the labor force and to discourage agitation and strikes as part of an economic development process. Thus, only exceptionally did they enjoy an independence from the government and the parties comparable to that of the United States and to a lesser extent the European unions.

Although the German socialist unions served as only a limited model for the non-Western unions, they did have a significant effect on other Western unions. Much can be gained by assessing the rise, fall, and rebirth of the German labor movement under a series of sharply contrasting political systems. Obviously, the movement will suffer or be extinguished in an unfavorable political climate (as in the Empire and Nazi eras), or suffer in an adverse economic climate (early and late Weimar), while it will prosper in a favorable political and economic climate (mid-Weimar, Federal Republic). Thus, for a labor movement the external conditions—the political, economic, and social milieu—rank among the crucial variables. To the average German worker, they spell deprivation or comfort.

APPENDIXES

Appendix A

List of Reich Chancellors

Chancellor	Terms of Office
Scheidemann (SPD)	February, 1919 - June, 1919
Bauer (SPD)	June, 1919 - March, 1920
Müller (SPD)	March, 1920 - June, 1920
Fehrenbach (Center)	June, 1920 - May, 1921
Wirth (Center)	May, 1921 - November, 1922
Cuno (Non-Party)	November, 1922 - August, 1923
Stresemann (People's Party)	August, 1923 - November, 1923
Marx (Center)	November, 1923 - January, 1925
Luther (Non-Party)	January, 1925 - May, 1926
Marx (Center)	May, 1926 - June, 1928
Müller (SPD)	June, 1928 - March, 1930
Brüning (Center)	March, 1930 - May, 1932
von Papen (Non-Party)	May, 1932 - December, 1932
von Schleicher (Non-Party)	December, 1932 - January, 1933
Hitler (NSDAP)	January, 1933

APPENDIX B

Reichstag Fraktionen

Union and Other Representation

TABLE 6
UNION REPRESENTATIVES IN THE REICHSTAG BY PARTIES, 1919-1924[*]

	1919	1920	May 1924	Dec. 1924
SPD				
Number of union representatives	58	33	26	30
Percent of Reichstag Fraktion	35.1	28.9	26.0	22.8
National People's Party				
Number of union representatives	4	5	10	8
Percent of Reichstag Fraktion	9.5	7.5	9.4	7.2
People's Party				
Number of union representatives	—	4	1	2
Percent of Reichstag Fraktion	—	6.4	2.3	3.9
Center & Bavarian People's Party				
Number of union representatives	18	15	18	12
Percent of Reichstag Fraktion	20.0	16.6	22.1	13.6
Democratic Party				
Number of union representatives	4	1	1	3
Percent of Reichstag Fraktion	5.3	2.2	3.6	9.4

[*] Source: Kamm, pp. 12-15.

TABLE 7
Occupations of SPD Deputies*

Occupations		1912	1919	1920	1924	1924	1928
Businessmen	Number	12	8	5	1	3	2
	Percentage	10.9	4.8	4.4	1.0	2.3	1.3
Government employees and teachers	Number	—	5	10	10	13	32
	Percentage	—	3.0	8.8	10.0	9.9	21.0
City officials	Number	1	1	5	3	2	—
	Percentage	.9	.6	4.4	3.0	1.5	—
Lawyers	Number	7	4	—	3	4	5
	Percentage	6.4	2.4	—	3.0	3.0	3.2
Private employees	Number	5	4	4	3	2	3
	Percentage	4.5	2.4	3.5	3.0	1.5	1.9
Party officials	Number	11	23	16	15	21	23
	Percentage	10.0	13.9	14.0	15.0	16.0	15.1
Union officials	Number	17	58	33	26	30	32
	Percentage	15.4	35.1	28.9	26.0	22.8	21.0
Doctors	Number	—	1	1	1	2	2
	Percentage	—	.6	.9	1.0	1.5	1.3
Editors and journalists	Number	44	39	23	34	39	39
	Percentage	40.0	23.6	20.2	34.0	29.7	25.6
Retired	Number	2	1	—	—	—	—
	Percentage	1.8	.6	—	—	—	—
Workers	Number	11	16	11	3	12	7
	Percentage	10.0	9.6	9.6	3.0	9.1	4.6
Others	Number	—	5	5	1	3	7
	Percentage	—	3.0	4.4	1.0	2.3	4.6
Total SPD deputies	Number	110	165	113	100	131	152
	Percentage a	100	100	100	100	100	100

*Sources: For 1912-1924 figures, Kamm, pp. 12-15; for 1928, RT, *Reichstagshandbuch 1928*, p. 474. Statistics for the periods after 1928 could not be calculated from available data. Percentage refers to proportion of entire SPD Fraktion.

   Rounded off.

a

Appendix C

List of Union Representatives in the SPD Reichstag Fraktion, 1928-1930*

1. *Union Representatives and their Offices*
   * Aufhäuser, Siegfried: President, AfA
   + Becker, Heinrich: District secretary, Mine Workers Union
   * Bender, Ferdinand: Member, Executive Committee, Transportation Workers Union
   + Bergmann, Paul: Regional leader, Food and Beverage Workers Union
   + Böckler, Hans: Regional secretary, ADGB
   * Brandes, Alwin: Member, Executive Committee, Metal Workers Union
   * Brey, August: President, Factory Workers Union
   * Girbig, Emil: President, Glass Workers Union
   * Grassmann, Peter: Vice-President, ADGB
   * Husemann, Friedrich: President, Mine Workers Union
   + Jäcker, Carl: Staff member, Agricultural Workers Union
   * Janschek, Alfred: Member, Executive Committee, Mine Workers Union
   + Kotzke, Franz: District leader, Textile Workers Union
   * Metz, Franz: Member, Executive Committee, Metal Workers Union
   * Müller, Hermann: Vice-President, ADGB
   + Nowack, Friedrich: Staff member, Factory Workers Union
   + Richter, Max: District secretary, ADGB
   * Scheffel, Franz: President, Railroad Workers Union

[188]

\#   Schlicke, Alexander: Former president, Metal Workers Union
\+   Schlüter, Wilhelm: District leader, Tobacco Workers Union
*   Schmidt, Georg: President, Agricultural Workers Union
\#   Schmidt, Robert: Member, Executive Committee, General Commission
*   Schumann, Oswald: President, Transportation Workers Union
*   Seppel, Max: Member, Executive Committee, Post and Telegraph Workers Union
*   Simon, Josef: President, Shoe Makers Workers Union
\+   Spiegel, Karl: District leader, Metal Workers Union
*   Tarnow, Fritz: President, Wood Workers Union
\#   Wissell, Rudolf: Former member, Executive Committee, ADGB

2. *Total number, by category:*
   \+ Minor union officials. 9
   * National union officials. 16
   \# Former national union officials. 3
   Total. 28
   The total represents 18.4 percent of the 152 members Fraktion.

3. *Other SPD representatives closely allied to the unions*
   Ansorge, Marie: Active in party and union movements
   Bock, Wilhelm: Founder, Shoemakers Union
   Bohm-Schuch, Clara: Active in party and union movements
   Graf, Georg: Head, Metal Workers Union School of Economics
   Hermann, Karl: Former district leader, Construction Workers Union
   Krätzig, Hermann: Former editor, Textile Workers Union journal
   Krüger, Richard: Former business agent, Metal Workers Union
   Limbertz, Heinrich: Editor, Mine workers union journal
   Lipinski, Richard: Former staff member, AfA
   Mache, Karl: Former district leader, Bakers and Confectioners Union. After 1919, party secretary
   Sauerbrey, Paul: Former district secretary
   Schreck, Carl: Active in party and union movements
   Sender, Toni: Trade union editor
   Thabor, Johannes: Former business agent, Construction Workers Union

*Sources: Horkenbach; RT, *Reichstagshandbuch* 1928, pp. 273 ff.

APPENDIX D

Position of Unionists
on the 1928 SPD Nomination Lists*

Election District	Number SPD Nominees Elected	Position of Unionists on List [a] Elected or not Elected	
1 Ostpreussen	4 out of 10	No. 2	Jäcker, yes
2 Berlin	6 out of 13	4	Aufhäuser, yes
		7	Breunig, no
3 Potsdam II	5 out of 12	10	Schneider, no
		11	Lehmann, no
4 Potsdam I	6 out of 10	1	Wissell, yes
		4	Müller, yes
5 Frankfurt/Oder	4 out of 10	2	Schumann, yes
		3	Kotzke, yes
		5	Reissner, no
		10	Sieloff, no
6 Pommern	4 out of 8	3	Schmidt, G., yes
7 Breslau	6 out of 14	4	Mache, yes
		5	Ansorge, yes
		6	Seppel, yes
		10	Bretthorst, no
8 Liegnitz	4 out of 8	4	Girbig, yes
9 Oppeln	1 out of 4	None	
10 Magdeburg	6 out of 13	2	Bender, yes
11 Merseburg	3 out of 6	None	
12 Thüringen	6 out of 12	8	Niewiera, no
13 Schleswig-Holstein	4 out of 8	3	Richter, yes
		5	Löhrke, no
14 Weser-Ems	3 out of 6	None	

Election District	Number SPD Nominees Elected	Position of Unionists on List [a] Elected or not Elected	
15 Osthannover	3 out of 8	2	Nowack, yes
16 Südhannover-Braunschweig	8 out of 15	1	Brey, yes
17 Westfalen Nord	4 out of 8	2	Schreck, yes
		3	Janschek, yes
		4	Schlüter, yes
18 Westfalen Süd	6 out of 13	1	Schmidt, R., yes
		2	Husemann, yes
		5	Brandes, yes
		6	Spiegel, yes
		7	Ottinghaus, no
		9	Bäcker, no
19 Hessen-Nassau	6 out of 12	No. 2	Metz, yes
		3	Becker, yes
		7	Hüttmann, no
		8	Hofacker, no
20 Köln-Aachen	3 out of 6	3	Böckler, yes
21 Koblenz-Prien	1 out of 3	2	Gruber, no
		3	Brand, no
22 Düsseldorf Ost	3 out of 6	None	
23 Düsseldorf West	2 out of 7	2	Thabor, yes
		3	Schatz, no
		6	Knops, no
24 Oberbayern-Schwaben	4 out of 8	None	
25 Niederbayern	1 out of 3	None	
26 Franken	5 out of 10	3	Simon, yes
		10	Schäfer, no
27 Pfalz	2 out of 6	6	Ludwig, no
28 Dresden-Bautzen	7 out of 16	2	Sender, yes
		4	Krätzig, yes
29 Leipzig	4 out of 8	1	Lipinski, yes
		4	Graf, yes
		7	Müller, G., no
30 Chemnitz-Zwickau	5 out of 10	6	Graupe, no
31 Württemberg	4 out of 8	4	Schlicke, yes
32 Baden	3 out of 8	None	
33 Hessen-Darmstadt	3 out of 6	6	Thomas, no
34 Hamburg	4 out of 8	1	Grassmann, yes
		4	Bergmann, yes
35 Mecklenburg	3 out of 6	None	
National Election List	9 out of 14	8	Scheffel, yes
		9	Tarnow, yes

*Source: RT, *Reichstagshandbuch 1928.*
[a] The number in front of the name signifies the position on the list.
"Yes" indicates election; "no" indicates failure to get elected.

APPENDIX D

TABLE 8

Membership in Trade Union Federations, 1931*

Federation	Manual Workers	Per cent	Salaried Employees	Per cent	Civil Servants	Per cent	Total	Per cent
Socialist	4,134,902	74.3	465,591	26.8	171,800	13.2	4,772,293	55.4
Christian	698,472a	12.6	593,800	34.1	10,336	0.8	1,292,272	15.0
Liberal	181,100	3.2	392,850	22.6			584,286	6.8
Syndicalist (1929)	20,000	0.4					20,000	0.2
Communist	347,774b	6.2					347,774	4.1
Nonpolitical	185,117	3.3	286,530	16.5	1,123,382	86.0	1,595,029	18.5
Total	5,567,365	100.0	1,738,771	100.0	1,305,518	100.0	8,611,654	100.0

*Sources: *Statistisches Jahrbuch, 1932*, pp. 555-561; syndicalist figure from *Statistisches Jahrbuch, 1929*, p. 498; communist figure, see b below. This table is adapted from Willey, *Trade Unions*, p. 8.

a Includes the General Association of German Transport and State Employees. In 1926, the Christian civil servant federation amalgamated with the DBB.

b Includes in addition to the *Jahrbuch, 1932* figure an estimated 312,000 RGO members. See Flechtheim, p. 172.

NOTES

PREFACE

1. There are two unpublished German studies of the socialist unions in the Weimar era, but they deal with only certain aspects of the subject matter: Ursula Hüllbüsch, "Gewerkschaften und Staat: Ein Beitrag zur Geschichte der Gewerkschaften zu Anfang und zu Ende der Weimarer Republik" (Unpublished Ph.D. dissertation, University of Heidelberg, 1961); and Rolf Thieringer, "Das Verhältnis der Gewerkschaften zu Staat und Parteien in der Weimarer Republik" (Unpublished Ph.D. dissertation, University of Tübingen, 1954). Many other studies cover the entire period from the birth of the unions to the present; hence devoting little space to the Weimar era.

2. In 1930, they had 5.3 million members, or 68 percent of all union members; the Christian unions had about 1,360,000, or 18 percent; and the Hirsch-Duncker unions 600,000, or 8 percent. Minor unions made up the remaining 6 percent (Statistisches Reichsamt, *Statistiches Jahrbuch für das Deutsche Reich, 1931* [Berlin: Hobbing, 1931], p. 557 [hereafter referred to as *Statistisches Jahrbuch,* year]).

According to other sources, in late 1930-early 1931, 22.3 million persons were employed in Germany, of whom about 9 million or 38 percent were organized. Among the 16 million manual workers, about 33 percent were organized, of whom 28 percent were in the ADGB, 4.5 percent in the Christian unions, and 0.5 percent in the Hirsch-Duncker unions. Among salaried employees, about 1.7 million out of 4 million, or 42 percent, were organized. Of the 1.7 million, about 592,000 were in Christian unions, 462,000 in the AfA, and 335,000 in the liberal Hirsch-Duncker unions. The remainder were scattered in smaller unions. Among civil servants, 90 to 95 percent of the 1.4 million were organized, of whom 1,030,000 were in the unaffiliated German Federation of Civil Servants (Deutscher Beamtenbund, DBB), 170,000 in the ADB, and 100,000 in the Reich League for Higher Civil Servants

(Maurycy Bergmann, Franz Schleiter, and Helmut Wickel, *Handbuch der Arbeit: Die deutsche Arbeiterklasse in Wirtschaft und Gesellschaft*, Abteilung III, *Die Koalitionen* [Jena: Karl Zwing, 1931], pp. 24, 29, 31; F. David, *Der Bankrott des Reformismus* [Berlin: Internationaler Arbeiterverlag, 1932; reprint, Erlangen: Politladen Reprint No. 4, 1971], pp. 254-255). See Table 8 for a 1931 tabulation, varying somewhat because of the use of different sources and time period.

3. The three federations collectively will be referred to hereafter as socialist or free unions. The Christian and Hirsch-Duncker unions will be referred to by name or by "other trade union federations."

4. For an interesting debunking of the "docile German" theory, see Charles Tilly, Louise Tilly, Richard Tilly, *The Rebellious Century, 1830-1930* (Cambridge: Harvard University Press, 1975), pp. 191-238.

CHAPTER I

1. Paul Göhre, "Three Months in a Workshop," *Industrialization and Industrial Labor in Nineteenth-Century Europe*, ed. James J. Sheehan (New York: Wiley, 1973), pp. 85-86.

2. For details see Harvey Mitchell, "Labor and the Origins of Social Democracy in Britain, France, and Germany, 1890-1914," in Harvey Mitchell and Peter N. Stearns, *Workers and Protest: The European Labor Movement, the Working Classes and the Origins of Social Democracy, 1890-1914* (Itasca, Ill.: F.E. Peacock Publishers, 1971), pp. 19-24.

3. Peter N. Stearns, "The European Labor Movement and the Working Classes, 1890-1914," in Mitchell and Stearns, p. 157; Hans Limmer, *Die deutsche Gewerkschaftsbewegung* (Munich: Olzog, 1966), pp. 8-14.

4. The organization was known as the German General Fraternity of Labor (Allgemeine deutsche Arbeiter Verbrüderung). For a survey of the labor movement (socialist and union) during the Imperial era, see Helga Grebing, *The History of the German Labour Movement* (London: Oswald Wolff, 1969), pp. 15-104; Hedwig Wachenheim, *Die deutsche Arbeiterbewegung, 1844 bis 1914* (Cologne and Opladen: Westdeutscher Verlag, 1967).

5. Vernon Lidtke, *The Outlawed Party: Social Democracy in Germany, 1878-1890* (Princeton: Princeton University Press, 1966), p. 80; Alfred Forster, *Die Gewerkschaftspolitik der deutschen Sozialdemokratie während des Sozialistengesetzes* (Berlin: Tribüne, 1971).

6. Paul Umbreit, *25 Jahre deutscher Gewerkschaftsbewegung, 1890-1915* (Berlin: Verlag der General Kommission, 1915) pp. 9-13.

7. Guenther Roth, *The Social Democrats in Imperial Germany: A Study in Working-Class Isolation and National Integration* (Totowa, N.J., The Bedminster Press, 1963), p. 268. See also John A. Moses: "Carl Legiens Interpretation des demokratischen Sozialismus: Ein Beitrag zur Sozialistischen Ideengeschichte" (Unpublished Ph.D. dissertation, University of Erlangen-Nuremberg, 1965).

8. Heinz Josef Varain, *Freie Gewerkschaften, Sozialdemokratie und Staat* (Duesseldorf: Droste, 1956), pp. 8, 35-36. The 1890 membership figures vary, partly because of a swift growth that year. Umbreit (p. 13) cites 228,000 members, while Wolfgang Hirsch-Weber refers to 300,000 members. (*Gewerkschaften in der Politik* [Cologne and Opladen: Westdeutscher Verlag, 1959], p. 5).

9. August Bebel, *Gewerkschaftsbewegung und Politische Parteien* (Stuttgart: Dietz, 1900), pp. 19-24. See also Gerhard A. Ritter, *Die Arbeiterbewegung im Wilhelminischen Reich: Die Sozialdemokratische Partei und die freien Gewerkschaften 1890-1900* (Berlin-Dahlem: Colloquium, 1959), pp. 107-175 and Manfred Scharrer, *Arbeiterbewegung im Obrigkeitsstaat— SPD und Gewerkschaft nach dem Sozialistengesetz* (Berlin: Rotbuch, 1976).

10. On the May Day issue, they agreed that funds for locked-out workers would be raised regionally and pro-rated among party and union members, and on the general strike issue they agreed that the party would assume leadership if a strike proved necessary, and the unions would pledge their neutrality. For details, see Otto Heilborn, *Die "freien" Gewerkschaften seit 1890* (Jena: Fischer, 1907), pp. 116-120; Sophie Klärmann, *Die Freien Gewerkschaften in Gesetzgebung und Politik* (Munich: Duncker and Humblot, 1912), pp. 49-74; Carl E. Schorske, *German Social Democracy, 1905-1917* (New York: Russell and Russell, 1955), pp. 91-97; Julius Braunthal, *History of the International, 1864-1914* (London: Nelson, 1966), pp. 285-304; Rosa Luxemburg, *Massenstreik, Partei und Gewerkschaften* (Leipzig: Vulkan, 1919; reprint of 1906 ed.).

11. Siegfried Nestriepke, *Die Gewerkschaftsbewegung* (2d ed.; Stuttgart: Ernest Heinrich Moritz, 1922), I, 431. In 1893, 5 out of 43 members (or 11.6 percent) in the SPD Fraktion were labor leaders; in 1912, the proportion had risen to 36 out of 110 (or 32.7 percent). Of the 36, 5 were members of the General Commission and 9 were chairmen of affiliated unions (Varain, pp. 44-45).

12. By 1906, the General Commission claimed 1,690,000 and the SPD 384,000 members. But if one compares union membership with the vote for the SPD in national elections, the gap narrowed as the SPD rapidly increased its vote. By 1912, the unions had 2,530,000 members and the SPD received 4,250,000 votes. Heinz Langerhans, "Partei und Gewerkschaften" (Unpublished Ph.D. dissertation, University of Frankfort, 1957), pp. 48-49. Cf. also August Mai, *Partei und Gewerkschaft in vergleichender Statistik* (Dresden: von Kaden, 1912).

13. Richard Seidel, *The Trade Union Movement of Germany* (International Trade Union Library, Nos. 7-8; Amsterdam: International Federation of Trade Unions, 1928), pp. 55-56; Schorske, pp. 49-53.

14. Schorske, p. 52.

15. According to one 1906 survey in Berlin, 80 percent of SPD workers were simultaneously trade union members (primarily in the skilled trades), while only one in six trade union members had joined the SPD (Langerhans, p. 28). Cf. Karl Kautsky, "Partei und Gewerkschaft," *Die Neue Zeit*, XXIV, Part II (1905-1906), pp. 749-754.

16. Grebing, p. 66, quoting a statement which appeared in a 1912 survey by Lewenstein, "Die Arbeiterfrage."

17. John P. Windmuller, *Labor Internationals: A Survey of Contemporary International Trade Union Organizations* (Bulletin No. 61, New York State School of Industrial and Labor Relations; Ithaca: Cornell University, 1969), p. 6.

18. Theodor Leipart, *Carl Legien: Ein Gedenkbuch* (Berlin: Verlagsgesellschaft des ADGB, 1929), pp. 38-39; Walther Schevenels, *Quarante cinq années: Fédération syndicale internationale, 1901-1945* (Brussels: Editions de l'Institut E. Vandervelde, 1964), pp. 5-30; Hans Gottfurcht, *Die Internationale Gewerkschaftsbewegung von den Anfängen bis zur Gegenwart* (Cologne: Bund, 1966), pp. 17-19.

19. The first congress of Chirstian trade unions (1899) set up an executive committee and in 1902 a permanent secretariat (Philip Taft, "Germany," *Comparative Labor Movements*, ed. by Walter Galenson [New York: Prentice-Hall, 1952], pp. 258-259.)

20. Manfred Gessner, "Wehrfrage und freie Gewerkschaftsbewegung in den Jahren 1918 bis 1923 in Deutschland" (Unpublished Ph.D. dissertation, Free University, Berlin, 1962), p. 39, citing Legien's address to the 1919 SPD Weimar Convention. See also Paul Umbreit, *Die deutschen Gewerkschaften im Weltkrieg* (Berlin: Verlag für Sozialwissenschaft, 1917).

21. It is not clear whether the meetings took place on August 1 and 2, or only on August 2 (*Correspondenzblatt*, August 8, 1914, p. 486 [hereafter referred to as *CB*]. Cf. also Langerhans, p. 52; General Commission, "Die Gewerkschaften und die Politik des 4. August 1914" [Flyer]).

22. At the Fraktion meeting of August 3, fourteen members voted against war credits. For details, see Varain, p. 72; John L. Snell, "Socialist Unions and Socialist Patriotism in Germany, 1914-1918," *American Historical Review, LIX (Oct. 1953), pp. 66-68; Gerald D. Feldman, Army, Industry and Labor in Germany, 1914-1918* (Princeton: Princeton University Press, 1966), p. 29. Susanne Miller states that the union decision played no role in the initial party discussions (*Burgfrieden und Klassenkampf: Die deutsche Sozialdemokratie im ersten Weltkrieg* [Duesseldorf: Droste, 1974], pp. 48-51).

23. *CB*, Feb. 6, 1915, p. 62. The new patriotism among the leaders was evident in a volume edited by Friedrich Timme and Legien, *Die Arbeiterschaft im neuen Deutschland* (Leipzig: Hirzel, 1915).

24. Paul Merker, *Sozialdemokratie und Gewerkschaften, 1890-1920* (Berlin: Dietz, 1949), pp. 176-177.

25. This manifesto was published in the *Leipziger Volks-Zeitung;* quoted in Selig Perlman, *A Theory of the Labor Movement* (New York: A.M. Kelley, 1949), p. 109. Among the SPD leaders were Bernstein and Kautsky, and among the union leaders was Robert Dissmann, Metal Workers Union (see Dissmann, *Die Kriegspolitik der Gewerkschaften* [Frankfort/Main: Oster and Munch, n.d.]).

26. Varain, pp. 79-81; Carl Legien, *Warum müssen die Gewerkschaftsfunktionäre sich mehr am inneren Parteileben beteiligen? Ein Vortrag*

(Berlin: Verlag der Gewerkschaftskommission Berlins und Umgegend, 1915); General Commission, "Beschlüsse der Konferenzen von Vertretern der Zentralverbandsvorständen" (1919), pp. 47-48; cf. also Johannes Timm, "Sozialdemokratie und Gewerkschaften," *Süddeutsche Monatshefte*, Nov. 1917, pp. 125-207.

27. Perlman, p. 109.

28. For instance, at the 1919 Congress of the Textile Workers Union, the left wing's resolution against the war won by 203,000 against 55,000 votes (Emil Lederer, "Die Gewerkschaftsbewegung 1918/19 und die Entfaltung der wirtschaftlichen Ideologien in der Arbeiterklasse," *Archiv für Sozialwissenschaft und Sozialpolitik*, XLVII [1920], pp. 263-264; Hellmut Kolbe, *Die beginnende Opposition in den deutschen Gewerkschaften im Jahre 1917* [Berlin: Tribüne, 1957]).

29. Arthur Rosenberg, *Imperial Germany: The Birth of the German Republic, 1871-1918* (Reprint of 1931 ed.; New York: Oxford University Press, 1970), pp. 210, 212; Werner Raase, *Zur Geschichte der deutschen Gewerkschaftsbewegung 1914-1917 und 1917-1919* (Berlin: Tribüne, n.d. [1968]), pp. 88-89.

30. Feldman, *Army, Industry and Labor*, p. 349; "Eine politische Streikbewegung," *CB*, Feb. 2, 1918, pp. 41-42. In the January 1918 strike the dissident leaders received reluctant support from the SPD, but only because numerous striking workers came from its own ranks.

31. Paul Lange, *Die Politik der Gewerkschaftsführer von 1914 bis 1919* (Berlin: Kommissions-Verlag Adolf Hoffmann, 1919), p. 14.

32. General Commission, "Beschlüsse der Konferenzen," p. 130; Merker, pp. 207-210.

Chapter II

1. *CB*, Nov. 2, 1918, pp. 407-409. At one meeting (Oct. 30), they requested General Hindenburg to remain in command in order to prevent chaos among the returning armies (Jürgen Kuczynski, *Die Geschichte der Lage der Arbeiter in Deutschland von 1917/18 bis 1932/33* [Berlin: Akademie, 1966], p. 117).

2. A. Joseph Berlau, *The German Social Democratic Party, 1914-1921* (New York: Columbia University Press, 1949), pp. 207-208. See also Prinz Max von Baden, *Erinnerungen und Dokumente* (Berlin: Deutsche Verlags-Anstalt, 1927), pp. 591-592; Dorothea Groener-Geyer, *General Groener: Soldat und Staatsmann* (Frankfort/Main: Societäts-Verlag, 1955).

3. H. G. Daniels, *The Rise of the German Republic* (London: Nisbet, 1927), p. 45.

4. Richard Seidel, *Die Gewerkschaften in der Revolution* (Berlin: Verlagsgenossenschaft "Freiheit," 1920); Karl Fugger, *Die deutschen Gewerkschafter und die November-Revolution* (Berlin: Die Freie Gewerkschaft Verlagsgesellschaft, 1948).

5. The eight-hour day provision was appended in a secret protocol. For general details, see Hans von Raumer, "Unternehmer und Gewerkschaften in der Weimarer Zeit," *Deutsche Rundschau*, Vol. LXXX, No. 5 (May, 1954), pp. 428-433; Feldman, "Die Freien Gewerkschaften und die Zentralarbeitsgemeinschaft 1918-1924," *Vom Sozialistengesetz zur Mitbestimmung: Zum 100. Geburtstag von Hans Böckler*, ed. Heinz Oskar Vetter (Cologne: Bund, 1975), pp. 229-259; "German Business between War and Revolution: The Origins of the Stinnes-Legien Agreement," *Entstehung und Wandel der modernen Gesellschaft: Festschrift für Hans Rosenberg zum 65. Geburtstag*, ed. Gerhard A. Ritter (Berlin: Walter de Gruyter, 1970), pp. 312-341; Heinrich Kaun, *Die Geschichte der Zentralarbeitsgemeinschaft der industriellen und gewerblichen Arbeitgeber und Arbeitnehmer Deutschlands* (Jena: Neuenhahn, 1938). Symbolic of the new management-union relationship, Stinnes named one of his ships "Carl Legien," several years after Legien's death.

6. Gewerkschaft der Eisenbahner Deutschlands, *Legien* (Frankfort/Main: GdED, 1950), p. 57.

7. The spirit of the Council did not die. In 1926, for instance, ADGB and the National Association of German Industry met secretly on a number of occasions to discuss common problems (Bundesarchiv, File R 43 I/2024, secret memorandum from a ministry [identification lacking] to Chancellor, April 22, 1926).

8. *CB*, Nov. 23, 1918, p. 436; General Commission (GGD), *Beschlüsse*, pp. 108-109; GGD, *Gewerkschaften und Arbeiterräte* (Berlin: GGD, 1919). For general works, see Dieter Schneider and Rudolf Kuda, *Arbeiterräte in der Novemberrevolution* (Frankfort/Main: Suhrkamp, 1968); Peter von Oertzen, *Betriebsräte in der Novemberrevolution* (Duesseldorf: Droste, 1963); Walter Tormin, *Zwischen Rätediktatur und sozialer Demokratie* (Duesseldorf: Droste, 1954); Eberhard Kolb, *Die Arbeiterräte in der deutschen Innenpolitik, 1918-1919* (Duesseldorf: Droste, 1962). For one local study, see Richard A. Comfort, *Revolutionary Hamburg: Labor Politics in the Early Weimar Republic* (Stanford: Stanford University Press, 1966), pp. 30-57.

9. Henryk Skrzypczak, "From Carl Legien to Theodor Leipart, from Theodor Leipart to Robert Ley: Notes on some strategic and tactical problems of the German free trade union movement during the Weimar Republic," *Internationale Wissenschaftliche Korrespondenz zur Geschichte der Deutschen Arbeiterbewegung*, XIII (Aug. 1971), p. 30.

10. A wing in the SPD, led by Max Cohen, advocated the formation of councils of labor to exercise political functions alongside parliamentary government, but could not receive General Commission support (*CB*, April 26, 1919, pp. 169-172).

11. von Oertzen, pp. 276-283; Gessner, p. 49.

12. Comfort, pp. 92-95.

13. Labor leaders claimed that they hardly influenced SPD politics during the war (*CB*, July 26, 1919, p. 338). For details of USPD strength in the free unions, see p. 211 below.

14. For details of the ADGB, see chapter IV.

15. For text of statute, see ADGB, *Satzungen und Richtlinien des ADGB* (Berlin: Verlagsgesellschaft des ADGB, 1925); for summary, Umbreit, "Allgemeiner Deutscher Gewerkschaftsbund (ADGB.)," *Internationales Handwörterbuch des Gewerkschaftswesens*, ed. Ludwig Heyde, Vol. I (1931), pp. 23-29. See also Arthur Dissinger, *Das freigewerkschaftliche Organisationsproblem: Eine soziologische Studie* (Jena: Gustav Fischer, 1929); Max Ziervogel, "Die Gestaltung der Organisationsform der freien Gewerkschaften" (Unpublished Ph.D. dissertation, University of Giessen, 1924).

16. ADGB, *Gewerkschaften, Friedensvertrag, Reparationen* (Berlin: ADGB, 1932), p. 6.

17. *Ibid.*, pp. 8; 12; GdEd, *Carl Legien*, pp. 48-49.

18. Harold J. Gordon, Jr., *The Reichswehr and the German Republic, 1919-1926* (Princeton: Princeton University Press, 1957), p. 114. The passive stance of the Reichswehr against a threat to the Republic from the Right was due to the conservatism of its officers and the failure of the SPD and unions to encourage workers to join it (*ibid.*, pp. 90-143; Francis L. Carsten, *Reichswehr und Politik, 1918-1933* [Cologne, Berlin: Kiepenheuer and Witsch, 1964], pp. 89-99).

19. According to Johannes Erger, the Chancellor's Office press chief apparently drafted the call for a strike, and appended the names of Ebert and the SPD ministers. But they never signed it, perhaps because they feared the strike would radicalize the workers. The public viewed the call, however, as an official government declaration (Johannes Erger, *Der Kapp-Lüttwitz Putsch* [Duesseldorf: Droste, 1967] pp. 193-194). See also Paul Loebe, *Erinnerungen eines Reichstagspräsidenten* (Berlin: Arani, 1949), p. 67; August-Günter Prinz, "Der Einsatz gewerkschaftlicher Macht in Konkretpolitischen Situationen nach 1918" (Unpublished Ph.D. dissertation, University of Cologne, 1957), pp. 31-69; Erwin Könnemann and Hans-Joachim Krusch, *Aktionseinheit contra Kapp-Putsch* (Berlin: Dietz, 1972); Hans H. Biegert, "Gewerkschaftspolitik in der Phase des Kapp-Luttwitz-Putsches," *Industrielles System und politische Entwicklung in der Weimarer Republik*, ed. Hans Mommsen, *et. al.* (Duesseldorf: Droste, 1974), pp. 190-205; Karl Schabrod, *Generalstreik rettet Weimarer Republik* (Duesseldorf: Carolus, 1960).

20. Wilfred H. Crook, *The General Strike* (Chapel Hill: University of North Carolina Press, 1931), p. 496.

21. *Korrespondenzblatt*, March 27, 1920, pp. 149-150 (hereafter referred to as *KB*); Erger, p. 196. In a Reichstag speech, Legien claimed that the ADGB Executive had made the decision to strike without knowing about the SPD call (Reichstag, *Verhandlungen des Reichstags*, Vol. 332, March 29, 1920, p. 4954).

22. *KB*, March 27, 1920, p. 151.

23. Franz Josef Furtwängler, *Die Gewerkschaften* (Hamburg: Rowohlt, 1956), p. 324. General Ludendorff, sympathetic at first to Kapp, reportedly asked Leipart whether the unions would be willing to join a government formed by the military and the unions. At the same time, the Christian labor

leader Adam Stegerwald asked Leipart whether he would favor the formation of a labor government. Leipart replied in the negative to both proposals
as being antidemocratic and not resting on any popular mandate
(Wachenheim, p. 622).

24. For full text, see Merker, p. 265.

25. Point 1: the unions no longer insisted in having a decisive influence on
the formation of governments, after having been told by government
spokesmen that such a demand was extraconstitutional. Point 2: the provision for the punishment of disloyal troops was eliminated. Point 7: the unions
accepted instead a proposal calling for the immediate socialization of
industries ripe for it, based on the recommendations of the Commission on
Socialization. Point 9: they accepted the proposal calling for the formation of
republican military units to include workers and other "trustworthy" elements. The government accepted points 4 and 6, and a modified point 8.
(For a verbatim account of the discussions see Erwin Konnemann, Brigitte
Berthold, and Gerhard Schulze [eds.], *Arbeiterklasse siegt über Kapp und
Lüttwitz* [Glashütten: Auvermann, 1971], I, 179-200. See also Merker, pp.
265-267; *London Times, Vorwarts*, March 22, 1920; Leipart, *Carl Legien*, p.
117).

26. *KB*, March 27, 1920, p. 154.

27. Rosenberg, *A History of the German Republic* (London: Methuen,
1936), p. 139; Fischer, p. 126.

28. *Rote Fahne*, March 17, 1920, cited by Flechtheim, p. 64; Rosenberg, *A
History of the German Republic*, p. 334.

29. Leipart, *Carl Legien*, pp. 118-119, 165, 167; Thieringer, p. 113; Varain,
pp. 180-181. It may be argued that when union leader Bauer was Chancellor,
the unions governed the country, but it was the SPD which nominated him
and upon which he relied in his government program.

30. The agreement had an effect in Prussia. The call by unions and the
SPD Reichstag Fraktion for a shake-up in the Prussian cabinet led to the
resignation of the cabinet. Otto Braun (SPD) formed a new one.

31. In the aftermath of the Putsch, only 174 officers were purged, while
the rest who participated escaped punishment. The Free Corps was not
dissolved, and the Reichswehr remained a state within a state (Wachenheim,
p. 622).

32. The agreement stipulated that workers were to surrender all weap-
ons within ten days, and return to their jobs, and that local defense corps and
a security committee composed of workers and party representatives were
to be formed in each district. On the relations of Reich Commissioner Carl
Severing, appointed as Ruhr supervisor, to the Reichswehr and labor, see
Friedrich Ebert archive (Bonn), Severing Nachlass, file 8, no. 6, 1920. See also
ADGB Board, 5th session, March 27, 1920; Erhard Lucas, *Märzrevolution im
Ruhrgebiet* (Frankfort/Main: März, 1970); Walter Neumann, *Die
Gewerkschaften im Ruhrgebiet* (Cologne: Bund, 1951).

33. ADGB Board, 1st session, June 29, 1922, p. 9.

34. Many unionists were rankled by conservative judges who meted out
harsh sentences against leftists and mild ones against rightists.

35. ADGB Board, 1st session, June 29, 1922, pp. 4; *Ist eine Einheitsfront mit den Kommunisten möglich?* (Berlin: ADGB, 1922), pp. 12-20.

36. ADGB Board, 1st session, June 29, 1922, pp. 5-9.

37. One law created a Reich criminal police to keep tab on antidemocratic elements; a second created a federal court, to be manned by judges committed to democratic principles; a third facilitated taking action against civil servants engaged in reactionary activities; and a fourth provided for amnesty for workers and salaried employees condemned to long sentences by reactionary judges (flyer, signed by ADGB, AfA, SPD, USPD, quoted in *Ist eine Einheitsfront mit den Kommunisten möglich?* pp. 3-6, 25-26).

38. *Ibid.*, pp. 24, 27.

39. Hans Spethmann, *Der Ruhrkampf, 1923-1925* (Berlin: Hobbing, 1933), p. 41; Paul Wentzcke, *Ruhrkampf* (Berlin: Hobbing, 1930), I, 176.

40. *KB*, Jan. 20, 1923, p. 25; Lothar Erdmann, *Die Gewerkschaften im Ruhrkampf* (Berlin: Verlagsgesellschaft des ADGB, 1924), p. 64.

41. ADGB, *Gewerkschaften, Friedensvertrag, Reparationen* (Berlin: ADGB, 1932), p. 14.

42. Friedrich Ebert archive, Severing Nachlass, file 19, no. 126, letter, IFTU to Dr. P. Nathan, Berlin, Feb. 9, 1923; Severing, *Mein Lebensweg* (Cologne: Greven, 1950), I, 374.

43. *KB*, Feb. 3, 1923, p. 53. The Second International, founded in 1889 and reconstituted after World War I, succeeded the defunct First International created under the influence of Marx and Engels. The International Workers Union (headquarters in Vienna), founded in 1921, was composed of left-wing socialist parties and merged in 1923 with the Second International (under the new name "Labor and Socialist International").

44. ADGB Board, 4th session, Jan. 24, 1923, p. 12; *KB*, Feb. 24, 1923, pp. 83-86. The IFTU, upon pressure of the German unions, formed a commission to study the economic conditions in the Ruhr (ADGB, *Bericht des Bundesvorstandes, 1919-1922* p. 110).

45. *KB*, April 28, 1923, p. 196. Leipart letter to British TUC, cited by *KB*, September 8, 1923, pp. 401-403. In May and June, the German government sought a diplomatic accord with the Allies, but the French and Belgian governments rejected any negotiations until passive resistance would end.

46. Gustav Stresemann, *Vermächtnis* (Berlin: Ullstein, 1932), I, 78.

47. Ossip K. Flechtheim, *Die Kommunistische Partei Deutschlands in der Weimarer Republik* (Offenbach: Bollwerk, 1948), p. 179.

48. Werner T. Angress, *Stillborn Revolution: The Communist Bid for Power in Germany, 1921-1923* (Princeton; Princeton University Press, 1963), pp. 442, 447.

49. ADGB Board, 2nd session, Feb. 8, 1926, pp. 3-7; SPD, *Jahrbuch 1926*, pp. 6-7, 15; *G-Z*, June 4, 1927, pp. 309-311; ADGB, *Kongress 1928*, p. 79.

50. For details, see Chapter V.

Chapter III

1. The cabinet included three SPD ministers: Hilferding, Minister of Finance (until Dec. 1929); Severing, Minister of Interior; Wissell, Minister of Labor. Schmidt became Minister of Economic Affairs in December, 1929.

2. ADGB, *Protokoll der Verhandlungen des Kongresses der Gewerkschaften Deutschlands*, 1928, p. 80 (hereafter referred to as ADGB, Kongress, year).

3. Friedrich Stampfer, *Die Vierzehn Jahre der ersten deutschen Republik* (Karlsbad: Verlagsanstalt "Graphia," 1936), pp. 561-562.

4. *Ibid.*, p. 561. According to Siegfried Aufhäuser (AfA President), Stampfer's account is too dramatic. Not only ADGB leader Müller, but other union deputies raised the same issue. Personal interview.

5. Statement by Aufhäuser, personal interview. See also ADGB, *Kongress 1931*, p. 132; Helga Timm, *Die deutsche Sozialpolitik und der Bruch der Grossen Koalition im März 1930* (Duesseldorf: Droste, 1952), pp. 182-187.

6. *Vorwärts*, March 29, 1930.

7. Unidentified journal, quoted in *G-Z*, April 12, 1930, pp. 236-237.

8. Stampfer, pp. 515-517.

9. Rudolf Hilferding, "Der Austritt aus der Regierung," *Die Gesellschaft* (May, 1930), pp. 385-392.

10. According to Otto Meissner, State Secretary in the Office of the Reich President, the SPD decided not to participate in the new government, partly because of persisting union dissatisfaction with former Chancellor Müller's economic policies (Meissner, *Staatssekretär unter Ebert-Hindenburg-Hitler* [Hamburg: Hoffmann and Campe, 1950], p. 187). No substantiation could be found in any other source.

11. See Gustav Stolper, *German Economy, 1870-1940* (New York: Reynal and Hitchcock, 1940), pp. 193-197; Fritz Sternberg, *Der Niedergang des deutschen Kapitalismus* (Berlin: Rowohlt, 1932), pp. 301-331.

12. Sturmthal, *The Tragedy of European Labor, 1918-1939* (New York: Columbia University Press, 1943), pp. 84 ff.

13. ADGB, *Jahrbuch 1930*, pp. 114-115.

14. *Ibid.*, p. 122. On June 15, Brüning claims to have met separately with all trade union federations, but Leipart rejected any accord (*Memoiren 1918 bis 1934* [Stuttgart: Deutsche Verlagsanstalt, 1970], p. 287).

15. *G-Z*, June 13, 1931, pp. 369-371; July 18, 1931, pp. 450-452; August 15, 1931, pp. 517-518; ADGB, *Jahrbuch 1930*, p. 126.

16. Brüning, *Memoiren*, p. 480. Brüning also writes that he was proud to have won over the unions and the workers to an acceptance of the wage cuts (*ibid.*). The statement is of course false.

17. *G-Z*, May 21, 1932, p. 335.

18. ADGB Board, 13th session, July 16, 1931.

19. Anderson, p. 146.

20. W.S. Woytinsky, *Stormy Passage* (New York: The Vanguard Press, 1961), pp. 460-472. Baade cites a sum of up to 4 billion RM, but that is in error ("Fighting Depression in Germany," *So Much Alive: The Life and Work of Wladimir S. Woytinsky*, ed. Emma S. Woytinsky [New York: Vanguard, 1962], pp. 61-68). See also Alfred Braunthal, "Adviser of the European Labor Unions," *ibid.*, pp. 78-87; Robert A. Gates, "German Socialism and the Crisis of 1929-33," *Central European History*, VII, No. 4 (Dec. 1974), pp. 332-359; Michael Schneider, "Konjunkturpolitische Vorstellungen der Gewerk-

schaften in den letzten Jahren der Weimarer Republik. Zur Entwicklung des Arbeitsbeschaffungsplans des ADGB," *Industrielles System,* pp. 226-237, and *Das Arbeitsbeschaffungsprogramm des ADGB* (Bonn: Neue Gesellschaft, 1975). Professor Emil Lederer and Aufhäuser presented two further public works programs but they only reached the discussion stage (*G-Z,* March 5, 1932, pp. 148-150; *Vorwärts,* February 18, 1932).

21. *G-Z,* February 20, 1932, pp. 114-120; Ferdinand Fried, "Das Arbeitsprogramm des ADGB," *Die Tat,* No. 12, March, 1932, pp. 1026-1028; Arkadij Gurland, "ADGB-Kongress, AfA Programm und Sozialismus," *Marxistische Tribüne für Politik und Wirtschaft,* II (May 1, 1932), 270-272.

22. Gates, p. 351. By then Leipart had changed his mind. In January 1931, he had still supported an antidepression program which reflected Napthali's proposals (John Price, *The International Labour Movement* [London: Oxford University Press, 1945], pp. 106-109).

23. No date is cited. Woytinsky, pp. 468-469.

24. No date is cited. *Ibid.,* p. 472.

25. Michael Schneider, p. 234; Gates, p. 354.

26. In March 1932, ADGB and SPD had to take a stand on the Reich Presidential election, in which Hindenburg was running for reelection against Hitler and Ernst Thälmann (KPD). According to Brüning, in January he held a conference with top SPD leaders to plead for their endorsement of Hindenburg. Refusing to back Thälmann, they had no choice but to reluctantly support Hindenbrug. Wels asked Brüning to talk also with the ADGB officers in order for the SPD not to receive any "flak" from that side. Thereupon Brüning met with Leipart and two associates who demonstrated a "high degree of political insight." SPD and ADGB issued appeals to their members to support Hindenburg, who did win reelection, but with only 53 percent of the votes in the second round (Brüning, *Memoiren,* pp. 501-502).

27. Sidney Pollard is critical of those writers who now criticize German labor and socialist leaders for failing to see the magnitude of the coming disaster. He argues that "they set out to deal with problems they knew or could recognize, not disasters that were truly unimaginable," and that "bereft of ideas by those whose duty it should have been to provide them, they advanced a long way toward evolving and supporting their own better ones, more appropriate to their predicament." ("The Trade Unions and the Depression of 1929-1933," *Industrielles System,* pp. 247-248).

28. *G-Z,* June 18, 1932, p. 385; June 25, 1932, p. 401; September 3, 1932; p. 561; September 17, 1932, p. 595; October 22, 1932, pp. 673-675. The Christian unions also assailed the new government as antilabor.

29. Arnold Brecht, *Prelude to Silence* (New York: Oxford University Press, 1944), p. 65. For Papen's version, see his *Der Wahrheit eine Gasse* (Munich: List, 1952), pp. 213-220.

30. Karl Rohe, *Das Reichsbanner Schwarz-Rot-Gold* (Duesseldorf: Droste, 1966), pp. 427-430; statement by Aufhäuser, personal interview.

31. Erich Matthias and Rudolf Morsey, *Das Ende der Parteien, 1933* (Duesseldorf: Droste, 1960), p. 135. According to the two authors, the SPD, also holding a pre-coup meeting on July 16, decided to stay on a legal course.

According to Wels' reconstructed notes, written in Prague exile, the date was July 18 (Hans J.L. Adolph, *Otto Wels und die Politik der deutschen Sozialdemokratie, 1894-1939: Eine politische Biographie* [Berlin: Walter de Gruyter, 1971], pp. 241-242).

32. According to Wels' notes, as cited by Adolph, p. 243.

33. *Ibid.*, pp. 242-246; statement by Tarnow, personal interview; Skrzypczak, pp. 37-38. On July 20 and 21, a joint meeting of the SPD, unions, and Reichsbanner may have been held, but details are not available (Rohe, p. 427).

34. Statement by Aufhäuser, personal interview; Matthias and Morsey, p. 139.

35. Severing, II, 355; statement by Richard Seidel, union writer, personal interview.

36. Von Papen, *Vom Scheitern einer Demokratie, 1930-1933* (Mainz: von Hase und Koehler, 1968), pp. 258-259; Hüllbüsch, "Die deutschen Gewerkschaften in der Weltwirtschaftskrise," *Die Staats- und Wirtschaftskrise des Deutschen Reichs 1929/33,* ed. Werner Conze and Hans Raupach (Stuttgart: Klett, 1967), pp. 139-147. For protocol of meeting, see Heer, pp. 157-158. In a pamphlet, the ADGB asserted that only trade union demands and the Nazi terror were discussed (*Klassenverrat* [Berlin: ADGB, n.d.]). But this statement seems to have been part of a cover-up.

37. Letter from SPD leader Hans Hirschfeld, Berlin, February 5, 1951. No substantiation can be found for British historian John Wheeler-Bennett's thesis that the SPD wanted a strike, but was overruled by the ADGB (*Hindenburg: The Wooden Titan* [London: Macmillan, 1936], p. 405). Erich Matthias calls this a legend (*Das Ende der Parteien,* p. 137).

38. Joseph Goebbels, *Vom Kaiserhof zur Reichskanzlei* (Munich: Zentralverlag der NSDAP, 1934), pp. 131-133.

39. Otto Braun, *Von Weimar zu Hitler* (New York: Europa, 1940), p. 410.

40. Stampfer, pp. 578-579; cf. Severing, II, 357; Brecht, p. 67.

41. Meissner, p. 257; Wheeler-Bennett, p. 404.

42. Hannes Heer, *Burgfrieden oder Klassenkampf* (Neuwied and Berlin: Luchterhand, 1971), pp. 87-89, 151-161. See also Papen, *Vom Scheitern einer Demokratie,* pp. 259-262. Papen, then Chancellor, claims not to have known of the details of the deliberations, although he had deputized a ministry official to represent him. The protocols came to his attention only during the writing of the book. He notes that had he known of Schleicher's plans, he would have opposed them (*ibid.,* pp. 262-263).

43. In July 1932, Franz Josef Furtwängler, head of the ADGB foreign affairs division, with the approval of top ADGB leaders, initiated secret contacts with Strasser. In late August, Tarnow was willing to meet with Strasser for a noncommittal talk. On August 24, Erich Lübbert, the economic consultant of the paramilitary, conservative Stahlhelm, and a friend of the Nazis, and ADGB officials Erdmann, Eggert, and Schlimme sought a common basis for national action (Heer, pp. 161-163; Skrzypczak, pp. 39-40; Prinz, pp. 95-96). The ADGB claimed rumors about direct negotiations with

Strasser were false (*Klassenverrat*). See also Bernhard Düwell, *Gewerk-schaften und Nationalsozialismus* (Berlin: E. Laubsche Ver-lagsbuchhandlung, 1931).

44. Gustav Noske, *Aufstieg und Niedergang der deutschen Sozialdemokratie* (Zurich: Aeroverlag, 1947), p. 311.

45. Leipart and Eggert, to placate the SPD, also demanded a socializa-tion of key enterprises, but dropped the demand when Schleicher reacted negatively (*G-Z*, Dec. 3, 1932, pp. 769-770; *Vorwärts*, Nov. 29, 1932).

46. Rosenberg, *A History of the German Republic*, p. 315; Loebe, p. 140. Schleicher reportedly also suggested to the unions that a general strike be called to be supported by the army (Wheeler-Bennett, p. 429).

47. According to Brüning, Guenther Gereke, Reich Commissioner for Federal Employment, formed an advisory council to study ways of enlarg-ing the cabinet to include officials from the ADGB and the Strasser wing of the NSDAP (Brüning, *Memoiren*, p. 642). See also Paul Gentz, "Les Pour-parlers entre von Schleicher et les Syndicats ouvriers," *Excelsior* (Paris), quoted in Robert Goetz, *Les Syndicats Ouvriers Allemands après la Guerre* (Paris: F. Loviton, 1934), p. 249; ADGB Board press release, Dec. 14, 1932; *G-Z*, Dec. 17, 1932, p. 811.

48. *G-Z*, December 31, 1932, p. 833.

49. *G-Z*, January 28, 1933, p. 52. A left-wing SPD journal concurred with Leipart's view that unions must negotiate with government no matter what its political complexion. But it argued that the unions still represent the shock troops of the socialist movement in any nonparliamentary struggle and must not stand aside in a conflict ("Das Experiment des Herrn von Schleicher," *Neue Blätter für den Sozialismus*, Vol. IV, No. 1 [1933], 7-8).

50. Karl Dietrich Bracher, *Die Auflösung der Weimarer Republik* (Stutt-gart and Duesseldorf: Ring, 1955), pp. 684, 699; Earl Beck, *The Death of the Prussian Republic* (Tallahassee: Florida State University Press, 1959), p. 182; Lothar Frey (pseud.), *Deutschland Wohin?* (Zurich: Europa, 1934), p. 21.

51. Heer, p. 100; Wheeler-Bennett, p. 432.

52. Bracher, *Die Auflösung der Weimarer Republik*, pp. 699-700. The historian Erich Eyck concurs (*Geschichte der Weimarer Republik*, Vol. II, *Von der Konferenz von Locarno bis zu Hitlers Machtübernahme* [Erlen-bach-Zurich and Stuttgart: Eugen Rentsch, 1956], pp. 564-565).

53. Adolf Hitler, *Mein Kampf*, Vol. I (1938 ed.), pp. 51 ff.; Vol. II (1927 ed.), pp. 49, 672; cited by Heer, pp. 102-103.

54. Personal interview with a former ADGB leader, Berlin.

55. Max Kele, *Nazis and Workers: National Socialist Appeals to German Labor, 1919-1933* (Chapel Hill: University of North Carolina Press, 1972), p. 170.

56. Heer, pp. 101-102, citing an unpublished report by Heinrich Schliestedt, Metal Workers Union Executive member, in DGB Archive, Nachlass Plettl. In letters to the ADGB, Käthe Kollwitz and Heinrich Mann urged action, but the ADGB did not reply to them (Furtwängler, p. 255). See also Bahne, p. 685.

57. Heer, p. 197. Wels reportedly stated that if the March 5 election

brings gains for the Nazis then a general strike should be called to change the political situation (Adolph, p. 251). According to Matthias and Morsey (p. 151), the ADGB Board and union functionaries from all areas of Germany also met then in separate sessions. See also Otto Buchwitz, *50 Jahre Funktionär der deutschen Arbeiterbewegung* (Berlin: Dietz, 1949), pp. 136, 142.

58. According to a letter of Breitscheid, July 23, 1935, cited by Wilhelm Hoegner, *Der schwierige Aussenseiter* (Munich: Isar, 1959), p. 154.

59. Adolph, pp. 251-252. See also Heer, pp. 102, 104, 197; Hans-Gerd Schumann, *Nationalsozialismus und Gewerkschaftsbewegung* (Hanover: Norddeutsche Verlagsanstalt O. Goedel, 1958), pp. 55-56; Peter Grassmann, *Kampf dem Marxismus!?* (Berlin: Verlagsgesellschaft des ADGB, 1933), p. 21.

60. According to Wels' notes, June 16, 1933, cited by Heer, p. 104 (full text of notes, pp. 190-193).

61. *G-Z*, Feb. 4, 1933, pp. 65-68.

62. Grassmann, p. 20; *Vorwärts*, Feb. 20, 1933.

63. SPD leaders Breitscheid and Stampfer were attempting to improve relations with the KPD. Stampfer reportedly held talks with Ernst Torgler, KPD head, concerning the possibility of a united front (Bahne, pp. 685-686). After the Reichstag fire on February 27, the KPD leadership sought contacts with the SPD and ADGB boards (Matthias and Morsey, p. 157).

64. Prinz, pp. 106-112; Schumann, pp. 16-17; Heer p. 192; Joachim G. Leithäuser, *Wilhelm Leuschner: Ein Leben für die Republik* (Cologne: Bund, 1962), p. 104; Erich Kosthorst, *Jakob Kaiser*, Vol. I, *Der Arbeiterführer* (Stuttgart: Kohlhammer, 1967), pp. 178-179.

65. In early April, Schleicher requested Leipart, Leuschner (ADGB), and Wels to meet with him. They were willing, but the meeting was canceled in the last minute when the Nazis began to trail him (Leithäuser, pp. 93-95; Heer, p. 191).

66. *G-Z*, March 18, 1933, p. 163; April 1, 1933, p. 205; April 8, 1933, p. 220.

67. Seelbach, *Das Ende der Gewerkschaften* (Berlin: Elsner, 1934), pp. 23, 26.

68. *G-Z*, Dec. 24, 1932, pp. 819-822. Two influential union writers took the same position: Clemens Nörpel, "Entwicklung und Rechtsstellung der Gewerkschaften bis zur Gegenwart," *Arbeit*, No. 3, 1933, p. 183; Karl Zwing, "Um die Zukunft der Gewerkschaften," *Gewerkschafts-Archiv*, IX, No. 6 (1932), pp. 241-244. See also AfA resolution of March 10; *G-Z*, March 18, 1933, p. 163. ADGB and SPD failed to protest the Nazi dissolution on March 7 of the Iron Front and the Reichsbanner (Hans Stadler, *Die Gewerkschaften: Ein Staat im Staate* [Munich: J.F. Lehmanns Verlag, 1965], p.57).

69. The document also noted the separate and different functions of parties and unions and the readiness of the ADGB to conclude a working agreement with employers (Frey, p. 114; *G-Z*, March 25, 1933, p. 177; Karl Dietrich Bracher, Wolfgang Sauer, and Gerhard Schulz, *Die nationalsozialistische Machtergreifung* [Cologne and Opladen: Westdeutscher Verlag, 1960], p. 179).

70. Stadler, pp. 57-58; Kosthorst, *Von der Gewerkschaft zur Arbeitsfront*

und zum Widerstand (Hamburg: Girardet, 1963), p. 19. According to Bracher, Sauer, and Schulz (p. 179), the letter was sent on March 28 and not 29. At an ADGB Board meeting on April 5, sentiments similar to those in the March communications were expressed (Heer, pp. 165-167).

71. DGB file, ADGB Vorstandskorrespondenz, letter, March 3, 1933.

72. Limmer, p. 66; *G-Z*, April 1, 1933, p. 207; April 8, 1933, p. 223; April 15, 1933, p. 239. On April 30, the AfA disbanded.

73. Frey, p. 116.

74. Among those consulted were Vice-Chancellor Papen and Minister of Labor Seldte. The latter, although an NSDAP member, was considered sympathetic to the unions (Frey, p. 114). There were alleged meetings between Nazi district leader Wagner of Munich and Leipart; between Nazis and Seelbach and Furtwängler through the latter's connections in the Association for the Germans Residing Abroad. The nature of the talks and their importance were not clear (Seelbach; Heer, p. 193; Abram Plotkin, "The Destruction of the Labor Movement in Germany," *American Federationist*, XL [Aug. 1933], 816-826; Stampfer, p. 601).

75. For protocol of meeting, see Heer, pp. 168-173. See also Frey, pp. 116 ff; Leopold Franz (pseud.), *Die Gewerkschaften in der Demokratie und in der Diktatur* (Karlsbad: Verlagsanstalt "Graphia," 1935), pp. 53-54.

76. Goebbels, p. 307. See also p. 299.

77. W. Schumann, "Arbeitertum," Folge II, 1933, p. 3, cited by Heer, p. 104.

78. Frey, p. 120. Seelbach (p. 29) claims that the Board decision represented a reversal of the Executive's decision.

79. Heer, p. 129.

80. *G-Z*, April 22, 1933, p. 259. Whether Leipart inspired this article, signed by Walther Pahl, is not certain.

81. According to an unconfirmed report, ADGB and SPD Executives met in separate secret sessions on May Day, but arrived at no decision on any counteraction (Heer, pp. 194-195).

82. Anderson, p. 155; Bracher, Sauer, and Schulz, pp. 182-184.

83. *Ibid.* p. 181; Schevenels, pp. 121-123. Most IFTU files were saved, having been removed abroad before April 30 or to the French Embassy in the last minute (*ibid.* p. 123).

84. For a discussion of the union stand in 1933, see contributions by Franz Spliedt, Wolfgang Abendroth, Otto Brenner, Irmgard Enderle in *Gewerkschaftliche Monatshefte*, Vol. VI, March, April, May, July, September 1955, and by Hans Mommsen, Henryk Skrzypczak, Bernt Engelmann in Vol. XXVI, July 1975.

CHAPTER IV

1. Umbreit, "Allgemeiner Deutscher Gewerkschaftsbund (ADGB)," pp. 24-25.

2. *Ibid.* p. 27.

3. Maurycy Bergmann, Franz Schleiter and Helmut Wickel, *Handbuch der Arbeit: Die deutsche Arbeiterklasse in Wirtschaft und Gesellschaft*, Abteilung III, *Die Koalitionen* (Jena: Karl Zwing, 1931), pp. 49-53.

4. *Ibid.*, p. 108.

5. Bundesarchiv, File R 43 I/2024, Nos. 312-317, 319, 321; correspondence, Chancellor's Office and ADGB, March 18, 21, 22; April 1, 6, 13, 1932.

6. ADGB Board, protocol, 17th session, May 2-3, 1922, pp. 24-25; 18th session, June 16-23, 1922, pp. 3-8; 18th session, June 12-13, 1925, p. 12, in ADGB, *Protokoll der 17. (18.) Sitzung des Ausschusses des ADGB, 2. Geschäftsperiode* (Berlin: Verlagsgesellschaft des ADGB, 1922, 1925), (hereafter referred to as ADGB, Board session, date).

7. Until 1928, unions with more than 500,000 members received more representation; thereafter, the figure was reduced to 300,000 (Statute, No. 20). Under special circumstances, editors of union journals and union treasurers could attend meetings, but in a nonvoting capacity.

8. Jack Schiefer, *Geschichte der deutschen freien Gewerkschaften, 1890-1932* (Aachen: Grenzland-Verlag Hollands, 1948), p. 42. Occasionally, a government official was invited to a Board session for a discussion of mutual problems. In October 1932, one such invitation went to Chancellor Brüning, who respectfully declined due "to the current situation." Instead he sent a Ministry of Labor official who was requested to report back to him (Bundesarchiv, File R 43 I/2024, No. 365; Chancellor letter to ADGB Executive, Oct. 17, 1932).

9. Schiefer, pp. 42-43.

10. In 1925, the sum was calculated on the basis of 2.5 pfennig (pf.) per each male member and 1.75 pf. per each female and youth member (*ibid.*, p. 50).

11. Richard N. Hunt, *German Social Democracy, 1918-1933* (New Haven: Yale University Press, 1964), p. 243; Stadler, pp. 48-50; Erich Roll, "Germany," *Organized Labour in Four Continents*, ed. by H.A. Marquand (London: Longmans, Green, 1939), p. 86.

12. In addition, a number of unions had an executive board, serving as a control organ and as the highest organ of appeal for grievances (Jeannette Cassau, *Die Arbeitergewerkschaften: Eine Einführung* [Halberstadt: H. Meyer's Buchdruckerei, 1927], pp. 60-66). For a history of two unions, see Fritz Opel and Dieter Schneider, *Fünfundsiebzig Jahre Industriegewerkschaft 1891 bis 1966: Vom Deutschen Metallarbeiter-Verband zur Industriegewerkschaft Metall* (Frankfort/Main: Europäische Verlagsanstalt, 1966); Karl Anders, *Stein für Stein: Die Leute von Bau-Steine-Erden und ihre Gewerkschaften, 1869 bis 1969* (Hanover: Verlag für Literatur und Zeitgeschehen, 1969).

13. In 1902 the unions had only 112 paid functionaries, but in 1912 the number jumped to 1937 (Langerhans, p. 48). After World War I there was a serious shortage of skilled cadre members; new ones had to be recruited from universities and eventually from labor institutes. Professor Parkinson's famous law on the proliferation of bureaucracies applied to the ADGB too.

14. Cited by Werner Richter, *Gewerkschaften, Monopol Kapital und*

Staat im ersten Weltkrieg und in der Novemberrevolution (1914-1919) (Berlin: Tribüne, 1959), p. 25.

15. ADGB Board, 11th session, Jan. 19-20, 1921, p. 607.

16. Furtwängler, p. 77; personal interview with former ADGB staff member, Berlin; Alphons Nobel, *Die Gewerkschaften: Die deutsche Wirtschaft und ihre Führer*, Vol. II (Gotha: Flamberg, 1925), p. 112; Wachenheim, p. 566.

17. For a list of Executive members selected at various congresses, see Salomon Schwarz, *Handbuch der deutschen Gewerkschaftskongresse* (Berlin: Verlagsgesellschaft des ADGB, 1930), pp. 203-205; *Geschichte der deutschen Arbeiterbewegung, Chronik, Teil II von 1917 bis 1945.* Published by Institut für Marxismus-Leninismus beim ZK der SED (Berlin: Dietz, 1966), pp. 130, 184-185, 274. See also Theodor Cassau, *Das Führerproblem innerhalb der Gewerkschaften* (Berlin: Verlag der Neuen Gesellschaft, 1925).

18. Theodor Cassau, *Die Gewerkschaftsbewegung: Ihre Soziologie und ihr Kampf* (Halberstadt: H. Meyer, 1925), pp. 126-141.

19. Executive members in 1928 were Bruns (Factory Workers Union), Heinrich Mahler (Leather), Georg Reichel (Metal), Georg Schmidt (Agriculture), Karl Schrader (Textile), in addition to Tarnow, Janschek, Bernhard, and the seven ADGB business staff leaders, headed by Leipart (Schwarz, p. 205).

20. *Ibid.* p. 203.

21. *Ibid.*, pp. 42-43.

22. Robert Michels, *Political Parties: A Sociological Study of the Oligarchical Tendencies of Modern Democracy* (New York: Collier Books, 1962), see especially, pp. 159-160, 217-218. Michels referred primarily to party bureaucracies, but Everett M. Kassalow notes, "Michels virtually made a sociological law out of the unions' right-wing, oligarchic-like force in the party-union relationship. He argues that the unions, with their day-to-day needs, inevitably became a conservative force undercutting any serious socialist, revolutionary appeals and programs" (*Trade Unions and International Relations: An International Comparison*, ed. by Solomon Barkin, et al. [New York: Random House, 1969], p. 44). Michels is partly correct, but it must be pointed out that the SPD developed a similar bureaucratic apparatus and in the Weimar era was hardly less conservative. As Seymour M. Lipset indicates, "The larger the size of a local union, or an international, the greater the need to establish a bureaucratic hierarchy" (Lipset, "The Political Process in Trade Unions: A Theoretical Statement," *Freedom and Control in Modern Society*, ed. by Morroe Berger, Theodore Abel, and Charles H. Page [New York: Van Nostrand, 1954], p. 83).

23. For instance, in the Metal Workers Union 1.2 million workers entered and 900,000 left between 1925 and 1931 (Hartmut Schellhoss, *Apathie und Legitimität: Das Problem der neuen Gewerkschaft* [Munich: Piper, 1967], p. 120).

24. See William Leiserson, *American Trade Union Democracy* (New York: Columbia University Press, 1959); and Seymour M. Lipset, Martin Trow, and James Coleman, *Union Democracy* (New York: Doubleday,

1962), for a study of the International Typographical Union, which is an exception.

25. Wachenheim, p. 564; Wolfgang Abendroth, *Die deutschen Gewerkschaften* (Heidelberg: Rothe, 1954), p. 18; Erich Winkler, *Organisations- und Werbetechnik in der Arbeiterbewegung*, Vol. I, *Die Politik und ihre Gesetze* (Jena: Karl Zwing Verlagsbuchhandlung, 1930), p. 38; Jeannette Cassau, pp. 110-112. Fritz Opel cites a similar bureaucratization process in the Metal Workers Union (*Der Deutsche Metallarbeiter-Verband während des Ersten Weltkrieges und der Revolution* [Hanover: Norddeutsche Verlagsanstalt O. Goedel, 1957], pp. 30-32).

26. Fritz Fricke, *Kampf den Bonzen!* (Berlin: Verlagsgesellschaft des ADGB, 1930).

27. In the formative decades, some unions had been organized on the basis of the production materials involved, such as wood and metals; by crafts, such as printing and bookbinding; or by general category, such as the factory workers. Alexander Wende, "Die Konzentrationsbewegung bei den deutschen Gewerkschaften" (Unpublished Ph.D. dissertation, University of Marburg, 1912), pp. 53-58.

28. Dissinger, pp. 179-180.

29. J. Cassau, p. 104; Fritz Tarnow, *Das Organisationsproblem im ADGB* (Berlin: Verlagsanstalt des Deutschen Holzarbeiter-Verbandes, 1925), pp. 35, 39.

30. J. Cassau, p. 108; Johann Fiedler, *Die Konzentrationsbewegung der Gewerkschaften* (Vienna, Leipzig: Holder-Pichler-Tempsky, 1924), p. 1; Hüllbüsch, "Die deutschen Gewerkschaften in der Weltwirtschaftskrise," pp. 126-154.

31. The leading theorists were Hugo Sinzheimer, Clemens Nörpel, Fritz Napthali, and Wladimir S. Woytinsky, and the leading publicists were Lothar Erdmann, Richard Seidel, and Karl Zwing.

32. According to delegate Heckert in KPD, *Bericht über die Verhandlungen des 11. Parteitages der KPD, 1927* (Berlin: Vereinigung Internationaler Verlagsanstalten, 1927), p. 358 (hereafter referred to as KPD, *Parteitag, year*); and letter of the KPD trade union section, KPD, *Parteitag, 1924*, p. 97. The economist Eugen Varga, however, estimated that only 150,000 KPD members and 800,000 sympathizers were in the communist bloc in the free unions (Varga [ed.], *Die Sozialdemokratischen Parteien* [Hamburg: Carl Hoym, 1926], pp. 49-50). The discrepancy may be due to the possibility that the KPD claimed USPD supporters in its bloc. For the ADGB position, see *Ist eine Einheitsfront mit den Kommunisten möglich?* (Berlin: ADGB, 1922).

33. Flechtheim, p. 136.

34. *Ibid.*, p. 82.

35. Willi Bredel, "Streik in der Maschinenfabrik," *Klassenbuch 3: Ein Lesebuch zu den Klassenkämpfen in Deutschland 1920-1971*, ed. by Hans Magnus Enzensberger, *et al.* (Darmstadt: Luchterhand, 1972), p. 45.

36. Flechtheim, p. 46; Varain, p. 162. Lenin labeled the free unions as "yellow, social-chauvinistic, counter-revolutionary," and assailed German

communists for their failure to bore from within through "Machiavellian, illegal" means (V.I. Lenin, *Über Deutschland und die deutsche Arbeiterbewegung: Aus Schriften, Reden, Briefe* [Berlin: Dietz, 1958], pp. 550,558).

37. The ADGB decision was made at a Board meeting on Jan. 16, 1924 (Perlman, p. 120).

38. Karl-Gustav Werner, *Organisation und Politik der Gewerkschaften und Arbeitgeberverbände in der deutschen Bauwirtschaft* (Berlin: Duncker & Humblot, 1968), p. 98.

39. KPD, *Parteitag, 1924,* pp. 316-336; Stalin letter of Feb. 28, 1925, quoted in Ruth Fischer, *Stalin and German Communism* (Cambridge: Harvard University Press, 1948), pp. 435-439; Heer, p. 65. See also Horst Bednareck, *Die Gewerkschaftspolitik der Kommunistischen Partei Deutschlands* (Berlin: Tribüne, 1969); Heinrich Farwig, *Der Kampf um die Gewerkschaften* (Moscow: Verlag der Roten Gewerkschafts-Internationale, 1929).

40. RGO strength was centered in Berlin, the Ruhr, the lower Rhine, and Saxony (Siegfried Bahne, "Die Kommunistische Partei Deutschlands," *Das Ende der Parteien, 1933,* p. 664). Another source estimates RGO strength at 350,000 members, of whom about 200,000 belonged to the KPD (*Rote Presse Korrespondenz*, No. 112, April 23, 1971, p. 9). See also *Die Revolutionäre Gewerkschafts-Opposition (RGO)* (Berlin: Rote Fahne, 1972), 2 vols.

41. Bahne, pp. 664, 682; Flechtheim, p. 171; Deutscher Metallarbeiter Verband, *Die Kommunisten und die Gewerkschaften* (Berlin: DMW, n.d. [ca. 1931]).

42. The USPD had 179 delegates who represented about 1.5 million workers; the reformist bloc had 445 delegates who represented 3.3 million workers (*CB*, July 12, 1919, p. 306). At the 1922 ADGB Congress, the USPD had 138 out of 691 delegates (Flechtheim, p. 82). See also Robert Wheeler, "Zur sozialen Struktur der Arbeiterbewegung am Anfang der Weimarer Republik: Einige methodologischen Bemerkungen," *Industrielles System*, pp. 179-190; David W. Morgan, *The Socialist Left and the German Revolution* (Ithaca, N.Y.: Cornell University Press, 1975).

43. Werner, p. 95.

44. Curt Geyer, *Der Radikalismus in der deutschen Arbeiterbewegung* (Jena: Thüringer Verlagsanstalt, 1923); Eugen Prager, *Geschichte der USPD* (2d ed.; Berlin: Verlagsgesellschaft "Freiheit," 1922), p. 192. In party councils, the left wing had limited representation. In 1925, for instance, none of its leaders was on the 20-member Executive; 7 were on the 42-member Board; and about 10 were in the 130-member Reichstag Fraktion (Varga, pp. 55, 64; Hunt, pp. 227-228). At SPD conventions, Aufhäuser and union editor Toni Sender introduced a few resolutions which passed if noncontroversial, or failed if controversial (SPD, *Sozialdemokratischer Parteitag, Protokoll mit dem Bericht der Frauenkonferenz* [Berlin: Dietz, 1927], p. 272 [hereafter referred to as SPD, *Parteitag, year*]). See also "Die Politische Bedeutung des Parteitages in Kiel, " *G-Z,* June 4, 1927, pp. 309-311.

45. Jürgen Kocka, "Zur Problematik der deutschen Angestellten 1914-1933," *Industrielles System*, pp. 792-811; Rudolf Jobst, *Die deutsche*

Angestelltenbewegung in ihrer grundsätzlichen Stellung zu Kapitalismus und Klassenkampf (Jena: Vopelius, 1930); Fritz Croner, "Die Angestelltenbewegung nach der Währungsstabilisierung," *Archiv für Sozialwissenschaft und Sozialpolitik*, LI (1928), pp. 103-146.

46. Siegfried Aufhäuser, "Allgemeiner Freier Angestelltenbund (AfA-Bund)," *Internationales Handwörterbuch des Gewerkschaftswesens*, ed. Ludwig Heyde, Vol. I (1931), pp. 31-34; citation, p. 34; Aufhäuser, *Gewerkschaften und Politik* (Berlin: Industriebeamten-Verlag, 1924).

47. Albert Falkenberg, "Allgemeiner Deutscher Beamtenbund (ADB.)," *Internationales Handwörterbuch des Gewerkschaftswesens*, ed. Heyde, Vol. I (1931), pp. 19-23.

48. ADGB Board, 12th session, March 22-23, 1921, pp. 73-74.

49. The three federations were known as the General Association of German Christian Unions (Gesamtverband der Christlichen Gewerkschaften Deutschlands), with a peak strength in 1922 of over 1 million, primarily Catholic, manual workers; the General Association of German Salaried Employees Unions (Gesamtverband deutscher Angestellten-Gewerkschaften), with 550,000 employees in 1922; and the General Association of German Civil Servant Unions (Gesamtverband Deutscher Beamtengewerkschaften), with 140,000 members in 1922. In 1926, the latter was renamed the General Association of German Transport and State Employees (Gesamtverband deutscher Verkehrs- und Staatsbediensteter) (Helmut Lenz, "Die Gesellschaftspolitische Stellung der Deutschen Gewerkschaften von 1918 bis 1933," *Die Neue Ordnung*, XIV, No. 2 [1960], p. 94; Josef Kurth, *Geschichte der Gewerkschaften in Deutschland* [Hanover: Norddeutsche Verlagsanstalt O. Goedel, 1957], p. 62).

50. See Iris Hamel, *Völkischer Verband und nationale Gewerkschaft: Der Deutschnationale Handlungsgehilfen-Verband 1893-1933* (Frankfort/Main: Europäische Verlagsanstalt, 1967).

51. Lenz, p. 94; Alfred Christmann, *Gewerkschaftsbewegung und Gewerkschaftstheorie* (Cologne: Bund, 1963), p. 89; Josef Deutz, *Adam Stegerwald: Gewerkschafter, Politiker, Minister, 1874-1945* (Cologne: Bund, 1952).

52. Bundesarchiv, File R. 43 I/2024, No. 287; letter, June 13, 1931. Yellow trade unions fared more poorly. They were deliberately not invited to government conferences because the ministries did not recognize them as legitimate trade unions. For a general study, see Klaus Mattheier, *Die Gelben: Nationale Arbeiter zwischen Wirtschaftsfrieden und Streik* (Duesseldorf: Schwann, 1973).

53. J. Cassau, p. 40.

54. *Sind die freien Gewerkschaften politisch und religiös neutral?* (Berlin: Christlicher Gewerkschaftsverlag, n.d.). See also *Die politische und religiöse Neutralität der "Freien" Gewerkschaften* (Berlin: Christlicher Gewerkschaftsverlag, 1923).

55. Aufhäuser refers to a Fulda Conference, but gives no date (*Gewerkschaften und Politik*, pp. 14-15).

56. DGB archive file, ADGB Vorstandskorrespondenz, ADGB

Ortsausschuss Trier, letter to Bishop Bornewasser, Trier, March 23, 1928; reply, letter, April 15, 1928.

57. Kurth, p. 60.

58. Philip Taft, "Germany," *Comparative Labor Movements*, ed. Walter Galenson (New York: Prentice-Hall, 1952), p. 256; Lenz, p. 97.

CHAPTER V

1. Leipart, *Carl Legien*, p. 90.

2. Varga, p. 42.

3. According to a 1924-1925 Bremen regional survey, 80 percent of its male members were enrolled in the unions. They represented seventy-three skilled and twenty unskilled trades, and belonged to thirty unions (*Jahresbericht 1924-1925*, issued by SPD Ortsverein Bremen; quoted in Varga, pp. 43-44). The 530,000 figure is estimated on the basis that perhaps 10 percent of the 84 percent did not actually join a union, leaving a total of about 75 percent or 500,000 of all male SPD members who were simultaneously union members. If an adjustment is made for the female enrollment, the total number of unionists in the SPD rises to 530,000.

4. Of the 120,000 members, 60 percent were workers, 14 percent were salaried employees, teachers, and civil servants, 17 percent were housewives, and 9 percent fell into miscellaneous classifications (SPD, *Jahrbuch 1930*, pp. 193-194 [figures rounded to the nearest percentage]). Thus, 74 percent of the members were possible unionists. If about 10 percent did not join a free union, that would leave a total of about two-thirds of SPD members holding a free union membership.

5. Varga, pp. 34-35, 42-43. A pamphlet issued by *Vorwärts* called on workers to join both the SPD and the ADGB in order to limit the power of the capital monopolists (*Sozialdemokratie, Gewerkschaft, Vorwärts* [Berlin: Vorwärts Buchdruckerei, n.d.]).

6. This figure is calculated on the basis of the ratio of union members in the SPD to total free union membership of about 4.4 million in 1926 and 5.2 million in 1930.

7. The adjustment is based on the omission of AfA and ADB members and the fact that, as estimated above, only two-thirds of SPD members were union members. In the pre-World War I era, the ratio of SPD to free union membership rose from 23 percent (384,000 SPD members to 1,690,000 union members) in 1906 to 38 percent (983,000 to 2,574,000) in 1913. The rapid rise in SPD membership as compared to a more gradual rise in free union membership accounts for the percentage increase (Langerhans, pp. 48-49).

8. Varga (pp. 34, 45) estimated that of 7.9 million votes cast for the party in the December 1924 election, about 6 to 6.5 million (75-80 percent) were from proletarian voters. If family members of workers and nonunion workers are excluded from his calculation, the result would approximate my estimate. Flechtheim, in an analysis of the SPD-KPD votes in industrial

centers, cites an indefinite voting trend, but notes SPD strength in city districts with a large working population. In 1928, the SPD received 70 percent of its votes in these districts, strongholds of ADGB-organized skilled and unskilled workers (Flechtheim, pp. 208-214).

9. The 65 percent estimate, which included the vote for the USPD until 1922, is derived as follows: from 100 percent must be subtracted about 8 percent of the union members who were of nonvoting age (Bergmann, Schleiter, Wickel, pp. 55-57); about 10 percent who did not vote (the nonvote of the total eligible population fluctuated from 17 percent to 25 percent in the Weimar period, excluding the March, 1933 election [*Statistisches Jahrbuch, 1933*, p. 539], but the political interest among unionists was higher than among others); and about 15-20 percent who voted for the KPD and other parties (according to the estimate of one ADGB staff member, personal interview). Langerhans estimates (p. 50) that in the pre-World War I era the percentage of unionists voting for the SPD increased from about 20 percent in 1890 to nearly 66 percent in 1912.

10. In 1927, the IFTU queried affiliated national federations on their links to political parties. The German federations described the "satisfactory" links to the SPD, and asserted that neither desired a change ("Relations between Political Labour Party and Trade Union Movement in various Countries," *The International Trade Union Movement*, VII [Aug., 1927], pp. 124-128; [Sept., 1927], pp. 133-137).

11. Hunt, p. 243.

12. Evidence is their failure to be selected as delegates at an ADGB Congress. This is established by comparing the list of delegates at party and union conventions.

13. SPD, *Parteitag 1927*, pp. 283-291 (list of delegates). The ten were Aufhäuser, Bergmann, Brandes, Brey, Husemann, Kotzke, Mache, Richter, Schmidt, J. Simon. At the 1929 and 1931 Conventions the proportion was nearly the same.

14. In 1921, one ADGB chapter passed a resolution requiring every union member to become a subscriber to a socialist newspaper (*Sind die freien Gewerkschaften politisch und religiös neutral?*, p. 25). See Wilhelm Sollmann, "Gewerkschaften und Tagespresse," G-Z, March 31, 1928, pp. 196-198.

15. G-Z, Oct. 25, 1924, pp. 412-413; Nov. 22, 1924, p. 459. The KPD press assailed the ADGB position, and reminded its readers of the 1919 ADGB neutrality policy. The ADGB retorted that the policy was no longer an issue after the SPD-USPD merger (*ibid.*).

16. See, for instance, ADGB, *Protokoll der Verhandlungen des 12. Kongresses der Gewerkschaften Deutschlands* (Berlin: Verlagsgesellschaft des ADGB, 1925), *inter alia* (herafter referred to as ADGB, *Kongress, year*).

17. G-Z, April 21, 1928, p. 241; May 12, 1928, pp. 289-291.

18. ADGB Munich, information sheet no. 34, May 17, 1928, quoted in *Sind die freien Gewerkschaften politisch und religiös neutral?*, p. 18.

19. *Ibid.*, p. 20.

20. G-Z, Aug. 16, 1930, p. 513; March 5, 1932, pp. 147-148; July 23, 1932, p. 477.

21. The union president, Nikolaus Bernhard, was nominated. Quoted in *G-Z*, Aug. 9, 1930, pp. 505-506.

22. Quoted in *G-Z*, Aug. 16, 1930, p. 520; Aug. 30, 1930, p. 558.

23. The planks, drafted by a union official active in the SPD, included those dear to the unions, such as protection of the right to organize and to strike, the raising of the workers' standard of living, equal job rights for women, and coparticipation of workers in the economy (SPD, *Jahrbuch 1929*, p. 509).

24. Leipart letter, quoted in Lothar Erdmann, "Nation, Gewerkschaften und Sozialismus," *Arbeit*, March-April, 1933, pp. 149-150.

25. *Ibid.*, p. 149.

26. *Ibid.*

27. *Ibid.*, p. 150.

28. Paragraph 9 was changed to 10 (SPD, *Jahrbuch 1929*, p. 507).

29. Paragraph 11 was changed to 12 (*ibid.*).

30. Seidel, *The Trade Union Movement of Germany*, p. 110.

31. SPD, *Parteitag 1927*, pp. 76-79, 83, 259; Theodor Kotzur, "Beamtengewerkschaftsfrage und SPD," *Klassenkampf*, Oct. 1, 1929, pp. 604-607. At the 1929 Magdeburg Convention, the Executive issued a declaration of amity toward the free unions, but failed to recognize specifically the ADB (SPD, *Parteitag 1929*, pp. 97-98). See also ADB, *Organisationsfrage der Beamten und Sozialdemokratische Partei* (Berlin: Verlagsgesellschaft des ADB, 1930); Kotzur, "Gewerkschaftsfrage und Leipziger Parteitag," *Klassenkampf*, Sept. 15, 1931, pp. 564-566.

32. Philip A. Koller, *Das Massen und Führer-problem in den freien Gewerkschaften* (Tuebingen: Mohr, 1920), pp. 23 ff.; Michels, "Die deutsche Sozialdemokratie, Parteimitgliedschaft und soziale Zusammensetzung," *Archiv für Sozialwissenschaft und Sozialpolitik*, XXIII (1906), pp. 471-556.

33. Hunt. p. 167; see also Wachenheim, p. 639.

34. Franz Neumann, *European Trade Unionism and Politics* (New York: League for Industrial Democracy, 1936), p. 24. Before the merger of SPD and USPD, some unions disbursed funds to both parties on a percentage basis (*Sind die freien Gewerkschaften politisch und religiös neutral?*, p. 14). The ADGB sensitivity on the subject of secrecy is revealed in the minutes of an ADGB Board meeting. Union leaders criticized Vice-President Grassmann for revealing at a meeting of SPD functionaries the existence of a union electoral fund; a Hamburg newspaper printed the news (ADGB Board, protocol, 8th session, Sept. 19, 1930, p. 177).

35. Personal interview, former ADGB leader.

36. Whether a similar procedure was used to raise money for the party's operating expenses could not be ascertained. As early as 1922, the ADGB Saxonian district committee officially asked its local branches to collect money for the regional election (*Die politische und religiöse Neutralitat der "freien" Gewerkschaften* [Berlin: Christlicher Gewerkschaftsverlag, 1923], p. 12).

37. ADGB Board, protocol, 8th session, Sept 19, 1930, pp. 177-178.

38. For instance, at its 1925 Convention, the SPD announced the receipt

of over 6 million RM, of which almost 1 million came from collections made at meetings and from "other income," for the one-year period, 1924-1925 (SPD, *Parteitag 1925*, pp. 41-73). For the Reichstag election of 1930, the party collected 2 million RM, including 250,000 RM from SPD-allied organizations (SPD, *Parteitag 1931*, p. 207). For the elections in 1930-1931, the party received 4.1 million RM, of which about 800,000 RM came from allied organizations (SPD, *Parteitag 1931*, p. 245).

39. DGB, archive file, ADGB Vorstandskorrespondenz, letter from Schulze (ADGB Executive member) to F. Kuhne, union member, Nov. 25, 1930. The communist local was the Leipzig branch of the Painters Union, which also complained that the ADGB was not supporting other parties (Verband der Maler . . ., 22. *Ordentliche Generalversammlung in Breslau, 1931.Protokoll* [Hamburg: Batz, 1931], pp. 58-59). Once in power, the Nazis claimed that the SPD had received 2 million RM from the ADGB for the Sept. 1930 election and 229,000 RM since Jan. 1, 1933 (Reinhold Muchow, *Nationalsozialismus und "freie" Gewerkschaften* [Munich: F. Eher, 1932], pp. 98-99; *Frankfurter Zeitung*, May 5, 1933, p. 2).

40. The record is not clear on this matter. To compound the confusion, the SPD spokesman believed, but was not certain, that the 384,000 RM collected represented contributions not only from ADGB national unions but also from its district organizations (ADGB Board, protocol, 10th session, Oct. 7, 1932, pp. 153, 158). According to ADGB Board protocols, only at the Oct. 1932 meeting were precise figures for union payments to the party cited.

41. *Ibid*. At the ADGB Board meeting in June 1932, Leipart indicated that for the July election, the SPD hoped that the national unions would donate additional funds from their central treasuries. Since previous elections had been a heavy drain on its coffers, the SPD also hoped that union officials would aid in the sale of stamps to help defray expenses. No objection was raised to the party's request (ADGB Board, protocol, 7th session, June 14, 1932, *passim*.).

42. ADGB Board, protocol, 8th session, Sept. 19, 1930, pp. 177-179. The Nazis claimed an AfA union had donated 50,000 RM to the Reichsbanner (*Frankfurter Zeitung*, May 12, 1933, p. 2).

Chapter VI

1. For instance, in the fourth legislative period (1928-1930), sixty-eight Reichstag members were simultaneously on corporation boards of directors (Richard Lewinsohn, *Das Geld in der Politik* [Berlin: S. Fischer, 1931], pp. 93-94). See also Gerard Braunthal. *The Federation of German Industry in Politics* (Ithaca: Cornell University Press, 1965), pp. 9-13.

2. Under proportional representation, Germany was divided into thirty-five electoral districts of about 1.7 million inhabitants each. A candidate was elected for every fixed number of votes that the party received in a district. If the required number of votes was not reached, or excess votes were cast for a

candidate, the votes would either be placed into one regional party list for several electoral districts or into a national list composed of all electoral districts.

3. SPD, *Parteitag 1925*, p. 12 (SPD Statute: section 6, para. 3,5; section 20, para. 2.).

4. James K. Pollock, *Money and Politics Abroad* (New York: Knopf, 1932), pp. 248-249.

5. SPD, *Jahrbuch 1926*, p. 11. These areas were Rhineland, Westphalia, Silesia, South Bavaria, Pommerania.

6. Statement by former AfA leader, personal interview.

7. Leipart did agree to serve from 1919 to 1920 as Minister of Labor in Wuerttemberg (Theodor Cassau, *Die Gewerkschaftsbewegung: Ihre Soziologie und ihr Kampf* [Halberstadt: H. Meyer, 1925], p. 127; ADGB Board, protocol, 1st session, July 6, 1919, p. 3, in ADGB, *Beschlüsse der 1. bis 12. Sitzung des Ausschusses des ADGB, 1919-1921* [Berlin: Verlagsgesellschaft des ADGB, 1928].

8. Such as in Berlin, Potsdam, Frankfurt/Oder, Westphalia, and Hamburg. See Appendix D for a list of unionists nominated, whether elected or not, in each district in the 1928 Reichstag election.

9. For instance, in the 1928 election, in the Westphalia-North district, Carl Severing, prominent SPD figure and erstwhile unionist, received first place. The other three members elected were all active unionists. In Westphalia-South, four out of six SPD candidates elected were union leaders, representing the key Mine and Metal Workers Unions (Reichstag [RT], *Reichstagshandbuch 1928* [Berlin: Reichsdruckerei, 1928], p. 265).

10. ADGB, *Jahrbuch 1924*, pp. 28-29.

11. Statement by Tarnow, personal interview.

12. ADGB Board, protocol, 10th session, Oct. 7, 1932, pp. 153, 158-159.

13. DGB file, ADGB Vorstandskorrespondenz, letters, Leipart to Wels, Feb. 29, 1932, Oct. 5, 1932; Wels to Erkelenz (copy to Leipart), Oct. 11, 1932.

14. See Appendix B for the number of union representatives in the Reichstag by parties. See also Thieringer, pp. 102-103.

15. The figures are approximations, since biographical data on Reichstag members is not always complete. See Cuno Horkenbach (ed.), *Das Deutsche Reich von 1918 bis Heute* (Berlin: Verlag für Presse, Wirtschaft und Politik, 1930), pp. 632-774 and later editions. I have excluded deputies who began their careers as unionists, but soon switched to party work; and those who were on the fringe of the union movement (for a list of the latter, see Appendix C3).

16. See Appendix B for a breakdown by occupation of SPD deputies; Hunt, pp. 93-94; Adolf Borell, "Die soziologische Gliederung des Reichsparlaments als Spiegelung der politischen und ökonomischen Konstellationen" (Unpublished Ph.D. dissertation, University of Giessen, 1933), p. 59.

17. *CB*, Feb. 22, 1919, p. 63.

18. Published estimates on the number of union leaders vary because of differences in the definition of "union leaders." See Goetz, p. 252.

19. ADGB Board, 10th session, Oct. 7, 1932, pp. 159-160. In addition,

Aufhäuser and ten ADGB national leaders held seats. For a complete list, see Appendix C.

20. Walther Kamm, *Abgeordnetenberufe und Parlament* (Karlsruhe: G. Braun, 1927), pp. 55-56.

21. In the first Reichstag session, the average age of 50.7 of SPD union members was ten years higher than that of USPD union members. Calculation from RT, *Reichstagshandbuch*, various eds.; Johann Dierkes and Erwin Rawicz, *Taschenbuch für die Sozialpolitik* (Munich: C.H. Beck, 1930), pp. 316-317.

22. The comparison follows:

Age Group	Unionists in SPD Fraktion	Nonunionists in SPD Fraktion
30-35	none	3
35-40	1	17
40-45	2	20
45-50	4	25
50-55	5	27
55-60	6	17
60-65	9	10
65-70	1	3
over 70	none	2
Total	28	124

Source: see note 21 above.

23. In the 1930 election, for instance, the ADGB, AfA, ADB, Factory, Communication, Agricultural, Wood, Metal, Mine, Construction, Railroad, and Post and Telegraph Workers Unions had prominent leaders in the Reichstag. As an illustration of longevity, Brandes held a Reichstag seat from 1912 to 1933, except for the 1924-1928 session when he declined candidacy because the SPD had nominated another top leader of his union (Paul Ufermann [ed.], *Alwin Brandes* [Berlin: Arani, 1949], p. 38).

24. Statement by a former SPD Reichstag member, personal interview.

25. SPD, *Parteitag 1929*, p. 165.

26. SPD, *Parteitag 1921*, p. 91.

27. Resolution no. 401, RT, *Verhandlungen des Reichstags*, Vol. 432, 4th el. period. See also SPD, *Parteitag 1921*, pp. 99-101.

28. Dierkes and Rawicz, pp. 87-88.

Chapter VII

1. English text of Constitution in Howard L. McBain and Lindsay Rogers, *The New Constitutions of Europe* (Garden City, N.Y.: Doubleday, Page, 1922), pp. 176-212.

2. Horkenbach, pp. 366-381.

3. Hans Staudinger, *Der Staat als Unternehmer* (Berlin: Gersbach, 1932), p. 52-89.

4. Meetings with Hindenburg were rare; more typical were instances in which a delegation of free union leaders attempted to see Hindenburg, but could only see his deputy (Bundesarchiv, File R 43 I/2024, Nos. 43-47, n.d.).

5. Hunt, p. 174. In Dec. 1919, the Berlin workers and soldiers council transmitted requests from the Berlin headquarters of national unions to Bauer urging him to clear any planned labor legislation with those unionists active in the SPD. Bauer answered in the affirmative (Bundesarchiv, File R 43 I/2023, No. 32, letters, Dec. 16, 26, 1919).

6. For example, the ADGB sent Chancellor Müller (SPD) a letter in June 1920, requesting an opinion on whether the unions should be subject to a capital gains tax as directed by a civil servant in the Ministry of Finance. When no answer was forthcoming, the ADGB sent two more letters to the Chancellor and the Minister of Finance. Finally, in early September, the latter insisted that the unions would have to pay, but the following day he changed his mind and stated that a Tax Court would have to make the decision. In late September, a state secretary in the Chancellor's Office, writing in behalf of the Chancellor, reaffirmed the Ministry's latest verdict (Bundesarchiv, File R 43 I/2023, Nos. 37, 136-139, letters, memoranda, June 19, Sept. 3, 4, 27, 1920).

In August 1921, the free union executives requested Chancellor Wirth to invite them to a cabinet meeting where they would discuss the steep price rises. The Chancellor, apparently not wanting to set a precedent of cabinets convening en masse with a national association, responded negatively, but was willing to meet the delegation privately with only the Minister of Economic Affairs present. (*Ibid.*, File R 43 I/2023, Nos. 136-139, letters, Aug. 28, Sept. 3, 1921).

7. ADGB Board, 12th session, June 4-5, 1928.

8. They were Gustav Bauer, Minister of Labor; Robert Schmidt (General Commission member 1903-1918), Minister of Nutrition; and Rudolf Wissell (General Commission and ADGB Executive member, 1919-1924), Minister of Economic Affairs. Alexander Schlicke (President, Metal Workers Union, 1895-1919) served in later cabinets. For a list of cabinets and members, see Horkenbach, 1st ed., pp. 517-520, and his later eds.

9. The free unions had seats in a few conservative cabinets: in Joseph Wirth's two cabinets (1921 to 1922), Bauer was Vice-Chancellor and Minister of Finance, and Schmidt was Minister of Economic Affairs. In Stresemann's cabinets (1923), Schmidt was Vice-Chancellor and Minister of Reconstruction.

10. Ernst Deuerlein, "Heinrich Brauns—Schattenriss eines Sozial-politikers," *Staat, Wirtschaft und Politik in der Weimarer Republik: Festschrift für Heinrich Brüning*, ed. Ferdinand Hermens and Theodor Schieder (Berlin: Duncker and Humblot, 1967), pp. 41-96.

11. "Fraktionspolitik und Regierungsbildung," *G-Z*, April 27, 1928, p. 260; ADGB, *Kongress 1928*, p. 80.

12. Personal interview, Berlin.

13. Bundesarchiv, File R 43 I/2023, No. 298, minutes, cabinet meeting, Oct. 15, 1923.

14. The unions had five out of thirty-five members on the Electricity Board, twelve out of fifty-four on the Water Supply Board, and twelve out of fifty on the State Railroad Boards (AfA, *Die Angestelltenbewegung, 1925 bis 1928* [Berlin: Freier Volksverlag, 1928], pp. 262-270; Nathan Reich, *Labour Relations in Republican Germany* [New York: Oxford University Press, 1938], p. 47).

15. Horkenbach, p. 498: Nörpel,, "Gewerkschaften-Wirtschaft-Politik," *Gewerkschafts-Archiv*, II (Feb. 1925), pp. 78-85; Georg Bernhard, *Wirtschaftsparlamente* (Munich: Rikola, 1923), pp. 59 ff.

16. *Soziale Praxis, XXXVIII, No. 48 (1929), pp. 1173-1174; Bernhard, pp.* 76-77. A list of members appears in Reichsamt des Innern, *Handbuch für das Deutsche Reich*, 1922, pp. 32-50.

17. Richard Seidel, *Gewerkschaften und politische Parteien in Deutschland* (Berlin: Weltgeist-Bücher, n.d. [ca. 1928]), p. 69; Goetz, pp. 163-164.

18. The number of enterprises covered by these agreements constantly mounted in the Weimar era until the advent of the Depression, although the number of workers covered reached a maximum of 17.4 million in 1922, thereafter fluctuating between 13.7 and 16.2 million. In 1925, the total industrial labor force was 26 million workers (*Statistisches Jahrbuch, 1931*, p. 21; Reich, pp. 63-64; Alexander Lorch, *Trends in European Social Legislation between the two World Wars* [New York: Éditions de la Maison Française, 1943], pp. 54-56).

19. According to ADGB statistics (Frieda Wunderlich, *Labor under German Democracy: Arbitration 1918-1933* [New York: New School for Social Research, 1940], pp. 61, 78). See also Reich, pp. 122-155; Schwarz, pp. 342-347; Hans-Hermann Hartwich, *Arbeitsmarkt, Verbände und Staat, 1918-1933* (Berlin: de Gruyter, 1967), pp. 348-355.

20. Hüllbüsch, "Der Ruhreisenstreit in gewerkschaftlicher Sicht," *Industrielles System*, pp. 271-289; Ernst Fraenkel, "Der Ruhreisenstreit 1928-1929 in historisch-politischer Sicht," *Staat, Wirtschaft und Politik*, pp. 97-117; Walter Neumann, pp. 207-218; Otto Bach (ed.), *Rudolf Wissell* (Berlin: Arani, n.d., ca. 1949), pp. 70, 72.

21. *Ibid.*, p. 80; Hartwich, pp. 67-80, 352.

22. Hartwich (p. 388), on the other hand, feels in retrospect that state intervention had the advantage of precluding traumatic social upheavals.

23. Wunderlich, *German Labor Courts* (Chapel Hill: University of North Carolina Press, 1946), pp. 55-56; Preller, pp. 343-344.

24. ADGB, *Jahrbuch 1931*, pp. 189-191.

25. Wunderlich, *German Labor Courts*, pp. 114-115, 125, 197.

CHAPTER VIII

1. Eduard Claudius, "Eben erst dreizehn," *Proletarische Lebensläufe: Autobiographische Dokumente zur Entstehung der Zweiten Kultur in*

Deutschland, Band II: 1914 bis 1945, ed. by Wolfgang Emmerich (Reinbek: Rowohlt, 1975), p. 229.

2. The decrees were dated November 23, 1918; December 17, 1918; March 18, 1919. Horkenbach, pp. 38, 63. See also Leipart (ed.), *Die 40 Stunden Woche* (Berlin: Verlagsgesellschaft des ADGB, 1931), p. 195.

3. Ludwig Preller, *Sozialpolitik in der Weimarer Republik* (Stuttgart: Franz Mittelbach, 1949), pp. 146-147.

4. Schwarz, pp. 88-89; ADGB executives met jointly to reiterate their request for ratification (ADGB Board, 16th session, March 18, 1925, p. 32). See also 14th session, July 22, 1924, p. 16.

5. Schwarz, pp. 88, 90; ADGB Board, 15th session, Jan. 27-29, 1925, p. 17; 17th session, May 19, 1925, p. 10.

6. Meetings of Oct. 12, 13, 1930, and March 10, 1931. The 1932 ADGB Emergency Congress issued a call for a forty-hour week as one remedy to end the Depression (Leipart [ed.], *Die 40 Stunden Woche*, pp. 201-203).

7. ADGB, *Jahrbuch 1922*, p. 73; *Jahrbuch 1923*, p. 52; Preller, pp. 280-282.

8. SPD, *Jahrbuch 1926*, p. 260: Preller, pp. 369-374, 510; Michael Stürmer, *Koalition und Opposition in der Weimarer Republik, 1924-1928* (Duesseldorf: Droste, 1967), pp. 210-212.

9. Claudius, "Ich will doch nur Arbeit," *Proletarische Lebensläufe*, p. 257.

10. In 1919 the Allies failed to agree on the details of reparations. The treaty stipulated that a later conference would determine the total sum that Germany would have to pay in reparations to them.

11. The 1921 Conference also required Germany to pay for occupation costs and to abide by an obligatory schedule of exports. German inability to accept and meet these demands led to Allied sanctions. The later debt settlement called for a total of 132 billion RM payable in thirty-seven yearly installments (ADGB, *Bericht des Bundesvorstandes, 1922*, p. 110; ADGB, *Gewerkschaften, Friedensvertrag, Reparationen*, pp. 9-10).

12. ADGB, *Jahrbuch 1928*, p. 43; DGB file, ADGB Vorstandskorrespondenz, letter, Hermann Müller (ADGB leader) to Foreign Minister Stresemann, Jan. 15, 1929; Bundesarchiv, File R 43 I/2024, No. 252, minutes, cabinet session, June 28, 1929; No. 253, ADGB letter to Chancellor Müller (SPD), June 26, 1929.

13. The Plan provided for fifty-nine more yearly payments until 1988, for a total of 111 billion RM (ADGB, *Jahrbuch 1930*, p. 112; ADGB, *Gewerkschaften, Friedensvertrag, Reparationen*, p. 18).

14. *Ibid.*, p. 20. On Dec. 4, 1931, all German trade union federations at a mass rally warned the Allied Reparations Commission that renewed payments would retard the economic development of Germany and the world (*ibid.*, p. 21; ADGB, *Jahrbuch 1931*, p. 46).

15. The dispute erupted again at a meeting of the SPD Fraktion executive where Grassmann (ADGB) urged the party to demand an end of reparations. When Breitscheid did not concur, Reichstag President Löbe (SPD) in a private session (Jan. 5, 1932) attempted, in vain, to reconcile their conflicting views (DGB file, ADGB Vorstandskorrespondenz, letter, Leipart

to Wilhelm Keil [SPD leader), Jan. 8, 1932). See also Keil, *Erlebnisse eines Sozialdemokraten* (Stuttgart: Deutsche Verlags-Anstalt, 1948), II, 428-431; Heer, pp. 41-42.

16. On Dec. 20, 1919, the first Congress of Workers' and Soldiers' Councils demanded the socialization of those industries suitable for it, especially the mining industry (Heinrich Stroebel, *Socialisation in Theory and Practice* [London: King and Son, 1922], p. 174).

17. *Ibid.*, pp. 175-176 (according to an unidentified newspaper of Dec. 8, 1918).

18. *Metallarbeiterzeitung*, Nov. 30, 1918. See also *Textilarbeiterzeitung*, Dec. 20, 1918; Lederer, pp. 252-253.

19. Bach, p. 29; Stroebel, pp. 209-210.

20. Merker, pp. 234-238.

21. The SPD, mirroring union views, repudiated Wissell's plan at the 1919 Convention and in a leaflet *Sozialisierung und Planwirtschaft* (Ralph H. Bowen, *German Theories of the Corporative State* [New York: Whittlesey House, 1947], p. 202).

22. Spectator (pseud.), *Sozialisierungsproblem in Deutschland* (Berlin: Seehof, 1920), p. 52.

23. Werner Mohr, "Sozialisierung und Wirtschaftsdemokratie," *Der Klassenkampf*, July 15, 1930, pp. 426-429. The Socialization Report was published in *Bericht der Sozialisierungskommission über die Frage der Sozialisierung des Kohlebergbaus vom 31. Juli 1920* (Berlin, 1920).

24. Evelyn Anderson, *Hammer or Anvil: The Story of the German Working-Class Movement* (London: Gollancz, 1945), pp. 68, 70; Rosenberg, *A History of the German Republic*, pp. 25-27. In April 1919, General Commission members established a commission to bring their views on the councils to the government's attention (*CB*, April 12, 1919, p. 150).

25. Wilhelm Romer, *Die Entwicklung des Rätegedankens in Deutschland*, cited by Lorch, p. 119.

26. Paul Fisher, "Labor Codetermination in Germany," *Social Research*, XVII, No. 4 (Dec. 1951), 451-453; Boris Stern, "Works Council Movement in Germany," *Bulletin of the U. S. Bureau of Labor Statistics*, No. 383 (1925), pp. 15 ff.; Marcel Berthelot, *Works' Councils in Germany* (Geneva; International Labor Office, 1924), pp. 27-39.

27. C. W. Guillebaud, *The Works Council: A German Experiment in Industrial Democracy* (Cambridge: University Press, 1928), p. 45; *Protokoll der Verhandlungen des Ersten Reichskongresses der Betriebsräte Deutschlands, 5.-7. Okt. 1920, Berlin* (Berlin: Gewerkschaftliche Betriebsrätezentrale des ADGB und der AfA, n.d.).

28. ADGB Board, 4th session, Feb. 24-25, 1920, pp. 13-14; 7th session, Aug. 17-18, 1920; 8th session, Oct. 4, 1920; Reich, pp. 167-168. According to Guillebaud (p. 120), the ADGB claim is too high. The remaining councilors were elected from the lists of other labor federations.

29. Taft, pp. 282-283; Dieter Schneider and Rudolf Kuda, *Mitbestimmung: Weg zur industriellen Demokratie* (Munich: Deutscher Taschenbuch Verlag, 1969), pp. 149-178.

30. David, pp. 85-108.

31. Johannes Herzig, *Die Stellung der deutschen Arbeitergewerkschaften zum Problem der Wirtschaftsdemokratie* (Jena: Fischer, 1933), p. 16; Gerhard Albrecht, *Vom Klassenkampf zum sozialen Frieden* (Jena: Fischer, 1932), pp. 51-67.

32. ADGB, *Kongress 1925*, pp. 206-207, 231-232; Schwarz, pp. 411-418; Leipart, *Auf dem Wege zur Wirtschaftsdemokratie?* (Berlin: Verlagsgesellschaft des ADGB, 1928); Alfred Kahler, "The Trade Union Approach to Economic Democracy," *Political and Economic Democracy*, ed. by Max Ascoli and Fritz Lehmann (New York: Norton, 1937), pp. 43-44; Tarnow, *Die Stellungnahme der Freien Gewerkschaften zur Frage der Wirtschaftsdemokratie* (Jena: Verlag des Bezirksausschuss des ADGB, Thüringen, 1929).

33. ADGB, *Kongress 1928*, pp. 170-190; Georg Decker, "Zum Begriff der Wirtschaftsdemokratie," *Arbeit*, No. 12, 1927, pp. 825-834; Fritz Napthali, *Wirtschaftsdemokratie* (Berlin: Verlagsgesellschaft des ADGB, 1928); Paul Hermberg, *Planwirtschaft* (Berlin: Verlagsgesellschaft des ADGB, 1933). For a critique, see Merker, pp. 274-275.

34. ADGB, Kongress 1919, p. 56. The AfA adopted a similar basic program at its first Congress (Oct. 1921): "They (AfA unions) consequently see in economic socialism rather than in the private capitalist economy the higher form of economic organization" (Croner, pp. 117-118). See also Rudolf Jobst.

35. *G-Z*, Dec. 31, 1932, p. 833; see Erdmann, "Nation, Gewerkschaften und Sozialismus," pp. 149-150.

36. SPD, *Parteitag 1931*, pp. 45-46; quoted in and translated by Sturmthal, *The Tragedy of European Labor, 1918-1939*, p. 83.

37. ADGB, *Jahrbuch 1924*, p. 28; F. Heinemann, "Neue Wege und Ziele der Arbeiterbewegung," *G-Z*, Feb. 14, 1925, pp. 91-93.

38. Erdmann, "Gewerkschaften und Sozialismus," *Arbeit*, No. 11, 1925, pp. 657-674. By 1933, Erdmann and Leipart, under the pressure of political events, shed their socialist views, and emphasized nationalism instead (Erdmann, "Nation, Gewerkschaften und Sozialismus," pp. 129-161).

39. Union theoreticians disagreed on tactics and goals. Labor historian Nestriepke urged the ADGB to stick to economic affairs, and let the SPD achieve a socialist society through political means (Nestriepke, pp. 49-50). Labor editor Karl Zwing called for a renunciation of union pressure on SPD and government, and the creation instead of a democratic industrial society based on management-labor parity (*Soziologie der Gewerkschaftsbewegung* [Jena: Verlag Gewerkschafts-Archiv, 1925], p. 22). Labor writer Richard Seidel, not in accord, called on the SPD to help change the structure of society (*Die Gewerkschaften nach dem Kriege* [Berlin: Dietz, 1925], pp. 29-30). Clemens Nörpel, a labor law specialist for the free unions, rejecting Zwing's positon too, argued that economic parity will never lead to the ultimate goal of socialism ("Gewerkschaften-Wirtschaft-Politik," *Gewerkschafts-Archiv*, II [Feb. 1925], pp. 78-85).

CHAPTER IX

1. Lipset, "The Political Process in Trade Unions," p. 116.
2. Laski, *Trade Unions in the New Society* (New York: Viking, 1949), p. 170. See also Mark van de Vall, *Die Gewerkschaften im Wohlfahrtsstaat* (Cologne and Opladen: Westdeutscher Verlag, 1966), p. 92.
3. For surveys of the Trade Union Federation and its politics, see Dieter Schuster, *Die deutsche Gewerkschaftsbewegung, DGB* (3rd ed., Duesseldorf: DGB Bundesvorstand, 1971), pp. 75-135; E.C.M. Cullingford, *Trade Unions in West Germany* (Boulder, Colo.: Westview Press, 1977); Hirsch-Weber; Richard J. Willey, "Labor and Politics in West Germany: The Deutscher Gewerkschaftsbund, 1949-1963" (Unpublished Ph.D. dissertation, Princeton University, 1964); Willey, "Trade Unions and Political Parties in the Federal Republic of Germany," *Industrial and Labor Relations Review*, XXVIII, No. 1 (October 1974), pp. 38-59; Theo Pirker, *Die blinde Macht: Die Gewerkschaftsbewegung in Deutschland*, Vols, I, II (Munich: Mercator, 1960); Günter Triesch, *Die Macht der Funktionäre (Duesseldorf: Karl Rauch, 1956)*.
4. There is a parallel to the British trade unions. As V.L. Allen notes, "With their nine million-odd members the unions cannot help but be among the most powerful groups influencing governments." (*Power in Trade Unions* [London: Longmans, Green, 1954], p. 339).
5. See *inter alia*, Kassalow, "Trade Unionism and the Development Process in the New Nations: A Comparative View," *International Labor*, Solomon Barkin, *et al.*, eds. (New York: Harper and Row, 1967), pp. 62-80; Bruce H. Millen, *The Political Role of Labor in Developing Countries* (Washington, D.C.: The Brookings Institution, 1963).

BIBLIOGRAPHY

GOVERNMENT PUBLICATIONS

Bundesarchiv, Koblenz. Files of Reich Chancellor's office, Lot R43 I, Folders 2023, 2024.

Reichsamt des Innern. *Handbuch für das Deutsche Reich*, 1922. Berlin: Reichsamt des Innern, 1922.

Reichstag. *Reichstagshandbuch*. Berlin: Reichsdruckerei, 1924-1933.

_____. *Verhandlungen des Reichstags. Stenographische Berichte*. Berlin: Reichsdruckerei, 1920-1932.

Statistisches Reichsamt. *Statistisches Jahrbuch für das Deutsche Reich*. Berlin: Hobbing, 1931, 1933.

OTHER PUBLICATIONS

Allgemeiner Deutscher Beamtenbund. *Organisationsfrage der Beamten und Sozialdemokratische Partei*. Berlin: Verlagsgesellschaft des ADB, 1930.

Allgemeiner Deutscher Gewerkschaftsbund. *Bericht des Bundesvorstandes an den Kongress in Leipzig, 1922, für die Zeit vom 1. Juni 1919 bis 31. Mai 1922*. Berlin: Verlagsgesellschaft des ADGB, 1922.

_____. *Beschlüsse der 1. bis 12. Sitzung des Ausschusses des ADGB, 1919-1921*. Berlin: Verlagsgesellschaft des ADGB, 1928.

_____. *Gewerkschaften, Friedensvertrag, Reparationen*. Berlin: Verlagsgesellschaft des ADGB, 1932.

———. *Jahrbuch des ADGB*. Berlin: Verlagsgesellschaft des ADGB, published for the years 1922-1931.

———. *Protokoll der Sitzung des Ausschusses des ADGB, 1. bis 5. Geschäftsperiode*. Berlin: Verlagsgesellschaft des ADGB, published for the years 1919-1932.

———. *Protokoll der Verhandlungen des Kongresses der Gewerkschaften Deutschlands*. Berlin: Verlagsgesellschaft des ADGB, published for the years 1919-1932.

———. *Satzungen und Richtlinien des ADGB*. Berlin: Verlagsgesellschaft des ADGB, 1925.

———. "Vorstandskorrespondenz, 1925-1933." DGB Archive files.

Allgemeiner freier Angestelltenbund. *Die Angestelltenbewegung, 1925 bis 1928*. Berlin: Freier Volksverlag, 1928.

Deutscher Gewerkschaftsbund, Duesseldorf. Archives. ADGB Vorstandskorrespondenz.

Deutscher Metallarbeiter Verband. *Die Kommunisten und die Gewerkschaften*. Berlin: Verlagsgesellschaft des DMV, n.d. (ca. 1931).

Friedrich Ebert Foundation, Bonn, Archives. Carl Severing file.

Generalkommission der Gewerkschaften Deutschlands. *Beschlüsse der Konferenzen von Vertretern der Zentralverbandsvorständen*. Berlin: GGD, 1919.

———. Gewerkschaften und Arbeiterräte. Berlin: GGD, 1919.

International Federation of Trade Unions. "Relations between Political Labour Party and Trade Union Movement in various Countries," *The International Trade Union Movement*, VII (August, 1927), pp. 124-128; (September, 1927), pp. 133-137.

Kommunistische Partei Deutschlands. *Bericht über die Verhandlungen des Parteitages der KPD*. Berlin: Vereinigung Internationaler Verlagsanstalten, 1924, 1926, 1927.

Protokoll der Verhandlungen des Ersten Reichskongresses der Betriebsräte Deutschlands, 5.-7. Oktober 1920, Berlin. Gewerkschaftliche Betriebrätezentrale des ADGB und der AfA, n.d.

Sozialdemokratische Partei Deutschlands. *Jahrbuch der deutschen Sozialdemokratie*. Berlin: Dietz, published for the years 1926-1931.

———. *Sozialdemokratischer Parteitag, Protokoll mit dem Bericht der Frauenkonferenz*. Berlin: Dietz, 1919, 1921, 1925, 1927, 1929, 1931.

Verband der Maler, Lackierer, Anstreicher, Tüncher und Weiss-
binder Deutschlands. 22. *Ordentliche Generalversammlung in Breslau, 1931. Protokoll.* Hamburg: Batz, 1931.

NEWSPAPERS AND JOURNALS

*Die Arbeit: Zeitschrift für Gewerkschaftspolitik und Wirt-
schaftskunde.* Berlin: ADGB journal. Monthly, 1924-1933.
Archiv für Sozialwissenschaft und Sozialpolitik. Tuebingen. Sociol-
ogy journal. Irregular, 1888-1933.
Correspondenzblatt. Berlin: General Commission journal. Weekly,
1891-1919.
Frankfurter Zeitung. Frankfort/Main. Daily.
Die Gesellschaft: Internationale Revue für Sozialismus und Politik.
Berlin. SPD journal. Monthly, 1924-1933.
*Gewerkschafts-Archiv: Monatsschrift für Theorie und Praxis der
gesamten Gewerkschaftsbewegung.* Jena. Monthly,
1924-1933.
Gewerkschafts-Zeitung. Berlin. ADGB journal. Weekly, 1924-1933.
Korrespondenzblatt. Berlin. ADGB journal. Weekly, 1920-1923.
Neue Blätter für den Sozialismus. Potsdam. Independent Left.
Monthly, 1930-1933.
Soziale Praxis. Zentralblatt für Sozialpolitik. Berlin. Weekly.
Vorwärts. Berlin. SPD newspaper. Daily, 1894-1933.

BOOKS AND ARTICLES

Abendroth, Wolfgang. *Die deutschen Gewerkschaften: Weg demo-
kratischer Integration.* Heidelberg: Rothe, 1954.
Adolph, Hans J.L. *Otto Wels und die Politik der deutschen
Sozialdemokratie, 1894-1939: Eine politische Biographie.*
Berlin: Walter de Gruyter, 1971.
Albrecht, Gerhard. *Vom Klassenkampf zum sozialen Frieden.* Jena:
Fischer, 1932.
Allen, Victor L. *Power in Trade Unions: A Study of their Organiza-
tion in Great Britain.* London: Longmans, Green, 1954.

Anders, Karl. *Stein für Stein: Die Leute von Bau-Steine-Erden und ihre Gewerkschaften, 1869 bis 1969.* Hanover: Verlag für Literatur und Zeitgeschehen, 1969.

Anderson, Evelyn. *Hammer or Anvil: The Story of the German Working-Class Movement.* London: Gollancz, 1945.

Angress, Werner T. *Stillborn Revolution: The Communist Bid for Power in Germany, 1921-1923.* Princeton: Princeton University Press, 1963.

Aufhäuser, Siegfried. "Allgemeiner Freier Angestelltenbund (Afa-Bund)," *Internationales Handwörterbuch des Gewerkschaftswesens.* Edited by Ludwig Heyde. Vol. I, 1931, pp. 31-38.

_____. *Gewerkschaften und Politik.* Berlin: Industriebeamten-Verlag, 1924.

Baade, Fritz. "Fighting Depression in Germany," *So Much Alive: The Life and Work of Wladimir S. Woytinsky.* Edited by Emma S. Woytinsky. New York: Vanguard, 1962.

Bach, Otto (ed.). *Rudolf Wissell.* Berlin: Arani, n.d. (ca. 1949).

Baden, Prinz Max von. *Erinnerungen und Dokumente.* Berlin: Deutsche Verlags-Anstalt, 1927.

Bahne, Siegfried. "Die Kommunistische Partei Deutschlands," *Das Ende der Parteien, 1933.* Edited by Erich Matthias and Rudolf Morsey. Duesseldorf: Droste, 1960.

Barkin, Solomon, *et al.* (eds.) *International Labor.* New York: Harper and Row, 1967.

Bebel, August, *Gewerkschaftsbewegung und Politische Parteien.* Stuttgart: Dietz, 1900.

Beck, Earl. *The Death of the Prussian Republic.* Tallahassee: Florida State University Press, 1959.

Bednareck, Horst. *Die Gewerkschaftspolitik der Kommunistischen Partei Deutschlands.* Berlin: Tribüne, 1969.

Bergmann, Maurycy, Franz Schleiter, and Helmut Wickel. *Handbuch der Arbeit: Die deutsche Arbeiterklasse in Wirtschaft und Gesellschaft.* Abteilung III. *Die Koalitionen.* Jena: Karl Zwing, 1931.

Berlau, A. Joseph. *The German Social Democratic Party, 1914-1921.* New York: Columbia University Press, 1949.

Bernhard, Georg. *Wirtschaftsparlamente.* Munich: Rikola, 1923.

Berthelot, Marcel. *Works' Councils in Germany.* Geneva: International Labor Office, 1924.

Biegert, Hans H. "Gewerkschaftspolitik in der Phase des Kapp-Lüttwitz-Putsches," *Industrielles System und politische Entwicklung in der Weimarer Republik.* Edited by Hans Mommsen, Dietmar Petzina, and Bernd Weisbrod. Duesseldorf: Droste, 1974.

Borell, Adolf. "Die soziologische Gliederung des Reichsparlaments als Spiegelung der politischen und ökonomischen Konstellationen." Unpublished Ph.d. dissertation, University of Giessen, 1933.

Bowen, Ralph H. *German Theories of the Corporative State,* New York: Whittlesey House, 1947.

Bracher, Karl Dietrich. *Die Auflösung der Weimarer Republik.* Stuttgart and Duesseldorf: Ring, 1955.

————, Wolfgang Sauer and Gerhard Schulz. *Die national-sozialistische Machtergreifung.* Cologne and Opladen: Westdeutscher Verlag, 1960.

Braun, Otto. *Von Weimar zu Hitler.* New York: Europa, 1940.

Braunthal, Alfred. "Adviser of the European Labor Unions," *So Much Alive: The Life and Work of Wladimir S. Woytinsky.* Edited by Emma S. Woytinsky. New York: Vanguard, 1962.

Braunthal, Gerard. *The Federation of German Industry in Politics.* Ithaca: Cornell University Press, 1965.

Braunthal. Julius. *History of the International, 1864-1914.* London: Nelson, 1966.

Brecht, Arnold. *Prelude to Silence.* New York: Oxford University Press, 1944.

Bredel, Willi. "Streik in der Maschinenfabrik," *Klassenbuch 3: Ein Lesebuch zu den Klassenkämpfen in Deutschland 1920-1971.* Edited by Hans Magnus Enzensberger, *et al.* Darmstadt: Luchterhand, 1972.

Brüning, Heinrich. *Memoiren 1918 bis 1934.* Stuttgart: Deutsche Verlagsanstalt, 1970.

Buchwitz, Otto. *50 Jahre Funktionär der deutschen Arbeiterbewegung.* Berlin: Dietz, 1949.

Carsten, Francis L. *Reichswehr und Politik, 1918-1933.* Cologne and Berlin: Kiepenheuer and Witsch, 1964.

Cassau, Jeannette. *Die Arbeitergewerkschaften: Eine Einführung.* Halberstadt: H. Meyer's Buchdruckerei, 1927.

Cassau, Theodor. *Das Führerproblem innerhalb der Gewerkschaften.* Berlin: Verlag der Neuen Gesellschaft, 1925.

————. "Die Gewerkschaften und die Politik," *Gewerkschafts-Archiv*, II (June, 1925), pp. 337-343.

————, *Die Gewerkschaftsbewegung: Ihre Soziologie und ihr Kampf*. Halberstadt: H. Meyer, 1925.

Christmann, Alfred. *Gewerkschaftsbewegung und Gewerkschaftstheorie*. Cologne: Bund, 1963.

Claudius, Edward. "Eben erst dreizehn," and "Ich will doch nur Arbeit," *Proletarische Lebensläufe: Autobiographische Dokumente zur Entstehung der Zweiten Kultur in Deutschland. Band II: 1914 bis 1945*. Edited by Wolfgang Emmerich. Reinbek: Rowohlt, 1975.

Comfort, Richard A. *Revolutionary Hamburg: Labor Politics in the Early Weimar Republic*. Stanford: Stanford University Press, 1966.

Croner, Fritz. "Die Angestelltenbewegung nach der Währungsstabilisierung," *Archiv für Sozialwissenschaft und Sozialpolitik*, LI (1928), pp. 103-146.

Crook, Wilfred H. *The General Strike: A Study of Labor's Tragic Weapon in Theory and Practice*. Chapel Hill: University of North Carolina Press, 1931.

Cullingford, E.C.M., *Trade Unions in West Germany*. Boulder, Col: Westview Press, 1977.

Daniels, H.G. *The Rise of the German Republic*. London: Nisbet, 1927.

David, F. *Der Bankrott des Reformismus*. Berlin: Internationaler Arbeiter-Verlag, 1932. Reprint, Erlangen: Politladen-Reprint No. 4, 1971.

Decker, Georg. "Zum Begriff der Wirtschaftsdemokratie," *Arbeit*, No. 12, 1927, pp. 825-834.

Deuerlein, Ernst. "Heinrich Brauns—Schattenriss eines Sozialpolitikers," *Staat, Wirtschaft und Politik in der Weimarer Republik: Festschrift für Heinrich Brüning*. Edited by Ferdinand Hermens and Theodor Schieder. Berlin: Duncker and Humblot, 1967.

Deutz, Josef. *Adam Stegerwald: Gewerkschafter, Politiker, Minister, 1874-1945*. Cologne: Bund, 1952.

Dierkes, Johann and Erwin Rawicz. *Taschenbuch für die Sozialpolitik*. Munich: C.H. Beck, 1930.

Dissinger, Arthur. *Das freigewerkschaftliche Organisationsproblem: Eine soziologische Studie.* Jena: Gustav Fischer, 1929.

Dissmann, Robert. *Die Kriegspolitik der Gewerkschaften.* Frankfort/Main: Oster and Munch, n.d.

Düwell, Bernhard. *Gewerkschaften und Nationalsozialismus.* Berlin: E. Laubsche Verlagsbuchhandlung, 1931.

Emmerich, Wolfgang (ed.). *Proletarische Lebensläufe: Autobiographische Dokumente zur Entstehung der Zweiten Kultur in Deutschland. Band II: 1914 bis 1945.* Reinbek: Rowohlt, 1975.

Erdmann, Lothar. *Die Gewerkschaften im Ruhrkampf.* Berlin: Verlagsgesellschaft des ADGB, 1924.

———. "Gewerkschaften und Sozialismus," *Arbeit*, No. 11, November 1925, pp. 657-674.

———. "Nation, Gewerkschaften und Sozialismus," *Arbeit*, No. 3, March 1933, pp. 129-161.

Erger, Johannes, *Der Kapp-Lüttwitz Putsch.* Duesseldorf: Droste, 1967.

Eyck, Erich. *Geschichte der Weimarer Republik.* Vol. II, *Von der Konferenz von Locarno bis zu Hitlers Machtübernahme.* Erlenbach-Zurich and Stuttgart: Eugen Rentsch, 1956.

Falkenberg, Albert. "Allgemeiner Deutscher Beamtenbund (ADB.)," *Internationales Handwörterbuch des Gewerkschaftswesens.* Edited by Ludwig Heyde. Vol. I, 1931, pp. 19-23.

Farwig, Heinrich. *Der Kampf um die Gewerkschaften.* Moscow: Verlag der Roten Gewerkschafts-Internationale, 1929.

Feldman, Gerald D. *Army, Industry and Labor in Germany, 1914-1918.* Princeton: Princeton University Press, 1966.

———. "Die Freien Gewerkschaften und die Zentralarbeitsgemeinschaft 1918-1924," *Vom Sozialistengesetz zur Mitbestimmung.* Edited by Heinz Oskar Vetter. Cologne: Bund, 1975.

———. "German Business Between War and Revolution: The Origins of the Stinnes-Legien Agreement," *Entstehung und Wandel der modernen Gesellschaft: Festschrift für Hans Rosenberg zum 65. Geburtstag.* Edited by Gerhard A. Ritter. Berlin: Walter de Gruyter, 1970.

Fiedler, Johann. *Die Konzentrationsbewegung der Gewerkschaften.* Vienna and Leipzig. Hölder-Pichler-Tempsky, 1924.

Fischer, Ruth. *Stalin and German Communism,* Cambridge: Harvard University Press, 1948.

Fisher, Paul. "Labor Codetermination in Germany," *Social Research,* XVIII, No. 4 (December, 1951), pp. 449-485.

Flechtheim, Ossip K. *Die Kommunistische Partei Deutschlands in der Weimarer Republik.* Offenbach: Bollwerk, 1948.

Förster, Alfred. *Die Gewerkschaftspolitik der deutschen Sozialdemokratie während des Sozialistengesetzes.* Berlin: Tribüne, 1971.

Fraenkel, Ernst. "Der Ruhreisenstreit 1928-1929 in historisch-politischer Sicht," *Staat, Wirtschaft und Politik in der Weimarer Republik: Festschrift für Heinrich Brüning.* Edited by Ferdinand Hermens and Theodor Schieder. Berlin: Duncker and Humblot, 1967.

Franz, Leopold (pseud.). *Die Gewerkschaften in der Demokratie und in der Diktatur.* Karlsbad: Verlagsanstalt "Graphia," 1935.

Frey, Lothar (pseud.). *Deutschland Wohin?* Zurich: Europa, 1934.

Fricke, Fritz. *Kampf den Bonzen!* Berlin: Verlagsgesellschaft des ADGB, 1930.

Fugger, Karl. *Die deutschen Gewerkschaften und die November-Revolution.* Berlin: Die Freie Gewerkschaft Verlagsgesellschaft, 1948.

Furtwängler, Franz Josef. *Die Gewerkschaften: Ihre Geschichte und internationale Auswirkung.* Hamburg: Rowohlt, 1956.

Galenson, Walter (ed.). *Comparative Labor Movements.* New York: Prentice-Hall, 1952.

Gates, Robert A. "German Socialism and the Crisis of 1929-33," *Central European History,* VII, No. 4 (December, 1974), pp. 332-359.

Geschichte der deutschen Arbeiterbewegung: Chronik. Teil II. *Von 1917 bis 1945.* Published by Institut für Marxismus-Leninismus beim ZK der SED. Berlin: Dietz, 1966.

Gessner, Manfred. "Wehrfrage und freie Gewerkschaftsbewegung in den Jahren 1918 bis 1923 in Deutschland." Unpublished Ph.D. dissertation, Free University, Berlin, 1962.

Gewerkschaft der Eisenbahner Deutschlands. *Carl Legien.* Frankfort/Main: GdED, 1950.

Geyer, Curt. *Der Radikalismus in der deutschen Arbeiterbewegung.* Jena: Thüringer Verlagsanstalt, 1923.

Goebbels, Joseph. *Vom Kaiserhof zur Reichskanzlei*. Munich: Zentralverlag der NSDAP, 1934.

Göhre, Paul. "Three Months in a Workshop," *Industrialization and Industrial Labor in Nineteenth-Century Europe*. Edited by James J. Sheehan. New York: Wiley, 1973.

Goetz, Robert. *Les Syndicats Ouvriers Allemands après la Guerre*. Paris: F. Loviton, 1934.

Gordon, Harold J., Jr. *The Reichswehr and the German Republic, 1919-1926*. Princeton: Princeton University Press, 1957.

Gottfurcht, Hans. *Die internationale Gewerkschaftsbewegung von den Anfangen bis zur Gegenwart*. Cologne: Bund, 1966. Revision of *Die internationale Gewerkschaftsbewegung im Weltgeschehen*. Cologne: Bund, 1962.

Grassmann, Peter. *Kampf dem Marxismus!?* Berlin: Verlagsgesellschaft des ADGB, 1933.

Grebing, Helga. *Geschichte der deutschen Arbeiterbewegung*. Munich: Nymphenburger Verlagshandlung, 1966. Translated into *The History of the German Labour Movement*. London: Oswald Wolff, 1969.

Groener-Geyer, Dorothea. *General Groener: Soldat und Staatsmann*. Frankfort/Main: Societäts-Verlag, 1955.

Guillebaud, C. W. *The Works Council: A German Experiment in Industrial Democracy*. Cambridge: University Press, 1928.

Hamel, Iris. *Völkischer Verband und nationale Gewerkschaft: Der Deutschnationale Handlungsgehilfen-Verband 1893-1933*. Frankfort/Main: Europäische Verlagsanstalt, 1967.

Hartwich, Hans-Hermann. *Arbeitsmarkt, Verbände und Staat, 1918-1933*. Berlin: de Gruyter, 1967.

Heer, Hannes. *Burgfrieden oder Klassenkampf: Zur Politik der sozialdemokratischen Gewerkschaften, 1930-1933*. Neuwied and Berlin: Luchterhand, 1971.

Heilborn, Otto. *Die "freien" Gewerkschaften seit 1890*. Jena: Fischer, 1907.

Hermberg, Paul. *Planwirtschaft*. Berlin: Verlagsgesellschaft des ADGB, 1933.

Herzig, Johannes. *Die Stellung der deutschen Arbeitergewerkschaften zum Problem der Wirtschaftsdemokratie*. Jena: Fischer, 1933.

Hilferding, Rudolf. "Der Austritt aus der Regierung," *Die Gesellschaft*, May 1930, pp. 385-392.

Hirsch-Weber, Wolfgang. *Gewerkschaften in der Politik: Von der Massenstreikdebatte zum Kampf um das Mitbestimmungsrecht.* Cologne and Opladen: Westdeutscher Verlag, 1959.

Hoegner, Wilhelm. *Der schwierige Aussenseiter.* Munich: Isar, 1959.

Horkenbach, Cuno (ed.). *Das Deutsche Reich von 1918 bis Heute.* Berlin: Verlag für Presse, Wirschaft und Politik, 1930, 1931, 1932, 1933.

Hüllbüsch, Ursula. "Die deutschen Gewerkschaften in der Weltwirtschaftskrise," *Die Staats- und Wirtschaftskrise des Deutschen Reichs 1929/33.* Edited by Werner Conze and Hans Raupach. Stuttgart: Klett, 1967.

_____. "Gewerkschaften und Staat: Ein Beitrag zur Geschichte der Gewerkschaften zu Anfang und zu Ende der Weimarer Republik." Unpublished Ph.D. dissertation, University of Heidelberg, 1961.

_____. "Der Ruhreisenstreit in gewerkschaftlicher Sicht," *Industrielles System und politische Entwicklung in der Weimarer Republik.* Edited by Hans Mommsen, Dietmar Petzina, and Bernd Weisbrod. Duesseldorf: Droste, 1974.

Hunt, Richard N. *German Social Democracy, 1918-1933.* New Haven: Yale University Press, 1964.

Ist eine Einheitsfront mit den Kommunisten möglich? Berlin: ADGB, 1922.

Jobst, Rudolf. *Die deutsche Angestelltenbewegung in ihrer grundsätzlichen Stellung zu Kapitalismus und Klassenkampf.* Jena: Vopelius, 1930.

Kähler, Alfred. "The Trade Union Approach to Economic Democracy," *Political and Economic Democracy.* Edited by Max Ascoli and Fritz Lehmann. New York: Norton, 1937.

Kamm, Walther. *Abgeordnetenberufe und Parlament.* Karlsruhe: G. Braun, 1927.

Kassalow, Everett M. "Trade Unionism and the Development Process in the New Nations: A Comparative View," *International Labor.* Edited by Solomon Barkin, et al. New York: Harper and Row, 1967.

_____. *Trade Unions and Industrial Relations: An International Comparison.* New York: Random House, 1969.

Kaun, Heinrich. *Die Geschichte der Zentralarbeitsgemeinschaft der industriellen und gewerblichen Arbeitgeber und Arbeitnehmer Deutschlands.* Jena: Neuenhahn, 1938.

Kautsky, Karl. "Partei und Gewerkschaft," *Die Neue Zeit*, XXIV, Part II (1905-1906), pp. 749-754.

Keil, Wilhelm. *Erlebnisse eines Sozialdemokraten.* Stuttgart: Deutsche Verlags-Anstalt, 1948.

Kele, Max. *Nazis and Workers: National Socialist Appeals to German Labor, 1919-1933.* Chapel Hill: University of North Carolina Press, 1972.

Klärmann, Sophie. *Die freien Gewerkschaften in Gesetzgebung und Politik.* Munich: Duncker und Humblot, 1912.

Klassenverrat. Berlin: ADGB, n.d. (ca. 1932).

Kocka, Jürgen. "Zur Problematik der deutschen Angestellten 1914-1933," *Industrielles System und politische Entwicklung in der Weimarer Republik.* Edited by Hans Mommsen, Dietmar Petzina and Bernd Weisbrod. Duesseldorf: Droste, 1974.

Könnemann, Erwin, Brigitte Barthold and Gerhard Schulze (eds.). *Arbeiterklasse siegt über Kapp und Lüttwitz.* 2 vols. Glashütten: Auvermann, 1971.

————, and Hans-Joachim Krusch. *Aktionseinheit contra Kapp-Putsch.* Berlin: Dietz, 1972.

Kolb, Eberhard. *Die Arbeiterräte in der deutschen Innenpolitik, 1918-1919.* Duesseldorf: Droste, 1962.

Kolbe, Hellmut. *Die beginnende Opposition in den deutschen Gewerkschaften im Jahre 1917.* Berlin: Tribüne, 1957.

Koller, Philip A. *Das Massen- und Führer-problem in den freien Gewerkschaften.* Supplement No. 17 to *Archiv für Sozialwissenschaft und Sozialpolitik.* Tuebingen: Mohr, 1920.

Kosthorst, Erich. *Jacob Kaiser*, Vol. I, *Der Arbeiterführer.* Stuttgart: Kohlhammer, 1967.

————. *Von der Gewerkschaft zur Arbeitsfront und zum Widerstand.* Hamburg: Girardet, 1963.

Kotzur, Theodor. "Beamtengewerkschaftsfrage und SPD," *Klassenkampf*, October 1, 1929, pp. 604-607.

————. "Gewerkschaftsfrage und Leipziger Parteitag," *Klassenkampf*, September 15, 1931, pp. 564-566.

Kuczynski, Jürgen. *Die Geschichte der Lage der Arbeiter in Deutschland von 1917/18 bis 1932/33.* Berlin: Akademie, 1966.

Kurth, Josef. *Geschichte der Gewerkschaften in Deutschland.* Hanover: Norddeutsche Verlagsanstalt O. Goedel, 1957.

Lange, Paul. *Die Politik der Gewerkschaftsführer von 1914 bis 1919.* Berlin: Kommissions-Verlag Adolf Hoffmann, 1919.

Langerhans, Heinz. "Partei und Gewerkschaften: Eine Untersuchung zur Geschichte der Hegemonie der Gewerkschaft in der deutschen Arbeiterbewegung, 1890-1914." Unpublished Ph.D. dissertation. University of Frankfort, 1957.

Laski, Harold J. *Trade Unions in the New Society.* New York: Viking, 1949.

Lederer, Emil. "Die Gewerkschaftsbewegung 1918/19 und die Entfaltung der wirtschaftlichen Ideologien in der Arbeiterklasse," *Archiv für Sozialwissenschaft und Sozialpolitik,* XLVII (1920), pp. 219-269.

Legien, Carl. *Warum müssen die Gewerkschaftsfunktionäre sich mehr am inneren Parteileben beteiligen? Ein Vortrag.* Berlin: Verlag der Gewerkschaftskommission Berlins und Umgegend, 1915.

Leipart, Theodor. *Auf dem Wege zur Wirtschaftsdemokratie?* Berlin: Verlagsgesellschaft des ADGB, 1928.

_____. *Carl Legien: Ein Gedenkbuch.* Berlin: Verlagsgesellschaft des ADGB, 1929.

_____. (ed.) *Die 40 Stunden-Woche.* Berlin: Verlagsgesellschaft des ADGB, 1931.

Leiserson, William. *American Trade Union Democracy.* New York: Columbia University Press, 1959.

Leithäuser, Joachim G. *Wilhelm Leuschner: Ein Leben für die Republik.* Cologne: Bund, 1962.

Lenin, W. I. *Über Deutschland und die deutsche Arbeiterbewegung: Aus Schriften, Reden, Briefe.* Berlin: Dietz, 1958.

Lenz, Helmut. "Die gesellschaftspolitische Stellung der deutschen Gewerkschaften von 1918 bis 1933," *Die Neue Ordnung,* XIV, No. 2 (1960), pp. 87-99.

Lewinsohn, Richard. *Das Geld in der Politik.* Berlin: S. Fischer, 1931.

Lidtke, Vernon. *The Outlawed Party: Social Democracy in Germany, 1878-1890.* Princeton: Princeton University Press, 1966.

Lipset, Seymour M. "The Political Process in Trade Unions: A Theoretical Statement," *Freedom and Control in Modern*

Society. Edited by Monroe Berger, Theodore Abel and Charles H. Page. New York: Van Nostrand, 1954.

———, Martin Trow and James Coleman. *Union Democracy: The Internal Politics of the International Typographical Union.* New York: Doubleday, 1962.

Loebe, Paul. *Erinnerungen eines Reichstagspräsidenten.* Berlin: Arani, 1949.

Lorch, Alexander. *Trends in European Social Legislation Between the Two World Wars.* New York: Éditions de la Maison Française, 1943.

Lucas, Erhard. *Märzrevolution im Ruhrgebiet.* Vol. I. Frankfort/Main: März, 1970.

Luxemburg, Rosa. *Massenstreik, Partei und Gewerkschaften.* Leipzig: Vulkan, 1919. Reprint of 1906 ed. Translated and expanded, *The Mass Strike: The Political Party and the Trade Unions and the Junius Pamphlet.* New York: Harper and Row, 1971.

McBain, Howard L. and Lindsay Rogers. *The New Constitutions of Europe.* Garden City, N.Y.: Doubleday, Page, 1922.

Mai, August. *Partei und Gewerkschaft in vergleichender Statistik.* Dresden: von Kaden, 1912.

Mattheier, Klaus. *Die Gelben: Nationale Arbeiter Zwischen Wirtschaftsfrieden und Streik.* Duesseldorf: Schwann, 1973.

Matthias, Erich and Rudolf Morsey (eds.). *Das Ende der Parteien, 1933.* Duesseldorf: Droste, 1960.

Meissner, Otto. *Staatssekretär unter Ebert-Hindenburg-Hitler.* Hamburg: Hoffmann and Campe, 1950.

Merker, Paul. *Sozialdemokratie und Gewerkschaften, 1890-1920.* Berlin: Dietz, 1949.

Michels, Robert. "Die deutsche Sozialdemokratie, Parteimitgliedschaft und soziale Zusammensetzung," *Archiv für Sozialwissenschaft und Sozialpolitik,* XXIII (1906), pp. 471-556.

———. *Political Parties: A Sociological Study of the Oligarchical Tendencies of Modern Democracy.* New York: Collier Books, 1962. Translated and reprint of *Zur Soziologie des Parteiwesens in der modernen Demokratie.* Leipzig: W. Klinkhardt, 1911.

Millen, Bruce H. *The Political Role of Labor in Developing Countries.* Washington, D.C.: The Brookings Institution, 1963.

Miller, Susanne. *Burgfrieden und Klassenkampf: Die deutsche Sozialdemokratie im ersten Weltkrieg.* Duesseldorf: Droste, 1974.

Mitchell, Harvey and Peter N. Stearns. *Workers and Protest: The European Labor Movement, the Working Classes and the Origins of Social Democracy, 1890-1914.* Itasca, Ill.: F.E. Peacock Publishers, 1971.

Mohr, Werner. "Sozialisierung und Wirtschaftsdemokratie," *Der Klassenkampf,* July 15, 1930, pp. 426-429.

Mommsen, Hans, Dietmar Petzina, and Bernd Weisbrod (eds.). *Industrielles System und politische Entwicklung in der Weimarer Republik.* Duesseldorf: Droste, 1974.

Morgan, David W. *The Socialist Left and the German Revolution: A History of the German Independent Social Democratic Party, 1917-1922.* Ithaca, N.Y.: Cornell University Press, 1975.

Moses, John A. "Carl Legiens Interpretation des demokratischen Sozialismus: Ein Beitrag zur sozialistischen Ideengeschichte." Unpublished Ph.D. dissertation, University of Erlangen-Nuremberg, 1965.

Muchow, Reinhold. *Nationalsozialismus und "freie" Gewerkschaften.* Munich: F. Eher, 1932.

Napthali, Fritz. *Wirtschaftsdemokratie: Ihr Wesen, Weg und Ziel.* Berlin: Verlagsgesellschaft des ADGB, 1928.

Nestriepke, Siegfried. *Die Gewerkschaftsbewegung.* 2d ed. Vol. I. Stuttgart: Ernst Heinrich Moritz, 1922.

Neumann, Franz. *European Trade Unionism and Politics.* New York: League for Industrial Democracy, 1936.

Neumann, Walter. *Die Gewerkschaften im Ruhrgebiet.* Cologne: Bund, 1951.

Nobel, Alphons. *Die Gewerkschaften: Die deutsche Wirtschaft und ihre Führer.* Vol. II. Gotha: Flamberg, 1925.

Nörpel, Clemens. "Entwicklung und Rechtsstellung der Gewerkschaften bis zur Gegenwart," *Arbeit,* No. 3, 1933, pp. 181-188.

_____. "Gewerkschaften - Wirtschaft - Politik," *Gewerkschafts - Archiv,* II (February, 1925), pp. 78-85.

Noske, Gustav. *Aufstieg und Niedergang der deutschen Sozialdemokratie.* Zurich: Aeroverlag, 1947.

Oertzen, Peter von. *Betriebsräte in der Novemberrevolution.* Duesseldorf: Droste, 1963.

Opel, Fritz. *Der Deutsche Metallarbeiter-Verband während des Ersten Weltkrieges und der Revolution.* Hanover: Norddeutsche Verlagsanstalt O. Goedel, 1957.

————, and Dieter Schneider. *Fünfundsiebzig Jahre Industriegewerkschaft 1891 bis 1966: Vom Deutschen Metallarbeiter-Verband zur Industriegewerkschaft Metall.* Frankfort/Main: Europäische Verlagsanstalt, 1966.

Papen, Franz von. *Vom Scheitern einer Demokratie, 1930-1933.* Mainz: von Hase und Koehler, 1968.

————. *Der Wahrheit eine Gasse.* Munich: Paul List, 1952.

Perlman, Selig. *A Theory of the Labor Movement.* New York: A.M. Kelley, 1949. Reprint of 1928 ed.

Pirker, Theo. *Die Blinde Macht: Die Gewerkschaftsbewegung in Westdeutschland.* 2 vols. Munich: Mercator, 1960.

Plotkin, Abram. "The Destruction of the Labor Movement in Germany," *American Federationist,* XL (August, 1933), pp. 811-826.

Die politische und religiöse Neutralitat der "freien" Gewerkschaften. Berlin: Christlicher Gewerkschaftsverlag, 1923.

Pollard, Sidney, "The Trade Unions and the Depression of 1929-1933," *Industrielles System und politische Entwicklung in der Weimarer Republik.* Edited by Hans Mommsen, Dietmar Petzina, and Bernd Weisbrod. Duesseldorf: Droste, 1974.

Pollock, James K. *Money and Politics Abroad.* New York: Knopf, 1932.

Prager, Eugen. *Geschichte der USPD.* 2d ed. Berlin: Verlagsgesellschaft "Freiheit," 1922.

Preller, Ludwig. *Sozialpolitik in der Weimarer Republik.* Stuttgart: Franz Mittelbach, 1949.

Price, John. *The International Labour Movement.* London: Oxford University Press, 1945.

Prinz, August-Günter. "Der Einsatz gewerkschaftlicher Macht in Konkret-politischen Situationen nach 1918." Unpublished Ph.D. dissertation, University of Cologne, 1957.

Raase, Werner. *Zur Geschichte der deutschen Gewerkschaftsbewegung 1914-1917 und 1917-1919.* Berlin: Tribüne, n.d. (ca. 1968).

Raumer, Hans von. "Unternehmer und Gewerkschaften in der Weimarer Zeit," *Deutsche Rundschau,*Vol. LXXX, No. 5 (May, 1954), pp. 425-434.

Reich, Nathan. *Labour Relations in Republican Germany.* New York: Oxford University Press, 1938.

Die Revolutionäre Gewerkschafts-Opposition (RGO). 2 vols. Berlin: Rote Fahne, 1972.

Richter, Werner. *Gewerkschaften, Monopolkapital und Staat im ersten Weltkrieg und in der Novemberrevolution (1914-1919).* Berlin: Tribüne, 1959.

Ritter, Gerhard A. *Die Arbeiterbewegung im Wilhelminischen Reich: Die Sozialdemokratische Partei und die freien Gewerkschaften 1890-1910.* Berlin-Dahlem: Colloquium, 1959.

Rohe, Karl. *Das Reichsbanner Schwarz-Rot-Gold.* Duesseldorf: Droste, 1966.

Roll, Erich. "Germany," *Organized Labour in Four Continents.* Edited by H.A. Marquand. London, New York: Longmans, Green, 1939.

Rosenberg, Arthur. *A History of the German Republic.* London: Methuen, 1936.

_____. *Imperial Germany: The Birth of the German Republic, 1871-1918.* New York: Oxford University Press, 1970. Reprint of 1931 ed.

Roth, Guenther. *The Social Democrats in Imperial Germany: A Study in Working-Class Isolation and National Integration.* Totowa, N.J.: The Bedminster Press, 1963.

Schabrod, Karl. *Generalstreik rettet Weimarer Republik.* Duesseldorf: Carolus, 1960.

Scharrer, Manfred. *Arbeiterbewegung im Obrigkeitsstaat—SPD und Gewerkschaft nach dem Sozialistengesetz.* Berlin: Rotbuch, 1976.

Schellhoss, Hartmut. *Apathie und Legitimität: Das Problem der neuen Gewerkschaft.* Munich: Piper, 1967.

Schevenels, Walther. *Quarante cinq années: Fédération syndicale internationale, 1901-1945.* Brussels: Éditions de l'Institut E. Vandervelde, 1964.

Schiefer, Jack. *Geschichte der deutschen freien Gewerkschaften, 1890-1932.* Aachen: Grenzland-Verlag Hollands, 1948.

Schneider, Dieter and Rudolf Kuda. *Arbeiterräte in der November-revolution: Ideen, Wirkungen, Dokumente.* Frankfort/ Main: Suhrkamp, 1968.

———. *Mitbestimmung: Weg zur industriellen Demokratie.* Munich: Deutscher Taschenbuch Verlag, 1969.

Schneider, Michael. *Das Arbeitsbeschaffungsprogramm des ADGB: Zur gewerkschaftlichen Politik in der Endphase der Weimarer Republik.* Bonn: Neue Gesellschaft, 1975.

———. "Konjunkturpolitische Vorstellungen der Gewerkschaften in den letzten Jahren der Weimarer Republik. Zur Entwicklung des Arbeitsbeschaffungsplans des ADGB," *Industrielles System und politische Entwicklung in der Weimarer Republik.* Edited by Hans Mommsen, Dietmar Petzina, and Bernd Weisbrod. Duesseldorf: Droste, 1974.

Schorske, Carl E. *German Social Democracy, 1905-1917: The Development of the Great Schism.* New York: Russell and Russell, 1955.

Schumann, Hans-Gerd. *Nationalsozialismus und Gewerkschaftsbewegung: Die Vernichtung der deutschen Gewerkschaften und der Aufbau der "Deutschen Arbeitsfront."* Hanover: Norddeutsche Verlagsanstalt O. Goedel, 1958.

Schuster, Dieter. *Die deutsche Gewerkschaftsbewegung, DGB.* 3rd ed. Duesseldorf: DGB Bundesvorstand, 1971.

Schwarz, Salomon. *Handbuch der deutschen Gewerkschaftskongresse.* Berlin: Verlagsgesellschaft des ADGB, 1930.

Seelbach, Herman. *Das Ende der Gewerkschaften.* Berlin: Elsner, 1934.

Seidel, Richard. *Die Gewerkschaften nach dem Kriege.* Berlin: Dietz, 1925.

———. *Gewerkschaften und politische Parteien in Deutschland.* Berlin: Weltgeist-Bücher, n.d. (ca. 1928).

———. *Die Gewerkschaften in der Revolution.* Berlin: Verlagsgenossenschaft "Freiheit," 1920.

———. *The Trade Union Movement of Germany.* International Trade Union Library, Nos. 7-8. Amsterdam: IFTU, 1928.

Severing, Carl. *Mein Lebensweg.* 2. vols. Cologne: Greven, 1950.

Sind die freien Gewerkschaften politisch und religiös neutral? Berlin: Christlicher Gewerkschaftsverlag, n.d.

Skrzypczak, Henryk. "From Carl Legien to Theodor Leipart, from Theodor Leipart to Robert Ley: Notes on some strategic and tactical problems of the German free trade union movement during the Weimar Republic," *Internationale Wissenschaftliche Korrespondenz zur Geschichte der Deutschen Arbeiterbewegung*, Vol. XIII (August, 1971), pp. 26-45; revised in "Zur Strategie der freien Gewerkschaften in der Weimarer Republik," *Vom Sozialistengesetz zur Mitbestimmung: Zum 100. Geburtstag von Hans Böckler*. Edited by Heinz Oskar Vetter. Cologne: Bund, 1975.

Snell, John L. "Socialist Unions and Socialist Patriotism in Germany, 1914-1918," *American Historical Review*, Vol. LIX (October, 1953), pp. 66-76.

Sozialdemokratie, Gewerkschaft, Vorwärts. Berlin: Vorwärts Buchdruckerei, n.d.

Spectator (pseud.). *Sozialisierungsproblem in Deutschland*. Berlin: Seehof, 1920.

Spethmann, Hans. *Der Ruhrkampf, 1923-1925*. Berlin: Hobbing, 1933.

Stadler, Hans. *Die Gewerkschaften: Ein Staat im Staate*. Munich: J.F. Lehmanns Verlag, 1965.

Stampfer, Friedrich. *Die Vierzehn Jahre der ersten Deutschen Republik*. Karlsbad: Verlaganstalt "Graphia," 1936.

Staudinger, Hans. *Der Staat als Unternehmer*. Berlin: Gersbach, 1932.

Stearns, Peter N. "The European Labor Movement and the Working Classes, 1890-1914." *Workers and Protest*. By Harvey Mitchell and Peter N. Stearns. Itasca, Ill. F.E. Peacock Publishers, 1971.

Stern, Boris. "Works Council Movement in Germany," *Bulletin of the United States Bureau of Labor Statistics*. No. 383, 1925.

Sternberg, Fritz. *Der Niedergang des deutschen Kapitalismus*. Berlin: Rowohlt, 1932.

Stolper, Gustav. *German Economy, 1870-1914*. New York: Reynal and Hitchcock, 1940.

Stresemann, Gustav. *Vermächtnis*. Vol. I. Berlin: Ullstein, 1932.

Stroebel, Heinrich. *Socialisation in Theory and Practice*. London: King and Son, 1922.

Stürmer, Michael. *Koalition und Opposition in der Weimarer Republik, 1924-1928*. Duesseldorf: Droste, 1967.

Sturmthal, Adolf. *The Tragedy of European Labor, 1918-1939*. New York: Columbia University Press, 1943.

Taft, Philip. "Germany," *Comparative Labor Movements*. Edited by Walter Galenson. New York: Prentice-Hall, 1952.

Tarnow, Fritz. *Das Organisationsproblem im ADGB*. Berlin: Verlagsanstalt des Deutschen Holzarbeiter-Verbandes, 1925.

————. *Die Stellungnahme der freien Gewerkschaften zur Frage der Wirtschaftsdemokratie*. Jena: Verlag des Bezirksausschuss des ADGB, Thüringen, 1929.

Thieringer, Rolf. "Das Verhältnis der Gewerkschaften zu Staat und Parteien in der Weimarer Republik." Unpublished Ph.D. Dissertation, University of Tübingen, 1954.

Thimme, Friedrich and Carl Legien. *Die Arbeiterschaft im neuen Deutschland*. Leipzig: Hirzel, 1915.

Tilly, Charles, Louise Tilly, and Richard Tilly. *The Rebellious Century, 1830-1930*. Cambridge: Harvard University Press, 1975.

Timm, Helga. *Die deutsche Sozialpolitik und der Bruch der Grossen Koalition im März 1930*. Duesseldorf: Droste, 1952.

Timm, Johannes. "Sozialdemokratie und Gewerkschaften," *Süddeutsche Monatshefte*, November 1917, pp. 125-207.

Tormin, Walter. *Zwischen Rätediktatur und sozialer Demokratie: Die Geschichte der Rätebewegung in der deutschen Revolution 1918/19*. Duesseldorf: Droste, 1954.

Triesch, Günter. *Die Macht der Funktionäre*. Duesseldorf: Karl Rauch, 1956.

Ufermann, Paul (ed.). *Alwin Brandes*. Berlin: Arani, 1949.

Umbreit, Paul. "Allgemeiner Deutscher Gewerkschaftsbund (ADGB.)," *Internationales Handwörterbuch des Gewerkschaftswesens*. Edited by Ludwig Heyde. Vol. I, 1931, pp. 23-29.

————. *Die deutschen Gewerkschaften im Weltkrieg*. Berlin: Verlag für Sozialwissenschaft, 1917.

————. *25 Jahre deutscher Gewerkschaftsbewegung, 1890-1915*. Berlin: Verlag der General Kommission, 1915.

Vall, Mark van de. *Die Gewerkschaften im Wohlfahrtsstaat*. Cologne and Opladen: Westdeutscher Verlag, 1966.

Varain, Heinz Josef. *Freie Gewerkschaften, Sozialdemokratie und Staat: Die Politik der Generalkommission unter der Führung Carl Legiens (1890-1920)*. Duesseldorf: Droste, 1956.

Varga, Eugen (ed.). *Die Sozialdemokratischen Parteien.* Hamburg: Carl Hoym, 1926.

Vetter, Heinz Oskar (ed.). *Vom Sozialistengesetz zur Mitbestimmung: Zum 100. Geburtstag von Hans Böckler.* Cologne: Bund, 1975.

Wachenheim, Hedwig. *Die deutsche Arbeiterbewegung, 1844 bis 1914.* Cologne and Opladen: Westdeutscher Verlag, 1967.

Wende, Alexander. "Die Konzentrationsbewegung bei den deutschen Gewerkschaften." Unpublished Ph.D. dissertation, University of Marburg, 1912.

Wentzcke, Paul. *Ruhrkampf.* Vol. I. Berlin: Hobbing, 1930.

Werner, Karl-Gustav. *Organisation und Politik der Gewerkschaften und Arbeitgeberverbände in der deutschen Bauwirtschaft.* Berlin: Duncker & Humblot, 1968.

Wheeler, Robert. "Zur sozialen Struktur der Arbeiterbewegung am Anfang der Weimarer Republik: Einige methodologischen Bemerkungen," *Industrielles System und politische Entwicklung in der Weimarer Republik.* Edited by Hans Mommsen, Dietmar Petzina and Bernd Weisbrod. Duesseldorf: Droste, 1974.

Wheeler-Bennett, John W. *Hindenburg: The Wooden Titan.* London: Macmillan, 1936.

Willey, Richard J. "Labor and Politics in West Germany: The Deutscher Gewerkschaftsbund, 1949-1963." Unpublished Ph.D. dissertation, Princeton University, 1964.

―――. "Trade Unions and Political Parties in the Federal Republic of Germany:" *Industrial and Labor Relations Review,* XXVIII, No. 1 (October 1974), pp. 38-59.

Windmuller, John P. *Labor Internationals: A Survey of Contemporary International Trade Union Organizations.* Bulletin, No. 61, New York State School of Industrial and Labor Relations. Ithaca: Cornell University, 1969.

Winkler, Erich. *Organisations- und Werbetechnik in der Arbeiterbewegung.* Vol. I, *Die Politik und ihre Gesetze.* Jena: Karl Zwing Verlagsbuchhandlung, 1930.

Wissell, Rudolf. "Einundzwanzig Monate Reichsarbeitsminister," *Arbeit,* No. 4, 1930, pp. 217-228.

Woytinsky, W.S. *Stormy Passage.* New York: The Vanguard Press, 1961.

Wunderlich, Frieda. *German Labor Courts.* Chapel Hill: University of North Carolina Press, 1947.

_____. *Labor under German Democracy: Arbitration 1918-1933.* Supplement II, *Social Research,* 1940. New York: New School for Social Research, 1940.

Ziervogel, Max. "Die Gestaltung der Organisationsform der freien Gewerkschaften." Unpublished Ph.D. dissertation, University of Giessen, 1924.

Zwing, Karl. *Soziologie der Gewerkschaftsbewegung.* Jena: Verlag Gewerkschafts-Archiv, 1925.

_____. "Um die Zukunft der Gewerkschaften," *Gewerkschafts-Archiv,* IX, No. 6 (1932), pp. 241-244.

INDEX